PHILO
SOPHY
@WORK

PHILO SOPHY @WORK

Reflections from the world's leading business thinkers

Curated by and featuring **ANDERS INDSET**

unbound

First published in 2022

Unbound

Level 1, Devonshire House, One Mayfair Place, London W1J 8AJ

www.unbound.com

Text design by PDQ Digital Media Solutions Ltd.

A CIP record for this book is available from the British Library

ISBN 978-1-80018-127-4 (special edition)
ISBN 978-1-80018-128-1 (paperback)
ISBN 978-1-80018-129-8 (ebook)

Printed in Great Britain by Clays Ltd, Elcograf S.p.A

1 3 5 7 9 8 6 4 2

Thank you to the following patrons for their generous support
of this book.

Andrea Allocco

Michelle Besier

Prince Boadu

Christian Böß

Jean-Marie Buchilly

Benjamin Buescher

Teodora Mona Croitoru

Sandeep Das

Guillermo De Haro

Nils Dudenhoefer

Signe Gammeltoft Frantzen

Hans Gallis

Jared Gil

Anna Görres

Simone Gross

Martin Heimers

Joern Herseth

Michael Hu

Barbara Hunter-Lemke

Hannah Indset

Jon Indset

Nikolaus Isele

Sanjin Kanesic

Michael Lefrancois

Mirja Linke

Matteo Lunardon Mr.

Reinhold W. Lutz

Lothar Mayer

Jan Mironiuk

Antonio Nieto-Rodriguez

Allan Rahn

Yannick Reiss

Benjamin Rohé

Arnaldo Romanos-Hofer

op 't Roodt Rudi

Bjarne Rugelsjoen

Professor Peter Sachsenmeier

Jim Savitz

Roger Spitz

Bridget Trusty

Olivier Van Duüren

Ute Wellenberg

Martin Whitworth

Beatrice Willmers

Frank Windau

With special thanks to Zigurat Global Institute of Technology
for helping to make this book happen.

CONTENTS

Part III – Coping with the Forces of Change and Exponential Technologies

Part IV – Philosophy Applied and in Action

INTRODUCTION

When I first started on this journey of pairing philosophy and business, more than a decade ago, it was all about building bridges and trying to rethink philosophical concepts in light of the twenty-first century.

In retrospect, it has been about what I now describe as 'practical applied philosophy'. I very much resonate with theoretical physicist Richard Feynman, who said, 'If I cannot build it, I cannot understand it.' In philosophical terms, he was rejecting a theoretical and an academic approach in favour of bringing philosophy to life. In other words, philosophy is something we do, something that can be applied to a practical purpose of improving our lives in order to reach a higher understanding and provide a pathway to acting by reason.

My passion for philosophy has followed me since my early childhood. *The art of being wrong.* That genuine curiosity and eagerness to understand 'everything' – which was not, however, always immediately relatable to my life. But it has helped me take a different perspective and to see things holistically. The search for wisdom and the willingness to share and grow together are essential values that can help give some kind of meaning to our 'wonderful journey to nowhere'.

Philosophy@Work does not attempt to cover every aspect of the topics it raises, but rather to provide the spark and the inspiration to think anew about philosophy in the context of doing business. Business leaders in the twenty-first century must have, on a fundamental level, a sense of curiosity and an open mind.

This book is a starting point for taking philosophy to work – seeing and learning how philosophical methods and thinking can be applied to the business world. It is a collection of articles and interviews by some of the leading business, leadership and/or management thinkers in the world today. It features intellectuals from the field of business thinking who have welcomed philosophical concepts and applied them to the world of business. It is a book to motivate the reader to take a different perspective and to be open to expanding their own models and to free themselves from what I refer to as our *Selbstverständlichkeiten* – ingrained ways of thinking. The reader should feel they can revisit what they take for granted today – the metaphors and terminologies that are anxiously and blindly used in everyday life without questioning.

The first part is 'Sparking Personal Development'. As interdependencies and collaborative approaches become more important and as projects drive companies, the role of the team member also requires ongoing learning. The well-being, self-reflection and growth of a leader are essential fields of all modern organisations. The second part covers various aspects of the Art of Leadership and how to become a leader of change. In the third section we take a look at how to cope with the Forces of Change – the underlying mechanisms impacting the world and driving external impulses for organisations. The fourth and final section of the book examines aspects of Applied Philosophy and how it is brought to life. How can philosophy be made part of action and how can it impact how we do business? Each of these four sections feature contributions from a range of leading thinkers and interviews with pioneers in their field.

Contributors

The contributions include an insightful interview with Megan Reitz, the professor of leadership and dialogue at Hult Ashridge Executive Education, UK, and a Zoom session in the Canadian mountains with Henry Mintzberg, the recipient of the lifetime achievement award from Thinkers50 for his long-term impact on the way people think about and practice management. There are chapters from the likes of international branding expert Martin Lindstrom, who has led deep research into the minds of buyers, applying insights from neuroscience to develop the concept of 'buyology'. You will also learn from Anil Gupta and Haiyan Wang, global strategists and experts on entrepreneurship and the transformational rise of emerging markets. The executive president of IE University, Spain, and winner of the first ever Thinkers50 founders' award, Santiago Iñiguez de Onzoño, brings 'If You Want to Be a Good Leader, You Had Better Understand Philosophy'. Dorie Clark, self-reinvention and branding expert, shares thoughts on how to take control of your professional life and make an impact on the world and Thinkers50 hall of fame expert in strategy, marketing, and pricing, Hermann Simon, writes on 'The Philosophy of Price'. The 'world's leading business coach', Marshall Goldsmith, together with many others, share their reflections on how they relate to philosophy in their particular field.

Philosophy@Work will give you a way to access new fields of interest by learning new leadership concepts for the twenty-first century. It will inspire you to approach personal development in a new way and teach you how to cope with the underlying forces of change by getting a better understanding of the world – your own, personal philosophy of the world, as defined in cognitive sciences through a German word, *Weltanschauung*.

Undressing the (business) world

*If change from a world of potentiality and infinity meet
a system of finitude, not only do tensions arise, but
fundamental changes in organised human life will follow.*

Davos, January 2020, and the sun is shining. I find myself amongst the 'financial elite' and a young generation of changemakers who have been invited to address and discuss the new world with the other attendees at the World Economic Forum. There is something of a new spirit in the air. There are the annual discussions about how to continue along the path of unlimited growth and prosperity, but these have been joined by real concerns about the sustainability of such a world. Such talks have long been on the table, but the young are now demanding change and the elite seems to finally be taking action.

Inviting young changemakers actually seems to be more than just a gimmick to get media attention. There is a willingness to take on the most pressing challenge for humanity – how to stave off ecological collapse while still trying to build a prosperous world; to find a way to unite economy and ecology. Philanthropists and their family offices are talking about 'impact investments' and 'sustainable technologies' and corporate leaders are striving for greater balance and more stakeholder management. In new, major investments, the concept of making the switch to a perfect, circular economy – a sustainable world – is making noise at this fiftieth anniversary summit in the Swiss Alps. The focus is not on prosperity for the elite but on shared prosperity.

Ever since Klaus Schwab gathered 444 business leaders back in 1971, to what has grown into the World Economic Forum, companies around the globe have failed to face up to the fact that our world has finite resources and to the danger of ecological systems that are increasingly breaking down. We live on a planet held hostage by absolute and finite thinking, by linear and slow development of the human understanding of the world, in direct conflict with the exponential development of technologies. The paradox is that the progress that has created a connected, more advanced world has also caused greater division and an increased gap between the rich and the poor – the lucky ones and those who were not born into systems of wealth and opportunity. It is true that humanity has made great progress, as described by the late Hans Rosling and more recently by Steven Pinker in his *Enlightenment Now*. However, behind the facade of growth and of globalisation and progress, underlying forces – hardly visible to the naked eye – have been boiling.

Little did we know, however, that following the anniversary summit and a serious call for action, the world would face the coronavirus pandemic and the associated lockdown. If the outbreak has taught us one thing, it is that our interconnected and interdependent society is a fragile one. We have built a society where we have neglected the weak links. Covid 19 has revealed the flaws in our systems and shown us a gordian knot of symptoms that has the potential to destroy our civilisation. History teaches us of such collapses – times when societies at their peak fall victim to their own ills, ranging from rapid expansion and growth to inequality, environmental and technological issues or lack of leadership and the failure to understand complexity. The beginning of 2020 might have been such a blindfolded, one-way journey towards collapse. Or perhaps it may be an alarm call that could be seen in a strange way to be fortunate. Coronavirus might have given us a window of opportunity to help us react, rethink and reshape our whole destiny.

We are confronted with a paradox: the only really impactful way forward to cope with the ecological collapse – namely, the rapid development of new technologies – also has the potential to destabilise society even further and threaten humanity. The looming ecological collapse cannot be tackled by re-education and recycling alone. Moving away from hypercapitalism and turbo-consumerism while building a 'perfect circular economy' are crucial tasks, but the real solution, going forward, is the rapid development of new technologies that help us rethink energy consumption and the usage of natural resources and to come up with business models that completely upend our perception.

With the decrease in birth rates in Western countries, the threat is not overpopulation, but rather the risk of underpopulation. New technologies are the only way forward to compensate for aging societies and to tackle the upside-down population pyramid. Despite its obvious potential to help humanity, the upcoming 'digital tsunami' is one of the most challenging developments humanity has ever faced; the linear and slow growth of our understanding cannot compete with the exponential progress in many fields of technology. The underlying financial system is being challenged by decentralised, digital structures with new technologies and new powerhouses. The blockchain revolution is ongoing while, at the same time, new quantum technological solutions – the second quantum paradigm – are entering the world and hundred-year-old theories from quantum mechanics are now being brought to life.

Quantum technology has already been mathematically proven capable of cracking any conventional security on a traditional computer. Although the computing power has not yet arrived at the time of writing, it is still a pressing challenge that needs to be tackled; the race for quantum-safe cryptography is on.

In the light of the changes to the financial markets – the switch to sustainable crypto/digital-currencies, the impact of blockchain and quantum technologies and the aim to 'wire up' our brains – we are most likely only at the beginning of what we are referring to as a digital transformation. Not only is humanity faced with complexities beyond our own understanding, but the speed of development means that there are fewer possibilities to readjust or learn from our mistakes. The pressure to solve issues the first time around is rapidly increasing. In other words, in a fluid and dynamic world, security and a fundamental understanding of potential consequences are essential.

Where are we today? Has our 'modern' civilisation peaked? It is now, at the intersection of technological progress and increasing complexity, that we can (re)define the role of the Mensch and how we live together in society. Not in an illusional sense of a perfect dreamworld of some utopian endstate but much more as a way of continuous progress for the status quo – a road towards a future worth working and striving for, a world of more balance. It is here and now that the economy can play a stabilising role rather than one of division. The economy can help us cope with societal challenges and avoid ecological collapse instead of being a root cause of that devastation. What is needed are 'leaders of change'.

Leaders of change are independent thinkers and interdependent doers and are freed from the ideas that most of us, and society as a whole, hold to be self-evident: our absolutes, our dogmas – our *Selbstverständlichkeiten*. Leaders of change are genuinely interested, strive for what I call *Weltverständlichkeit* – a higher understanding of the world – and therefore challenge the paradoxes of our time in search of wisdom.

Each individual is tied to their subjective view of the world, based on their own journey and the knowledge they have gathered along the way. If you want to change your view or bend your own reality and accept new and other views as a (business) leader and a human being, it should not be through your job title or your educational attainment, nor should it solely be based on the hours you put in. *Philosophy@Work* is also about the balance between your 'inner world' and your experienced 'external world' in striving for more balance. It is about your willingness to learn

7

something new. As a leader you must have the courage to move from the known to the unknown; to free yourself from taking things for granted, as they have always been, and instead to seek greater understanding of the world.

As I write, almost two years after the last physical Davos gathering of 2019, I believe coronavirus is not the most pressing problem; it is our thinking that is infected. Companies today must be built on the premise of serving future generations while still being profitable in the short term. Leadership must tackle ecological regulation and the goal of reducing emissions. Leaders should not see a circular economy as a limitation but as potential for growth. It is not about ecology or economy, but both at the same time. It is not about global or local, but both at the same time. It is not about stability or chaos, but both at the same time. We live in a parallel and simultaneous society, and we must free ourselves from borders and limiting thinking and open our minds to an infinite mindset.

What is now needed is a holistic, stakeholder-driven approach towards greater balance. It is not about building a new operating system but much more about upgrading, about adding compassion to capitalism, aiming for a humanistic approach to business in which the economy and the business world serve humanity and not the other way around. It is about building prosperity for posterity ('prosterity') – striving to create a dynamic balance of peace and wealth for future generations – while securing economic stability in the short term. This portmanteau, prosterity, symbolises such a vision for a new generation of leaders – prosterity leadership. Prosterity describes the essence of twenty-first century leadership in business, politics and society as a whole. Prosterity leaders are stakeholder-driven and strive towards a dynamic equilibrium. They build for future generations, grow as human beings and shape the world around them – including people, communities, resources, and the planet. Prosterity is a way of life and a guiding principle for shaping a holistic, humanistic and compassionate capitalism.

We can all be navigators and leaders of change, with our action and our thinking based on reason. We can all serve as guides to create a society of understanding and a humanistic capitalism in which prosperity for the few turns into shared prosperity for all. I am a believer in technology, the progress of science and the mathematical and structural understanding of the world. But, underneath, filling the void between us – describing the ways in which we organise human life, our relationships and how we reach some higher symbiosis, combining our inner and outer worlds – we find philosophy.

This book does not aim to be an absolute guide. Feel free to see this as forming your starting point – a contribution from management thinkers around the globe, bringing completely different backgrounds and relationships to the art of philosophy. Let us call them 'sparks'. I encourage you to apply *Shoshin* (初心) – a mind open to learning. Enjoy the freedom to test what you hold to be absolute – self-evident – and we will embark on a journey together to bridge business and philosophy.

CHAPTER 1: THERE CAN BE NO POST-HUMANISM WITHOUT HUMANISM

Manfred Geier's book *The Last Philosophers*, about Wittgenstein and Heidegger, is lying on my desk. The book starts by examining their origins and homeland. As Heidegger put it, a hundred years ago, 'It is necessary to reflect on whether and how a homeland is still possible in the age of the technologised uniform global civilisation.' Does this seem familiar, in our own, technologically disorienting lives?

We realise that the challenges we currently face are not disparate and isolated. How can we reconcile a simultaneous belief in decline (the disintegration of the economy) and prosperity (the further growth of the economy)? The world is full of such paradoxes. But we always insist on the primacy of our own certainties, of what we hold to be self-evident. The result is that the contradictory narratives simply collide and disintegrate through their absolute nature. Our identity is bound up with our relation to our homeland but we are also dependent on a larger, world society and on our planet itself. We must accept the concept of parallel societies on our path to seek wisdom and equilibrium.

With the increasing speed of technological development we must question what we are and what we want to become. After exploiting resources such as trees, animals and plants, the Mensch – the human being – has now become the product, exploited by algorithms and recommendation engines. We are confronted with two fundamental philosophical questions. What is a Mensch and how do we (re)organise our society with humans at the centre? How can we create new forms of living in a technological age, e.g. how can we be assured of a stable operating system – the economy – so that we can focus on our societal challenges?

Hegel reloaded – a new understanding of freedom for the twenty-first century

In our fragile construct – our created society – we have a weak link. Our thinking is infected and this vulnerability risks greater destruction. When the coronavirus pandemic broke out in late 2019, it turned out that many societies hadn't even invested in adequate supplies of surgical masks and, once we did, wearing masks was pretty much still the only answer we had on how to tackle a pandemic. Yet we have been investing billions of dollars in printing body parts and extending our lives, trying to optimise ourselves in the cause of survival of the species. This has led humanity into a state of living simply to avoid dying, rather than for living in itself. It hasn't had the desired effect; we are alive, but not truly living.

We are stuck in an ever-faster spinning wheel and are losing the ability and freedom to navigate and create. What we need is a revolutionary shift towards more collective thinking and action. All of our systems – be they educational, political, or economic – are interconnected and interdependent. As they are now falling apart it becomes clear to us that these systems are also only as strong as their weakest link. We have been isolated together, cut off from one another while at the same time connected to a global community of shared suffering. For many, however, the question is whether this is a time of suffering or the start of taking a path to somewhere better. We can only satisfy our desire for individual freedom if it is done in harmony with what leads to the collective good.

On 27 August 2020, German philosopher Georg Wilhelm Friedrich Hegel would have turned 250 years old. His thinking has never been more relevant. Hegel explained that freedom doesn't mean that we can do whatever we want, but rather that we can only enjoy individual freedom in relation to (and together with) other people. Today, our task is not, however, about understanding what such a genius thinker meant to the society in which he was born. We must find a way to read and reflect on his great work in regard to the development of the world we now live in. Hegel teaches us what the essence of philosophy should be – namely, to gather our thoughts in the time that we live. Even Hegel himself was shaped by his environment and path and – despite his visionary outlook and understanding – his own limits on how far he could foresee the consequences of 250 years of exponential technological progress.

The English version of Hegel's text throws up valuable lessons about the nature of words and terminology. Even in the best rendering, much is lost in translation. Certain words cannot be grasped – even in the original German, you only get a sense of the stream of thinking which is hard enough to grasp and as a consequence impossible in English. This journey into the art of thinking even unfolds to a paradoxical anti-climax, where Hegel himself might not have even managed to be Hegelian enough, at times getting stuck in words or his own assumptions or absolutes about his time, leaving out the potential development of a world we have built, beyond the imagination of thinkers from past centuries.

But what does this have to do with today's business world, with models, management and leadership, you might ask? It is not so much the analysis of the actual work done centuries ago by various outstanding intellectuals that counts, but their path of thinking, in the context of our lives and society today, that is relevant. Given the current ethical challenges regarding coping with technology, finding meaning and navigating paradoxes has become essential to the business world.

Hegel himself put it very clearly. 'Philosophy is the understanding [Hegel says *Erkenntnis* in the original] of now gathered in thoughts.' What does this mean? Here we need a reference point for the German word. *Erkenntnis* means more of an experience or the lived realisation of an understanding. In other words, our own thoughts will, and must, be redefined depending on the context in which they emerge.

We go wandering and wondering in our strange lives in an abnormal world. The underlying operational system of our society – the economy – has shown us again and again how little we actually understand the interdependencies, how much we rely on our own sense of absolutes and how fragile everything has become due to the complexities of the systems we have built. Yet, at the same time we have, paradoxically, also increased stability and now relate everything with technology to support us on our journey. What is self-evident today can be changed by a new world view that will lead to a new sense of the absolute for the future.

Philosophical zombies or the path to global understanding?

'*Deus ex machina*' – 'the god in the machine'. With incredible scientific and technological breakthroughs, we have strengthened the strong in society and made the vulnerable even more vulnerable. Our own quest to reach the superhuman through technological progress, our curiosity about godliness, bliss, and immortality has manifested in the development of digital superintelligence. We are on the brink of a new paradigm shift, driven by a wiring of our own brains and the potential fusion of the world of objects with our subjective experiences to create a new, symbiotic form of intelligence. However, it won't be Nietzsche's superhuman who emerges, but rather some kind of synthesis of the last human with that superhuman. Not even Nietzsche himself could have imagined how the collapse of the structure of exploitative society and the 'fall of the conscious man' could lead to such a construct. If we want to connect our brains to external devices, we urgently need to deal with our concept of what it is to be human and figure out what humans, whether in this final expression or in some kind of super-godlike form, really are and should become. In other words, we can only create something that is posthuman if we are first clear about what it means to be human.

Technology must (and will) save humanity. The question is: what will it save us from? If technology is going to save humanity, then we must first understand the essence of what it means to be a human being and from there develop an increasing global understanding, including an understanding about what we are doing now and what we as a global society want. The only way to do this – in my opinion – is if we, together with our technological development, seek answers and the help within the fields of deep art, psychology and philosophy.

What is a human? What do terms like 'intelligence', 'consciousness' and 'sub-conscious' refer to? In developed regions of prosperity around the world, people are newly confronted with old philosophical questions. 'What can I hope for?' 'What can I know?' 'What ought I to do?' The aim is not only to reach understanding, but also to optimise and shape our species to live by reason and what the German philosopher Immanuel Kant referred to as the 'categorical imperative' – even if that means merging with technology. The cornerstone of Kant's moral philosophy – 'Act only according to that maxim whereby you can, at the same time, will that it should become a universal law' – today plays an essential role in building tomorrow's technologies. Dealing with the problems of phenomenology and 'thinking as such' (as Hegel puts it), is more important than ever today. If we are going to get past hypercapitalism, it is not just through our actions and thoughts, but also through our thinking in itself: looking at why we think and act as we do. My academic background may not qualify me to be a professional Hegelian, but I strongly believe that we can only consciously survive the technological journey ahead of us if we travel along the border between 'objective reality' and 'transcendental subjectivity', as thinking beings – a lesson from Hegel for all of us to ponder – and for this we can all be professional amateurs.

At the same time, neither Kant nor Hegel can offer us any hard and fast solutions for the challenges we face today, and that is also not the point. Our task is not to understand past philosophical works as absolutes, but rather to apply the essence of the thinking to the world we live in today. Against the backdrop of Einstein's theory of relativity and today's practical implementation of theoretical breakthroughs in modern physics from the 1920s, it is up to us to reignite philosophy. Kant, Hegel, Nietzsche and even Einstein could not have imagined a world such as the one we live in today. We now have a window of opportunity to rediscover and reconceptualise the thinking of great philosophers for the twenty-first century or, as Hegel himself put it – getting down to the very essence of the matter – 'Philosophy is its own time apprehended in thoughts.'

Our task must now be to address the root causes of the symptoms that have been revealed by the pandemic that began in late 2019 and aim to begin the healing process. Throughout history, times of crisis – whether large or small – can teach us something about the underlying problems of our time. The way forward is not to lapse into reactionism or act opportunistically in the short term, but to build something for posterity. We need to gain a greater understanding of the interconnectedness of all things; to achieve a level of global understanding and free ourselves from old certainties. That means that we need to confront our thinking itself. Again, returning to Hegel, philosophy comes to the surface when we experience moments of doubt and despair. Ubiquitous paradoxes, the fatal information society that we have built and a broad uncertainty about how we should best organise our social systems have led us into a state of desperation. The coronavirus was and is therefore not the problem, it is merely a catalyst. A new era of philosophy has begun.

A holistic philosophy

In recent years, the search for fundamental truth and underlying principles has led more and more thinkers and practitioners to look at blending theories from various fields, seeking truth in the spaces between the borderlines of rigidly separated disciplines. Instead of accepting dividing lines between natural sciences and human sciences, we should be open to searching for unifying approaches.

More physicists have become open to theories that link transcendental meditation and old Indian practice with modern quantum physics. In the science of consciousness, philosophy, spiritual and natural experiences look for new pathways to meet science. Adherents of eastern philosophical concepts have also found inspiration in modern physics and quantum theory. Which of these various approaches to gaining knowledge and enlightenment are to be categorised as voodoo science and which represent some kind of unifying, fundamental theory? I am not one to take stands.

Underneath – or should I say within? – the world of subatomic particles of neutrinos, quarks and gluons, where the laws of the physical world become funky and turn into a nothingness, the underlying structure of our perceived reality and our metaphysical basis – a void or a oneness of unification, in which, potentially, one scientific theory of everything can be found – is now the focus of research for various disciplines.

No one can currently describe, reliably and seriously, how the world is tied together but, during the past decade, public interest has been ignited by the idea of a unifying theory of everything. There now seems to be a positive spirit and a sense of progress in finding something that debugs our current views about how the world works, or at least unites many different ideas.

There are theories of fields of energy with beliefs of a fundamental consciousness that knits everything together. Other approaches have suggested that there are attributes or variables that are yet to be discovered, remaining hidden for now. One thing is for sure – the questions are still plentiful. From a philosophical standpoint it seems as if we could be moving in a direction that frees ourselves from the absolutes.

When physicists are searching for a unifying theory of everything, describing the relationship between Einstein's theory of general relativity and the contemporary physics of quantum theory, then it is just that which is the path – the search for one fundamental component, one simplified theory or something 'mystical' and/or hidden, that unifies what we have discovered. And, as we are still very much in the dark, we should be open to anyone who makes a thoughtful and serious approach to help us along the journey. We need holistic philosophy to support this search for wisdom.

I have great respect for the academics and philosophers who have dug deep into the thoughts of the many minds who have pondered the existential questions. These thoughts serve as inspiration for us, and provide a theoretical framework to cope with every aspect of life as technology affects fundamental parts of what it means to be Mensch.

Today, the rapid progress of technology pushes the boundaries of trying to understand what we are and how we function. It is the responsibility of the field of philosophy to try to keep up with progress in science and technology. One aspect that, to me, has become fundamental for life as a human being and how we experience and relate to the world we perceive, is the field of phenomenology: the philosophical study primarily related to the structures of human consciousness and the phenomena related to the experiences of consciousness. By following the progress in the science of consciousness, one can't help but wonder if consciousness, in fact, may be a fundamental component of this soup of funky surprises that gives rise to the very essence of having an experience of being something.

The consciousness of reality

At the surface of our perceived reality, we experience diversity and complexity and find mathematical descriptions to teach us how the fundamental entities of our reality relate to each other. In a business and work essence this means tying together and understanding our interdependencies with everyone and everything.

This present chapter is not meant as a complete metaphysical journey, nor is it an attempt to provide conclusions and a sense of completeness. Instead, this should provide you the background to understanding the sources of inspiration; some starting points, if you like, and some initial thoughts that can help spark a journey towards seeing and feeling the interconnectedness and interdependence that we all share in this world.

There is most certainly beauty found in these mathematical formulae and the complex models created by so many thinkers throughout history. Many people still believe what Pythagoras postulated 2,500 years ago; that our universe is a universe of mathematics and is entirely based on numbers. But how can complex phenomena emerge from simple ingredients and create such wonders? Have we created maths to describe the world around us or are mathematical structures there for us to discover something yet more fundamental?

These are questions that have driven various fields of study for centuries and still lead many philosophical discourses. They have brought us all the way into the twenty-first century and modern physics, with completely new discoveries attracting a new group of followers who are convinced that the laws of physics are built or described by mathematical equations.

The field of quantum mechanics – derived in the 1920s with the famous equation of Austrian–Irish physicist Erwin Schrödinger – has given birth to various theories of hidden variables and deterministic and non-deterministic views of the world. The equation itself seems to be a description of how the physical world is perceived. Beyond its fascinating world of numbers and symbols, however, one is tempted to believe that there must be something that has ignited the magic, something that sparks the 'it'. This is the challenge for physicists and mathematicians – finding explanations for how something seemingly mystical becomes a measurable and calculable piece of information.

Twenty-first century progress in physics seems, however, to show that, at the subatomic level, everything comes together in a unifying field: from a fluid world of waves and energy to the world of solid particles. It is this complexity, showing through measurement that particles can be waves *and* particles at the same time, a seeming absurdity – that particles are actually waves. Even without a deeper understanding of the underlying maths, it seems that quantum physics has revealed some kind of fundamental unity of life.

This world of potentiality is what one hundred years ago drove Albert Einstein crazy, making even one of the greatest analytical minds of all time into that of a philosopher during his last years. Einstein tried to unite the description of the world based on the underlying maths and the experience of the actual world. The funky new kid on the block – quantum theory – did not match with Einstein's own theories in his search for a unifying theory of everything. One hundred years later we are left with a very strange puzzle – having to describe the diversity we experience in the world and connect the theory of general relativity and quantum mechanics.

As long as there is no such unification, no underlying mathematical description, the belief can, and maybe even should, be that there is some non-mathematical nature that is even more fundamental than math. More recently, physicists such as Stephen Wolfram with his cellular automata, Eric Weinstein with his geometric unity and Michio Kaku with his God equation have taken the search to mainstream media, where they lead the expedition for greater knowledge.

One belief is that consciousness does not emerge out of the physical models, but is in itself fundamental. One of the twenty-first century's leading philosophers, David Chalmers, is among those who believe that consciousness may play a fundamental role in our reality and says that philosophy is even more fundamental in its nature than scientific models. Within the science of consciousness, multiple theories and views keep philosophers and scientists around the world up at night. Is consciousness a consequence of evolution or simply a – yet-to-be-understood – information processing phenomenon? Do physical bits of matter, at some point, become conscious under conditions of particular complexity or structure? Or are they things that emerge out of nothingness? If so, how can something emerge out of nothing? Or is there, maybe, something very simple at the very bottom teaching us the way in which simplicity creates complexity?

Physicalism or materialism holds with the belief that the emergence of perceived consciousness comes out of matter. More and more materialists, however, are coming out of the closet, showing at least an openness to accepting spiritual and theological concepts and the history of such thinking – where, of course, there is very little room for absolute explanatory models – and proposing questions that might even lead to finding bridges between various *Weltanschauungen* – between contradictory world views. The challenge for materialism is to show how specific compositions can produce mental experiences; in other words, why any physical state would be conscious rather than non-conscious. How does it feel to be something? The explanation of why and how we have experiences or *qualia* (subjective, conscious sensation) – is what David Chalmers referred to as the 'hard problem of consciousness'.

The philosophical teaching of mind-body dualism stands in opposition to the scientific view of materialism and physicalism, in which the brain – through physical states – produces consciousness. Dualism, by contrast, tells us that mental and physical states are distinct from one another, that the mind and the body are separable. French philosopher and mathematician René Descartes addressed the separation of the physical body in the seventeenth century. This gave rise to the early problem of how mind, thought and consciousness relate to the physical body – described as the famous mind-body problem or 'Cartesian dualism'.

This philosophical contemplation on the science of consciousness has, over the past decades, led to something of a revival of one of the oldest concepts in the field of the philosophy of mind, namely 'panpsychism'. Panpsychism has been on trend of late, although it actually dates all the way back to the works of Thales and Plato. It has found sympathy with philosophers and psychologists alike as a way to relate to consciousness. Panpsychism can be seen as encompassing a family of theories that hold our minds are fundamental and omnipresent features of reality. Everything in nature, from a teaspoon and a pebble on the beach to our own mystical minds, has some kind of consciousness, from the most primitive formation all the way up to the most highly developed human.

Maybe consciousness is the missing building block of the understanding of our universe – or even universes – or maybe it is, in itself, *the* fundamental building block of our reality. Whichever way it is approached, there seems to be something more to the story than simply information processing. If everything can be reduced to a simple world of material and we crack the code and reach some kind of explanatory end game we could, at first glance, seem to end up in a dystopia. On the other hand, we could also, of course, find ourselves on a path to some kind of eternal realm of bliss and divinity. Can we become aware of awareness itself? Can we tune into consciousness and bend our own reality? Can the stuff of consciousness evolve by itself or is it a fundamental truth that bits of information give birth to consciousness? One may come to the conclusion that, if we believe in consciousness, and then take it away, there would be nothing left.

Swedish philosopher Nick Bostrom has been among recent thinkers who have breathed fresh life into what has been dubbed the 'simulation hypothesis' or 'simulation theory'. Its popularity is illustrated by the increasing number of sci-fi movies, including *The Matrix*, tackling philosophical concepts such as the allegory of the cave and various historically driven theories of sceptical hypotheses, mysticism and illusionism – from 'Zhuang Zhou Dreams of Being a Butterfly' by Zhuangzi to the Indian philosophy of Maya. The modern version, revitalised by Bostrom, proposes that all of reality, including the Earth and the totality of the whole universe, could in fact be artificial and simulated; a giant virtual simulation running on some kind of quantum super-computer. As difficult as it is, in our everyday experience of the strangeness of reality, to find arguments against not living in a simulation, the proposal merely moves the problem up one more level. This is best expressed through the simple comment made by Tesla founder Elon Musk while discussing reality, the simulation theory and technology with podcaster Joe Rogan. Rogan confronted Musk with the question of what he would ask the machine if he knew that we were all living in a simulation. Musk's answer was simply, 'What is outside of the simulation?'

With so many differing viewpoints, it becomes obvious that we still have many mysteries to solve. And so, disciplines move closer together, more people join the journey of research and discovery and technology speeds up. The importance of gaining a greater understanding of the nature of what it is to be human will also increase. The demand for people who have a deeper understanding of human beings will increase in step with new breakthroughs in engineering and technology. Art, psychology and philosophy become even more relevant.

Over the past years there has also been, after decades of neglect, an increased emphasis on experimenting with substances both synthetic and natural to go beyond the senses of our perceived reality. The field of deep meditation has rapidly gained public attention – the practice of directing awareness from the outside world to the interior world, in order to access what people refer to as higher levels of consciousness and a deeper state of mind.

Whichever way we lean, it has implications for how we operate and organise our society. One can sympathise with a mentally constituted world view – in which ideas about what it is to be human fuse with our perception and understanding of the wider world. A diverse group of metaphysical views may provide a plausible way in which to interpret the theories of relativity and evolution, revolving around the connection between minds. Yet, still, our acceptance of hard facts leads us to an intuition, a gut feeling, that we just can't convince ourselves, as George Orwell suggested, that two plus two could be five. The answer does actually seem to be four, leading us to the conclusion that maths could be fundamental. Objective truth would then be detached from the truth of our minds.

In the business world, in which consumerism flourishes and individualism and materialism are driving forces, it is easy to forget that the underlying forces that hold everything together are not detached from the models and systems we have created, be they the market economy, money, stocks or capitalism. The business world makes no sense without human beings to perceive and to build stories around it.

Now is the time to move towards a more holistic view of how we build our society through our economic systems. We need digital enlightenment to guide us when, often, we get the feeling that we are rather heading towards some kind of 'endarkenment'. But it is just this – how we feel, our emotions, and our sensory experiences – that lie at the very heart of how we organise human life, arrange trade and manage businesses. The taste of a strawberry, the feeling of a paper cut; our anxiety, fear and arousal. All this is a part of being a Mensch – a conscious, creating and participating being.

If we simply do not know which one path to follow, we should be open instead to looking at various disciplines as we continue our journey towards wisdom. We should welcome new participants to the debate.

In engaging in philosophical contemplation we can free ourselves from what we hold to be self-evident – our *Selbstverständlichkeiten*, and move on to understand the world we live in.

CHAPTER 2: IN SEARCH OF A NEW STORY

We should all start with an intrinsic interest in growing and developing – to learn how to learn.

For that we need a new *Weltanschauung* – a different way of perceiving the world. We should open our senses to the obvious and pay attention to the signals in the ordinary. *What is going on right now and right here*? If we tune in, there is a chance that we can become aware of the paradoxes of our time and see the underlying forces of change in the making.

The world becomes more local and yet, at the same time, we desperately need more globalisation to counteract ecological collapse and the challenges of the digital tsunami. As the trust in traditional systems falters – be it in educational models, outdated party-political structures or an economy built around finite structures and models – we must seek a new understanding. Only if we understand the underlying forces at work in our world can we think and act. A new digital enlightenment, paired with new political and educational structures, must lead us to create a society of understanding in order to cope with the forces of change.

The problem is that many people get stuck in *Selbstverständlichkeiten*, their own absolutes. Experts in a particular subject matter can't look beyond their own field; they get tied up in their own view of the world, in trying to become a master of a particular discipline. But nothing can be taken in isolation today; everything is connected. The moment you claim to be an expert, you are stuck in the past. Instead, you must seek to follow a much broader approach and be open to new ways of learning and embrace the art of being wrong. One of the most crucial skills you can learn is that of permanently challenging your own knowledge and being open to new views. As mentioned earlier, this is all about keeping an open mind, feeling like a beginner. I have often referred to this as being a 'professional amateur'. You put in the work of a professional, yet retain the curious playfulness of being an amateur seeking to progress. We can also examine what underpins this idea.

Elon Musk has recently breathed fresh air into what has been called 'first principle thinking', which has also become his underlying philosophy for success. The media has also picked up this old philosophical tradition practised by Musk and other visionary entrepreneurs. First principle thinking derives from ancient philosophy and proposes a basic proposition or an assumption that cannot be deduced from any other proposition or assumption. In the school of Aristotle the first principle comes from the 'first cause', referring to the underlying physics of the material world. 'Something coming out of nothing'; an idea that takes us on the philosophical journey of physicalism, idealism, panpsychism and various views of how the world came to be, as we discussed in the previous chapter.

It is this search that takes us beyond physics and mathematics to the field of philosophy that is again becoming a fundamental tool for our progress in the world, one that can help us free ourselves from our old ways of thinking in order to get a fresh perspective on the world. From here we can create new stories. We can shape our own future. 'To future' is now a verb, it is something we do.

Business as (un)usual

Everything in the business world is built on a story. It is the story that we are buying when we purchase a product. When I grab my Coke Zero at Zurich airport that, by the time you read this, probably costs almost ten euros, it is me buying into the story of Coke. It is an agreement between me, the sales department and marketing division and the brand that is corporate Coke. It is not real, it is fiction – a story in which I drink some kind of dark soup (most likely not the healthiest alternative out there). It is a story I buy into, an agreement with the corporate structure, the legal department and the complete tale of Coke. Today, the product alone is not enough. If the stories, however, are based on the true account of a journey of creating value and solving problems, then you are on to something. That is why, now, we need a new story to believe in.

Most of us, however, don't dare to talk about our own visual images, those that take up space in our heads, and we don't bring our story to life with our pictures. But you should remember this: no story is born perfect. Your story will grow stronger with every telling and soon people will follow you on your journey. We must believe in something bigger. At first this story is small and flawed and then, as we shape and adapt, it gets stronger and stronger. It is this story – not the 'b2b' or 'b2c', the products and services and various buzzwords we come up with – is what humans buy into. *It is the relationship, the story and the magic.*

Crucial to our success is defining which problem we want to solve. Very often the economic impact – what can be sold – is the sole focus of the story, rather than solving problems and trying to improve the state of the world. There is an emphasis on innovation, true, and we do need innovation to make progress. But what is innovation? In simple terms it can be defined as doing more with less – an efficiency game or the core of an action economy, if you like. Innovations change the world, as we adapt and adopt and develop products, model by model. So, yes, innovation is crucial and it is the one part of change that we are actually pretty good at. Technology is continuously updated by new ways of doing things, creating attributes that follow a path and make our lives easier.

But what is also needed is the second, essential, part of change. This part tackles the way in which we see the world. It is all about our perception and how, by reframing how we look at the world, we can carve out a completely new approach. Innovation requires action, while changing perception – reframing – needs *thinking*. Do you have a regular 'thinking hour'? The one time, set in stone, that you block in your diary? Just as you make your regular visits to take care of the 'physical scum' – the body, as described by the late Stephen Hawking – you also need time for exercising the mind. We run a marathon, we go to the gym, we drink smoothies and do yoga. But are we doing any bench pressing for our minds? Just as we set our daily or weekly sessions of physical exercise in our diaries, we should set aside time for practising thinking, even if it means just sitting for one hour and staring at a white piece of paper. The point is this – we can actually learn and practise this thing called 'thinking'.

We are caught up in reactive mode – adapting and adding – but to make fundamental progress through a new way of perceiving the world, we must also learn to slow down. In practising the 'thinking hour', just as an artist works at their canvas, we will learn to master the art of doing nothing. Of course, this, like anything else, is not accomplished overnight. But in practising the art of thinking, it is essential that we actually set aside time to do nothing.

The world is not always logical, nor is it at its core explicable; sometimes things make no sense at all. We need a functioning preparation mode to improve our adaptability, to make ourselves more resilient and to find the courage to move from the known to the unknown, to discover the 'unknown unknowns' hidden in plain sight in the absoluteness of the ordinary. This is the essence of what we can and must seek. This is when philosophical contemplation is helpful and applying regular 'thinking hours' can be helpful.

It is not that management methodologies, strategies, KPIs and structures, leadership training and various tools for business success are not needed. It is just that they are not enough. There are also new paths to be explored.

Today, the role of the controlling and overseeing manager is obsolete. So many middle and senior managers find themselves in this position right now. They ask themselves, 'What am I actually doing?' Technology is taking over management and the only real boss is the project. We are only as successful as the project we are working on. There is no top or bottom in the modern organisation, just a front and a back. We collaborate on making our input as good as it can be and – through being culturally strong and agile (meaning having a stable and clear process rather than opting for chaos and absolute freedom) – comes high-quality output.

Leadership is everywhere, as are playgrounds that enable exploration and mistakes – very much like the practice field for a soccer team; a place for staff to try out new ideas without existential consequences. You can't have a disruptive doctor taking on open-heart surgery, nor can you have a hyper-creative pilot trying out new landing techniques on a plane full of passengers, but we all need a space to practice, room for exploration and play. We need somewhere where the process is trusted and the result is an outcome rather than being pre-defined. It is not about one thing or the other, but both at the same time. We need management, technology and stability – but also new horizons and more chaos.

Building the quantum economy

The fall of the Berlin wall symbolised the end of the cold war and the triumphant advance of liberal democracies. Nineteen-ninety might have been the year of freedom, but today we see that time as not marking the freeing of humanity, but more as creating a burden. We are now stuck with what we thought at the time would be our freedom. Social media portals and communication channels flood our lives with information and we are the ones left screaming for attention. We have become exploiter and exploited in one single person. We have become the product we are consuming, and the third parties – advertisers – finance our self-exploitation while triggering our consumption. Needless to say, when the efficiencies of exponential technologies put pressure on old business models, the outcome can be a barbaric and raw form of hypercapitalism. A modern-day Robin Hood is required to reduce the gap between rich and poor and move the world towards dynamic equilibrium. We must take on a new path towards caring for all stakeholders, our society and our planet as a whole, as opposed to living in this winner-takes-all scenario – with the finite loss being borne by the many.

We have built a fragile society – a house of cards that is falling apart due to the conditions we ourselves have imposed, stuck in our *Selbstverständlichkeiten*. Traditional structures and institutions have been confronted with the birth of new structures, models and systems. The outcome may be that they tear down the house altogether. The lack of trust in traditional institutions comes from the fact that they are set in a rigid and finite form – the world and the economy must now be seen as something infinite.

We live in the action economy, the attention economy, the new economy: there have been many terms used over the years, but now we need a (new) new model for our economy. The economy is the operating system of society and should serve as a stabilising factor. Today's form needs to aim for some kind of dynamic balance. We experience depression alongside prosperity and we need more local identification and regional self-sufficiency and, at the same time, we need hyper-globalisation, connecting the world to work better together. It is a complex dynamic. What was once one or the other is now both at the same time. This is how the world operates; the economy cannot simply be reduced to numbers. It is a pendulum that swings continuously between extremes yet, at the same time, it is something fluid and lively. We live in parallel in our society. When economists say, 'Times ahead look great,' often the next crisis will hit. Now is not the time to set out long-term visions and strategic plans or, at least, not that alone; we need a positive, 'infinite' vision and, at the same time, we need to take short-term action.

If we want to understand society, we must rethink the economy.

The old economy is dead, but so is what was called the 'new economy'. The Silicon Valley dream – of infinite growth with luxury objects and heroes of economic freedom and independence – cannot and will never work for everyone. What we need to do is to strive for a more balanced society; a humanistic approach to upgrading capitalism and a model that is built on the belief of working for the future – a new model for posterity. This is what I call the 'quantum economy'. But why should we stick with capitalism, though, one might ask? Isn't there another option?

Capitalism has been a working model. It has provided growth and prosperity in so many ways, but it undoubtedly has its limitations and flaws in its current form and needs to be re-balanced. We should upgrade the economy – ensure it serves society and becomes humanistic. Or, as the Dalai Lama famously put it, 'Capitalism is a working model, but it lacks compassion.' This new, humanistic capitalism is what I believe can help us reconnect to what it means to be a human being and to secure stability and support in redistributing wealth and resources for all. Our world is not finite and absolute; it is fluid and its possibilities are limitless. It is an 'inter-world', a world of interconnectivity and interdependence. The economy is not a game to be played in terms of winning and losing but it should be one you can play as long as you are able.

In the quantum economy – at least, in affluent, western, welfare states – we will reduce our consumption and learn how to cherish what we have and practise modesty. We will aim to recycle materials by cutting the distance between customer and producer, putting the pressure on the producers to own their product throughout its life-cycle, reintroducing every part of it back into a new life-cycle – cradle to cradle – as we now see the emerging perfect circular economy as the only way forward. Anything finite must be made infinitely usable.

Lightbulbs with limited lifespans will be replaced by long-lasting products that can be recycled and even the energy costs will be calculated for each model. In the future, we will pay for the light used rather than for the lightbulb – energy will form part of the sustainable economic model. Everything will be paid for as a service, as responsibility is transferred from the product to the provider.

The third part of the quantum economy (after reduce and re-use) will be the main driver of new jobs – the creation of new business models. We will need a completely new perception of how to operate and how to see the world. A utopian dream? No. More a call to action. Out of the many inspiring stories that I have heard during my endeavours in creating *Philosophy@Work*, one particularly fascinating example is that of the owner of a market-leading producer of chemical pesticides in Germany – Reckhaus. The company are expert in killing bugs but decided to confront themselves with the question of how much the life of a fly is worth. After a long night the company's ethos was turned upside-down. The boxes of its product were marked 'Caution – product kills valuable life' and with that, they began to change. Reckhaus went on to be nominated for a German sustainability award in 2021 and, today, they are still doing well and operating by asking themselves just one question: 'What can insects do for *us*?' Reckhaus had realised insects are highly valuable and threatened. The focus of the company is now to raise awareness of insects. Today the company – building on its sixty-year tradition – has one target: saving more than killing.

The quantum economy is not finite. Just as professor of history and religion James P. Carse described in his 1986 book, *Finite and Infinite Games* – the quantum economy is about continuous posterity – infinity. It is about playing as long as you can. Carse uses the example of the game of soccer, in which eleven players meet and play against each other for ninety minutes. There is a finite result with a set of rules. The business world – and society in general – is completely unlike that clearly defined game. Some companies bring 400,000 players, others twenty. Some define the rules in months, others in years. The business world is funky and much more like quantum physics than the fixed and rigid linear and finite models we have, to date, built the economy around. We, human beings, are the gluons that tie it all together. The strong forces that are pushing and pulling. We live in a state of interdependence, in which everything is connected to everything. The declaration of independence turns into a declaration of interdependence. The economy and our world in general are not predictable and explainable. Companies are innovative until they stop being innovative. The world that we experience – and the business world itself – follows more our understanding of quantum physics. We do not live in a deterministic world, but rather a world of potentiality.

The art of doing business must be re-discovered and we need new stories that we can believe in. We are now all story-makers. What we need are true, bold and courageous entrepreneurs setting out on journeys to solve problems, re-frame and re-form, and create new stories. Instead of layering complexity through middle-man structures and various sales-driven, 'value-adding' attributes and transaction-driven models, we must find new ways to capitalise. We must leave the weeds behind. I envision a new journey, like that taken in the post-World War II era in Germany, that gave birth to so many world-class companies – the hidden champions – and the 'economic miracle' that was sparked by a hacker-like mentality of real entrepreneurship. The goal must be to build something not for the sake of the pitch deck or the early exit, but for the sake of true, pure entrepreneurship and for making a contribution of value and for building prosperity for posterity.

Becoming a leader of change

Start with why – as many know, this is also the title of Simon Sinek's bestseller. Everyone should start by defining their own purpose, a 'why'. Something to believe in. When your 'why' is authentically lived and communicated, others will join you. How does this work in relation to corporate life? If you hire people to make money, they will leave you when they can make more money or as Sinek himself puts it, 'If you hire people just because they can do a job, they'll work for your money. But if you hire people who believe what you believe, they'll work for you with blood and sweat and tears.' You need to have a vision and a purpose for people to buy into.

But we also need 'why' in the other sense, that of the art of asking questions. We do not only need more information and big data, we also need more questions. In the time of absolutes the expectation is that everyone should have the answer; the one, defining response – look important, make sure you have an answer. That is business as usual, as it's always been done. Instead, you should dare to be the one asking questions. If you do, you will discover that you weren't the only one who didn't know, but you were the only one who admitted it. Others answer for answering's sake, trying to look important. They want to fill what they believe their role to be and hustle, trying to reach the top of the value chain by destroying others or by sitting it out, just waiting. The simple art of asking questions can and will change your life for ever.

As a leader, being genuinely interested and open to other views must lie at the core of striving for growth. As all voices get louder, we all realise that being a human means more than acquiring the next fancy car or eating the next meal. Everything is connected and the business world is not detached from life in general. Love, compassion, unity, togetherness; something to believe in is part of the totality of living in the world of business. Today, business it is not about managing your work-life balance but establishing your life-life balance.

Leadership is also about 'soft skills'. But what is described as 'soft' is actually hard: showing emotion, opening up, standing in front of a group of people and feeling that weird tickling in the stomach when you are caught off-guard or simply do not understand what the other person is talking about; that is the real deal. How you handle such a situation is essential in defining your business culture. Saying the words, 'I don't know,' is really tough in an environment in which you are supposed to show power and to know it all. Forget domination and power – concentrate on *strength*. Showing the strength and courage to say, 'I have no idea, I really need to look into this and read up. Can we meet tomorrow and discuss again as this is new to me?' *That is real strength*. Opening up this vulnerability is the key to developing new relationships and trust. It is where creativity and radical innovation are born. Tapping into human factors – what it means to be a Mensch – will be essential for leadership and the success of any organisation in the future.

Do you have the courage? The courage and the strength to create, build and strive? The courage and the strength to empower people and enter the unknown? What is it that is holding you back? What are we afraid of? What would you do if you were not afraid? Many of the things that we consider frightening actually turn out to be a source of growth. We often look back at what we thought were terrifying moments in life and realise they weren't actually that bad and we would have been better off embracing the situation and taking it as a cue to grow.

The good thing is that there seems to be something going on. A slow waking up and transition to some kind of conscious revolution. We are now facing a window of opportunity as more and more of us start to look inwards for answers and try to balance our internal world with the external world. Even top executives now turn inwards and ask themselves fundamental philosophical questions: 'What is a Mensch?' 'Is this all there is to life?' 'Why do I see the world as I do?' 'What can I really know and what is there to hope for?' From a world of technological reactionaries, there is a wave of real, purpose-driven leaders emerging.

Becoming a leader of change is a journey for all of us, characterised by a process of constant trial and error on the path towards growth as a human being. We can look at this as a never-ending journey; along the way, we tackle the world we live in by getting a better understanding of how we see it.

We are handed two lives. The first one ends when we realise life is finite. Then we understand that we are all privileged to share valuable moments on this planet, to exploit its infinite wonders and possibilities.

The first step is to seek to understand, to be open to other perspectives. This is when we have a chance to develop a greater *Weltverständlichkeit*. We question our path and choose our reality. We can rethink our definition of wealth, value and growth; for many of us, this process provides a reality check or simply a chance to achieve a conscious awakening. Following such experience, we tap into our interior life – what it means to be a human being. In connecting the outside world with the inside world, we build a symbiotic relationship to reach a flow state of connectedness and interdependence.

We can then cope with what, in quantum physical terms, can best be referred to as the collapse of the wave function – the outside and inside world are brought together in a state of unity. This is the fundamental challenge in life. It is in doing this that we experience how we can change our reality and become leaders of change.

You can develop the art of leadership by serving as a mentor and helping your fellow human beings to cope with the challenges life throws at us. Leaders of change are practising how to learn while, simultaneously, teaching their peers how to teach.

Change follows when we take care of the little things and understand that the little things are actually the big things that make a real difference. I love technology and strongly believe we are at the beginning of a second quantum paradigm – bringing quantum theory to life – that will take us to places we cannot even imagine. Yet still we, the Mensch, form the basis of it all, little gluons that tie together those strong forces that push and pull at everything. Creating your own future means you should go beyond – or should I say underneath? – laws of maths, and physics. You should be seeking something more fundamental – namely, *philosophy*. This doesn't just mean taking an analytical journey to interpret the works of the great philosophers of the past. It is more about learning their way of thinking and applying that to your current time. Your essential task is to apply these ways of thinking to what we call our everyday reality. This is taking philosophy to work; this is practical applied philosophy.

Why Philosophy@Work matters

A couple of years ago, Stuart Crainer (the co-founder of Thinkers50) and I reached out to a group of the world's leading management and business thinkers, many of whom are listed among the Thinkers50 bi-annual awards, the Oscars of management thinking. We wanted to see if there was a narrative within the field regarding the way that the business world relates to philosophy. We were surprised by how many of these leading intellectuals have applied philosophical concepts to their work over the years.

We have begun seeing relationships between business and philosophy and it becomes clear that the old certainties – the fixed, defined world, based on its set models and the structures that we have bought into – can be replaced by a fluid, dynamic, unpredictable – and more confusing – interconnected set of relations, more similar to the underlying laws of modern physics than the given models we have been used to. In order to navigate and unpack our discoveries, it is helpful to engage in philosophical contemplation. We can then better cope with ethical questions, with seeking a new perspective and, basically, we can bring more of an open mind to our work, to question everything in our corporations.

As I have already stated in this introduction, philosophy is something practical, it is something we *do* and it is about activation – the art of being wrong. While I have great respect for analytical and academic forms of philosophy, to me philosophy is something fundamental underlying our physical laws and mathematical structures. Philosophy is that space in which ideas, the mental world and our vision of our reality are brought to life or, at least, where we are supported to continue our search for wisdom in various disciplines. My goal is to breathe life into a new form of continental philosophy, a Europeanism building on great thinkers of the past and their attempts to find explanations through philosophical concepts. Kant, Hegel, Nietzsche, Arendt – even Heidegger and Wittgenstein; the list is long.

The whole concept of learning underpins my life and is based around my general curiosity and interest. It is true that if you approach things with interest you automatically become interesting. It is a proven fact that interesting people are loved – we all like to work with and share with interesting people. It is therefore those who are interested – the conscious and aware – those of us with the habit of always seeking out new learning – who act as a sponge for talent, connecting people and acquiring the most useful knowledge. The challenge in today's world is not learning how to do things – there are thousands of books and pages of content devoted to how-to guides. It is much more today about *what* to do and *why* do it?

The articles you will read here are designed to inspire and you can return to them or simply let them serve as a first encounter with new ideas and thoughts. This book also sets out to be a source of inspiration for aspiring entrepreneurs and leaders looking for guidance on their journey through the twenty-first century. I have left it up to each author to start the dialogue in the way they want and together they will provide a spark for holistic thinking and a starting point for developing new questions in the world of business.

You will find contributions that have been made not by philosophers but management practitioners, leaders in academia and some of the most sought-after thinkers in their fields. Together, our job will then be to expand on these ideas, write more essays and think further, bridging the philosophy of the past with our challenges in the business world of today. Along with the science and technology of tomorrow, we will all move towards a humanistic and sustainable capitalism.

This journey has been filled with laughter and inspiration and I have enjoyed gathering the thoughts you are about to read. Some of the conversations went on for hours and the interviews in the book reflect the edited essence of our dialogues. Other, short encounters sparked new discussions and further collaboration that has led to new paths of thinking which will be represented in future works.

What is *Philosophy@Work*? It is a concept that helps us to cope with change and supports business leaders in navigating and creating in the twenty-first century. It also provides analytical skills and takes the approach of building upon a revitalised continental European tradition of thinking. It offers a holistic approach to deal with both the challenges of the world and our own perceived reality. The result is an analytical approach combined with holistic understanding that relates to humanity as a whole, as much as for each of our own, individual developmental journeys.

PART I

SPARKING PERSONAL DEVELOPMENT

BECOMING AWARE THAT THE PATH IS EVERYWHERE

Ayelet Baron

This is dedicated to the millions and millions of people on this planet of ours who have yet to find their bold and beautiful voice and feel trapped in a world that forces them to merely survive when the opportunity is there to thrive.

> To obtain the truth in life, we must discard all the ideas we were taught and reconstruct the entire system of our knowledge.
>
> René Descartes (1596–1650)

Today, we have thousands of experts predicting what the future of work will look like – and the impact of the next industrial revolution – but most of us no longer know what 'work' means in a digital world. Many have been led to fear our jobs will be replaced by technology and robotics. But we are having very limited conversations about how all of our systems need to shift for us to have healthy and fulfilling lives as human beings rather than just as workers.

Over the past decade, we have been reporting trends such as the advent of the sharing economy. But, in essence, many of the companies that have been hailed as part of this progressive new economy, still commoditise their workers. The sharing that is taking place is still stuck on an old business model that provides an illusionary sense of progress. And if you talk to someone in a country that is having huge economic challenges, like Greece, they would tell you that sharing – opening their homes to strangers – is simply part of life and not a massive monetisation model.

And, of course, companies like Uber, Airbnb and others have transformed our lives. If I had told you, just ten years ago, that you would get into a stranger's car, having given them your credit card information, and they would take you to your destination, and that you would entrust your children's safety to that stranger, you would have told me I was insane. But when you use such sharing platforms yourself and talk directly to the workers, you understand the need for better financial sharing business models that respect everyone's lives, not just the company's bottom line. There is hope with the rise of cryptocurrencies, but only when we put the human in the centre of the model.

I was invited to be on a panel at a conference for investors and, when the moderator reached out to me to discuss what I planned to share, he made it clear that his audience did not want to hear about the human aspect except in terms of the cost of recruiting and retaining talent. He said that there was no room to discuss the impact on society and people on his panel.

The longer we try to kill or suppress our humanity in the name of business and profit, the further we get from building a healthy world in which we could thrive. That moderator's audience may only be interested in the bottom line today, but how long will it take people to speak out about what truly matters? How many systems will need to collapse before we infuse ourselves with common sense? What will take each of us to realise that life is a daring adventure in which work and the bottom line are merely part of a much bigger whole?

Modern-day addictions are available to all

So many people today have been inflicted with the infectious disease of busyness that is spreading like wildfire. They blame technology for accelerating the pace of their lives and believe they need a detox to have a life. We have become an increasingly busy and lonely society, forgetting how to connect deeply with ourselves and each other.

Levels of loneliness and depression around the world are sadly at an all-time high. In 2017, the UK government appointed a minister of loneliness, as more than nine million people in the country admitted feeling lonely, according to a report published by the Jo Cox Commission on Loneliness. The study found that loneliness is worse for your health than smoking fifteen cigarettes a day. It was determined that loneliness is associated with the greatest factors leading to cardiovascular disease, dementia, depression and anxiety. Dr Vivek Murthy, a former US surgeon general, wrote an article for the *Harvard Business Review* in 2017 arguing that loneliness needed addressing in the workplace.*

So, what is loneliness? The *Oxford English Dictionary* defines it as being solitary, without companionship and isolated. An article in *Psychology Today* in 2014 addressed more deeply the impact on the psyche: loneliness does not depend on how many friends or relationships you have but whether you feel emotionally and/ or socially disconnected from those around you. It distorts our perception of relationships; devaluing them and making us withdraw even further. The article even stipulated that loneliness

---

* Vivek Murthy, 'Work and the loneliness epidemic', *Harvard Business Review*, 26 September 2017, available at www.hbr.org/cover-story/2017/09/work-and-the-loneliness-epidemic

is contagious in social networks and attracts and compounds the misery of seclusion and exclusion.

How do you become lonely and isolated? You cut yourself off from your family, you are not able to express your feelings and you feel as if you are not being heard. You are not feeling part of the team at work and you are unsafe in expressing or contributing to the group effort in your department. This leads to feelings of being unrecognised or unacknowledged and therefore unable to enjoy the celebration of success with your colleagues. You withdraw from society as you feel invisible and overlooked. These compounded feelings build and perpetuate as you feel you are the only one feeling this way. You are too busy or embarrassed to understand that you are not alone.

Feeling alone is the first place to start, believe it or not. Acknowledging where you are at in the moment is where you begin.

There is a magic pill for everything

Society readily medicates us whenever we slip off the page of the manual. We live in a world in which more and more people function on antidepressants to get through their daily lives. If you feel lonely or sad, there is a pill to take to help you take the edge off. There is an expectation and pressure to find a quick and speedy solution for whatever bothers you. There are hundreds of different types of antidepressants on the market that try to fix what ails you.

Why isn't anyone asking, 'Why are you feeling this way?' Socrates taught us centuries ago the power of asking questions. It is so important to identify the root cause, before reaching for a prescribed generic answer, to heal a deeper issue.

We have been taught to cherish the material world and anything tangible. We are conditioned to respect and take care of what is physical and real. Many people consume drugs like painkillers, swallowing a pill to take care of a headache. It is a quantifiable act because the headache disappears after a while. Pop a pill and it can perform and take care of invisible pain. Over a period of time, you form the belief that every time you get a headache you grab an Aspirin to deal with it. Now society has a pill or supplement for almost anything that ails you. Did you ever stop and think that maybe you are simply dehydrated? Perhaps the headache is information, trying to tell you that you need to drink more water and nurture your body.

What's your story?

Every feeling comes from a story. A story in this respect is an incident or episode in your life that made a huge impression on you. Healing yourself following a personal story that impacted you negatively can be extremely difficult and, sometimes, very painful.

We are creatures of habit and, if you are willing to look back, you will see a pattern emerge in the form of the kind of romantic partner, friend and organisation to which you gravitate; the same being true of the communities in which you live, your workplaces – as well as the conflicts you attract.

To take responsibility for your happiness you need to go back and look for the cause of your pain – the original wound – and see how it is repeating in the present moment. This is imperative if you want to heal, or interrupt and stage an intervention to prevent the pattern repeating again. The process requires of you that you revisit and confront one of the most difficult times in your life and challenges you to look at the incident from a different perspective. Being able to look honestly at your problems and see the opportunities within them allows you to have a greater understanding of the lesson you need to learn.

Society teaches us that being angry is not acceptable. But anger is a fundamental emotion, along with sadness, happiness and love.

It is absolutely OK to feel angry but it is important to monitor how you express your anger. It is very healthy to understand your anger and it is crucial to become aware of what triggers it. Suppressing anger and storing it inside is very unhealthy; like a pressure cooker, contained anger can explode at any moment.

Being sad is part of being human, like being happy, but you don't have to live in your house of sadness forever. You can become aware of why you feel sad by going back to that original wound and healing yourself. You can also control the amount of hurt you are exposed to. Take a note of the news programmes you are watching, the stories you are listening to and the friends and colleagues you are hanging out with. Do these sources share stories of inspiration? Are they relating stories of sadness about atrocities and injustices in the world? By changing the channel or selecting different people to befriend you make the choice of what kind of information you would like to receive.

Feel fear, but don't cultivate fear. Become aware of the difference between rational and irrational fear. Rational fear is one of the basic human necessity survival instincts. It will help protect you from touching a hot stove, stop you walking into oncoming traffic on a busy street or assist in avoiding a wild bear in the forest.

Irrational fear is the perceived fear inside your head that has been conditioned since childhood by family, friends, teachers and other authority figures; anyone who triggered the recording, 'You are not good enough' or, 'You don't have enough' in your mind. Fear has become an unspoken epidemic from which many want release – but don't know how.

Some people are learning to step out of their box of conformity and you too may be yearning to break free. But that feeling of freedom, which is totally unknown after so many years in captivity, can be scary.

It can be like being a wild animal that has adapted to being taken care of while being nursed back to health. It is then very unsure and fearful of being set free after months of rehabilitation. The open plains or the majestic mountains are very daunting. It feels uncertain of being able to find its flock or herd and doesn't know how it will survive when it crosses the invisible line from its confinement. Ultimately, however, its instincts kick in and it runs towards freedom.

Do you remember the source?

When you look at nature, you see change happens constantly as the animal and plant kingdoms interact every second. It is a natural process, but one that humans try to manage and control. For example, think about the billions of dollars that have poured into parts of the world for humanitarian aid during your lifetime. Safe water continues to be a scarce commodity, one in five children go to bed hungry, and disease and suffering is still very prevalent on our planet. It is not something that can be addressed by writing a cheque every year. Yes, cash helps, but it does not yield sustaining and lasting results as charities still operate within a very broken system that is dispensing Band-Aid solutions. There are approximately ten million NGOs worldwide operating in the humanitarian sector and, while we have seen vast improvements around the globe, the number of people suffering from hunger, disease and homelessness is still staggering.

We have to go deeper. It begins with the self – you, me and I. We have to change. We have to be the change before we can see the change in the world. Why? Because life is changing every second of every day and we are the point of reference from which our life flows. We therefore need to adapt and change to be able to make a difference in our lives and in our communities. We need to change our mental models and remember that each of us is a strong creator and we are here to thrive, not merely survive.

No one wants to be saved or fixed and yet that is what we practise and teach. The hardest work you will ever do starts with you – self-examination. No robot, software program, or app will be able to take on this task for you. The buck stops with you! When you can stop warring with yourself you will be able to reach a healthier vantage point and can then step out in the world and create better systems and structures that take into account every living being on the planet. When you stop consuming unhealthy beliefs and products, you will be able to create new paths with other pioneers who want to co-create a better world.

More and more people of all ages are seeking greater purpose and meaning in their lives. The material things no longer seem enough to satisfy or bring lasting happiness. How many people wake up every day and sit in traffic to arrive at a job that does not fulfil them? All because they need to pay their bills and feed their families. Was this the purpose – to raise kids to be held hostage by duties and obligations so they can be labelled responsible adults? Do we not realise that, once we join a highly congested route to work, we ourselves are the traffic we complain about?

There are many unspoken addictions all around us in our society today. One of the most prevalent is the addiction to drama. We are constantly fed excitement through television shows, news media, film and social media platforms. Why? Because it feeds the adrenaline that makes us feel alive. It connects us with other human beings as we interact to share the thrill. Yet, how many of us pause to consider what this does to us as individuals and our lives?

We feel a constant yearning for more thrills to feed the high and increase our sense of exhilaration. The body reacts the same to fear and to excitement. Next time you watch a tragedy on the news or an amazing sporting feat, notice if there is any difference in your emotional body. Is there any contrast in the sensations?

So, like any addict, the focus becomes a need to find the next high and what can be more stimulating than to share our own personal dramas with others? Yes, the stories meet a need to vent and be heard but they also provide the addictive high as we relive the incident or event that created the sense of excitement or fear in the first place. Notice, also, how your stories become embellished as you go deeper into how you were wronged or the need to blame someone else for your circumstances.

Addiction is addiction. It does not matter if it is coming from outside or from your personal life. There is no difference. What matters is that you take responsibility for creating a more fulfilling life. You can teach yourself to stop the cycle of drama, blame and judgement. You can cease looking for meaning in drama and find a new meaning that invigorates you. Life will become purposeful and being high on life itself will give you a whole new reason for living.

Every thought, every action and every reaction matters more than you can imagine. Within each moment, you hold immense power to change your reality, not solely by what you do, but through who you are becoming.

Everything is here to be discovered

We are living in extraordinary times and what seems too often to be impossible can become possible. There are no manuals or roadmaps to where we are headed. You have already been given abundant tools, including imagination, courage, fear and hope and the rest is up to you to create and produce.

Our world continues to go through dramatic change, improbable advancements, and game-changing breakthroughs. Public personalities will continue to be hailed or criticised. Internal wars will be won and lost. And, at the same time, there will be a growing realisation that people, like you, can transform the world, when you start seeing the invisible line that is holding you hostage – a line created by fear, sadness or loneliness.

Many of us are now realising that we have been living inside a prison of invisible walls that has either been constructed through years of societal conditioning of how life should be, or has been self-inflicted through our own belief systems and stories. There is an increasing desire to break free from this prison. For many, it is hard to admit how stuck they are through fear – a fear of being judged by others. Yet those they fear, who criticise them, are also incarcerated by their fears. It takes courage to break free from the walls manufactured by society and discover who you truly are outside the lines.

Unlike most jails, being stuck in life does not include guards or physical bars to keep you imprisoned. The only person who can release you or give you parole is you. But the box is not really a jail; you don't have to ask anyone for permission. This is the time to be curious, to get in touch with your imagination and to find your courage and boldness. It is about finding your path, your deep purpose that will propel you and find a way out of the insane rat race that humanity has constructed, telling you how to live your life.

No one really knows. No one has the answers. No matter how much they will try to convince you they have the answer to reach nirvana.

It is part of our deep societal conditioning not to question but to accept the lifestyle we were born into. Yet it is your right to find your voice and take the life you choose. Of course, you cannot snap your fingers and overnight become a professional golfer or chef. You must first become aware of why you may be feeling trapped. When you can ignore your irrational fear, you will find a way to break out and explore the life that is calling you.

And is it easy? How can it be, when from an early age, you are told by those older and more experienced than you to listen and do what the teacher says? If you were programmed to be good and do your homework and you were rewarded for following instructions, it will be more difficult to cross the invisible line.

This programming becomes instilled and rooted in your psyche while you develop, earning more praise with your parents' joy and happiness as you excel at school and they continue to share your achievements with friends and family.

No wonder as adults that we are scared to think for ourselves. We have been conditioned to feel responsible for our parents' happiness by being 'good' and are terrified of losing their love and appreciation if we do something different and outside the norm. Independence is dangerous and unsafe. What normal person likes danger?

The world is changing fast and providing you with abundant opportunities to become an empowered leader in your own life. The new, conscious leaders are starting to emerge around the world. They are rewriting the established code to create responsible companies with purposeful systems to generate industries that can contribute positively to sustain communities and lives.

These new CEOs acknowledge the fact that we cannot continue to pollute the Earth and the environment that supports our very existence. It is not sustainable, practical or wise. We have gone too far and now find ourselves in a state of fighting for survival.

The big question, the most important one, is how can we ensure financial sustainability with our ever-increasing population, to produce more humane practices for the collective good?

We can no longer prioritise profitability at the expense of poisoning and polluting the very environment that sustains all living beings on this planet. The Earth is the source of our life, not a resource to be exploited. And there is a growing awareness that it is not prudent to breathe polluted air, drink impure water, eat cancerous foods and think unhealthy thoughts. It is the acceptance of harmful and false beliefs that most urgently needs your attention.

Be careful not to remain stuck, waiting for instructions and hanging out on the sidelines, watching life go by. The path is open and freely accessible now to each of us. Don't believe the fallacy that someone else has the answers for you. Like any journey, the key is to begin. It doesn't really matter where, as there is no perfect entry point. When you have the mindset and curiosity of an adventurer, your world will be far easier to steer as you know there will be trial and errors along the way. You will be alert to the lows so they are not so low and the highs will not be so high; you can find a balance on the middle path with harmony.

The path is here

Our world needs you to be fully awake so you can live a life that matters to you and supports our collective on this beautiful planet. It requires an upgrade of your operating system to reject beliefs that pollute your mind and heart so you can free yourself from someone else's story of how you should show up. It is time for a revolution in the mindset of humanity and this begins with you! It is not so much that your body needs to be freed, but your mind and spirit together are eager to dance with nature and explore new opportunities.

There is no one else – each of us must come together to express our collective humanity. Wars break out, terrorist attacks occur and crime proliferates throughout our cities. This is happening in our world and it is created by us. We can sit back and ask for a meeting with the architects of humanity or we can reflect deeply on this one question, of what our own role is in the world. If we lead together, humanity can achieve unity.

We have been given this precious gift called life to explore our purpose and create what is meaningful, with authenticity and a sense of responsibility. We are architects of our own human life. It does not need to be a burden. That is always a choice.

When you awaken to your voice and purpose in life, reach out and connect. You never need to be alone – unless you choose to be – despite all the stories our current conditioning tells us in this regard. Paint your canvas with beautiful colours and find the other architects and twenty-first-century leaders who have given themselves permission to play on this abundant and beautiful planet with open hearts, a vivid imagination, and a belief that business is one of the biggest forces in the world that can start us on a journey to bring us together like never before.

SOCIAL FORENSICS: WHY A SELFIE IS MORE THAN JUST A PICTURE

Martin Lindstrom

A murder scene could be harder to crack without the presence of DNA. A single hair, a fingerprint, a skin flake; all form the minutiae that reveal a person's identity.

But did you know that our homes are filled with emotional versions of DNA? Namely, the way we place our shoes in the hallway, fill our fridge, hang our paintings and even use our toilet paper? All these and other, seemingly insignificant, clues, which I call 'small data', reveal an astonishing amount of information about our genuine selves.

Small data not only shows whether or not an individual is extroverted, self-confident, embarrassed about their lack of education or in ongoing battle with the people they live with, but it can also help determine the future of an entire company.

Small data is visible not only in our homes, but also online, on social media – especially Facebook. Alongside status updates, comments, videos, photos and the inspirational quotes we share on our homepages, is the sense of how our posts make us feel about ourselves. Any Facebook user who has ever scanned a friend's page knows how rarely it matches the reality of their life, but instead serves up an idealised image – how that person wants others to perceive them. Even if you don't know another Facebook user well, small data often serves up clues about that person's true self. For example, if in their profile picture the person is glancing away from the camera, nearly a decade of experience has taught me that they are more or less self-confident. A selfie profile picture, by contrast, typically implies that the person is lacking self-esteem. As for our Facebook cover photos, they reveal the places in which we find our peace, our oasis, the settings where, it might be said, we live out our dreams.

More intriguing yet, Facebook homepages have their literal counterparts in our physical houses or apartments, specifically in that part of the home I call the 'perception room'. Whether it's a living room or a kitchen, the perception room is generally located in a public area. It's where you find coffee-table books, sculptures, candles and other knick-knacks placed as conversation pieces. Women, specifically, will often hang things or create areas around the house for the very simple reason that they want to be asked about them – objects pertaining to their work or interests outside of the home. (This suggests to me that they feel unheard or in some other way excluded and that, rather than giving their opinions directly, they have to rely on a painting, a memento or even a fridge magnet to ignite a conversation they would otherwise feel too shy to initiate themselves.) In short, our perception rooms serve as our display windows for the world, in the same way Instagram, Pinterest, Twitter and Facebook accounts represent the digital equivalent of the inside of homes glimpsed from the street.

Entering a perception room, you'll invariably find it often reveals more about its owner than they want to admit and that may be the opposite of what they hope to convey. Is there an enormous shelf packed with hardcovers and paperbacks and wouldn't you conclude that its owner is probably exceptionally literate? In fact, in my experience, an ostentatious and over-crammed bookshelf reveals just the opposite – that the owner fears they are poorly read and the sheer number of books they have on display serves to compensate for their own insecurities. If, on the other hand, you come face to face with a colourful, oversized painting hanging from a prime wall, chances are good that you're dealing with a person with a high degree of self-confidence.

Where does the person keep their television remote control? If it's situated inches away from the television, either they are fearful of losing it or they are duplicating standard hotel room décor out of fear they are not 'doing the right thing'.

What about the way toilet paper hangs in a bathroom? Well, if the paper hangs from the top down, the man is usually in charge of domestic decision-making; if it is accessible from the bottom up, it's the woman.

As I've travelled around the world and had the opportunity to visit or live in thousands of consumers' homes, I've come to realise that, in a world punch-drunk on big data, we believe that the truth about anyone and everything can be revealed via terabytes and kilobytes. Yet an entire, equally valuable, world still remains accessible via smaller, more personal variations of data. Small data, in fact, arguably represents the next logical step on from big data in that, underneath all these bytes, we can now study up close what our digital and non-digital habits – Facebook postings, tweets, music and television consumption as well as every square inch of our homes, including our kitchens, bathrooms and clothing drawers – really say about us.

There's an old saying that if you want to study animals, don't go to the zoo, go to the jungle. It's time for us to open our eyes again, visit the places in which we live and observe the apparently insignificant – but altogether profound – small data that is right in front of us, right now. Can you see it?

The decisive moment

In a digital universe in which three hundred million Instagram photos are tagged with the word 'selfie', the practice of snapping our own photos has both cheerleaders and critics. Selfies are either harmless or they're apocalyptically ghastly. Selfie taking is a symptom of millennial self-absorption or precisely how an older generation would have behaved if they, too, had been armed day and night with a lightweight, portable camera.

What's less apparent to most digital commentators is the damage our global selfie-taking habit has done to the way in which we remember the signature emotions of our lives. Mostly shot at the moment of an emotional high, selfies not only freeze that moment, but they also compromise how we remember – or believe we remember – the past.

I spend three hundred days a year travelling from country to country, interviewing consumers for their insights on brands ranging from beer to detergent to cereal. In the course of my home visits – and with the owners' permission – I open drawers, peer inside refrigerators and analyse everything from their music to the television shows they watch to their photo libraries. Everywhere I look, of course, selfies flourish. But when I ask interviewees of all ages to go into further detail about the photos or to fill in missing context – what were you feeling? Why did you take that cheeseburger photo? Who is the boy in the green sweater? – I am always slightly shocked by how they remember almost nothing.

How did human memory work in the days before selfies?

Well, there are two kinds of memory – short-term and long-term. The former lasts anywhere from fifteen to thirty seconds. Long-term memory creation requires more work. The brain has to create new links between synapses. Lasting memory is either implicit, which refers to those things we know instinctively how to do – drive a car, brush our teeth – or explicit, which refers to things we are actively trying to recall. Explicit memory is broken down further into semantic memory (e.g. we know the capital of Maine is Augusta) or episodic (we remember the moment we saw that moose outside Augusta). The brain's storage area for new memories, the hippocampus, encodes whatever memories have a strong emotional content in ways that generally involve several of our senses, at which point these memories migrate further into the cortex where, whenever ignited, they gain in strength.

In contrast to everyday photos, which are about capturing memories, we take selfies to capture emotions – primarily our own – with the crucial extra consideration of how good we looked at the time. The problem is that, by starting and stopping in that moment, selfies suggest and inspire no more than the peak high of that moment itself. In a climate of instant gratification, there is no room for wider complexities of desire or anticipation. When we try to retrieve further memories of our vacation or the last two weeks of high school, we hit a wall. All those funny, random details and sensory impressions – that is to say the natural emotional feedback created by a multi-sensory experience and by time passing – are no longer there. Why? Because our emotional highs never made their way into our brains in the first place. They were uploaded instead onto a phone, the cloud or a hard drive where a program filed them automatically under 'Moments'.

Many people have observed that we no longer need to remember information. If the name of the second president, the third Teletubby, the fourth Supreme or the fifth Temptation escapes us, a cursory Google search resolves all. The problem is that we don't merely outsource political and pop-culture information to our devices – we are now outsourcing the core emotions of our lives.

Along the way, our imaginations take a beating too. A good analogy is the process whereby a book – say, *Gone Girl* or *The Hunger Games* – turns into a movie. If we find ourselves rereading the book, what happens? We envisage the characters with the bodies and gestures of Ben Affleck or Jennifer Lawrence. The more we tell someone a story, after all, the more fantastical yet bizarrely real it becomes. Real life suggests, whereas selfies freeze-dry experience. It's no wonder the people I asked about their selfies, from Brazil to Indonesia, looked back at me mostly blankly.

How does this affect how we recall the past? A middle-aged friend of mine who had a difficult, complicated relationship with her father has taken, since his death, to recalling the good times, the same process by which our memories allow us to recall our childhoods in a mostly flattering light. What happens if, thanks to selfies, those good times are pushed out of reach forever, frozen in the image of a fallen Christmas tree or a father's eternally disapproving frown?

HAPPINESS AT WORK

Henry Stewart

Happiness has been at the centre of philosophical discourse for over two thousand years. As André Comte-Sponville has written, 'If philosophy doesn't help to make us happy, or less unhappy, what's the use of philosophy?'

Buddha is quoted as saying, 'There is no path to happiness. Happiness is the path.' For Aristotle, happiness was the 'supreme good'. Plato wondered whether the question was even worth asking. 'What human being is there who does not desire happiness?'

Does happiness also have a role to play in business? In April 2005, investor Jerome Dodson decided, on the advice of the creator of CNN's 'best companies to work for' list, to create 'a fund that only invested in organisations where employees were really happy'.

Over the ten years to September 2018 the Parnassus Endeavor Fund has shown annual growth of 12.3 per cent a year, putting it in the top one per cent of US mutual funds. It has at times been the single best performing fund out of 1,303, according to ratings agency Morningstar.

Its stated focus is clear, 'The Parnassus Workplace Fund invests in companies with outstanding workplaces. The philosophy behind this fund is that companies whose employees love going to work will do better than companies with poor workplaces.'

Is it possible that this is the secret to business success? Never mind the business school focus on strategy and finance or the endless tomes on leadership. Could the route to success be to create an organisation in which people are happy and love coming to work?

At my company, Happy, our core principle is, 'People work best when they feel good about themselves.' And it is rare to find anybody who disagrees with that statement.

For me, it is therefore clear that the key focus of leadership in an organisation should be to create an environment in which people are able to feel good about themselves. When I ask audiences how many of them work in organisations where that is the case, I am lucky to get more than one in fifty to raise their hands.

I asked that question while on a panel with the chair of one of the UK's biggest retail companies. He instantly raised his hand and stated that was indeed the main focus of leadership in his 85,000-strong organisation. The company was John Lewis and Charlie Mayfield went on to explain that, at their last board meeting, they spent twenty minutes discussing the numbers and three hours discussing people and how to help them feel valued and motivated.

The John Lewis Partnership was set up by John Spedan Lewis in 1929 as a company owned by its workers. He set a constitution that states 'the happiness of its members' (its staff) is the partnership's ultimate 'purpose'. It is with that principle at its core that the partnership has grown from its London stores to occupy almost fifty sites across the country (and many more Waitrose outlets) and has been rated as the most admired company in the UK.

I like to ask people what their organisation would be like if the focus of leadership was indeed on making people feel good about themselves. The answers paint a positive picture: 'less office politics', 'more innovative', 'less sickness', 'people would stay longer', 'just a better place to work in'.

I do add a caveat about what we mean by 'happiness at work'. One of our clients delegated an individual to 'make people happy'. He brought in hula hoops and games and made people have fun. He measured happiness before and after and discovered that levels had gone down. The reasons are perhaps obvious. People do not like being made to have fun. And the happiness literature draws a distinction between hedonism, happiness in the moment (a fine glass of wine, a good piece of music) and eudemonism, which is more about long-term fulfilment.

At Happy, our aim is that our employees find joy in their work at least 80 per cent of the time. We ask people to measure their fulfilment and report it in their quarterly check-ins. I'm delighted to be able to say that some report they are getting to 90 per cent happiness.

We have found the key factors to be that people are playing to their strengths, being stretched and are trusted to make their own decisions. To enable that trust, one key factor we have adopted is pre-approval. It is common in most organisations for an individual or team to be asked to find a solution to a problem or to come up with a new service idea and report back for approval. We miss out the last step – we approve the solution before they have thought it.

An example: we had a youngster called Libby in charge of our café and she asked if she could change the whole look and feel. We didn't ask for a set of proposals or set up a group to work on it together. Instead, we agreed a budget and checked she'd understood the look and feel of the company and then left her to it, with support. The first I saw of the new look was when I walked in after she implemented it. It was fabulous, colourful and welcoming. But more important was the effect on Libby. How do you think she – nineteen years old and three months into her first job – felt walking into her café each morning? That certainly gave her a sense of joy.

What people don't like is being told what to do and neither do they appreciate micro-management or blame culture. What we believe makes people happy at work is to be doing something they are good at, having the freedom to make their own judgements and having managers who coach rather than tell; to feel listened to and valued.

All this is in line with the philosophy of happiness, which talks about using your strengths and about being stretched and challenged.

We live in a world of work where everybody seems busy, needs to be always available and suffers from an overload of information. Does philosophy have anything to teach us about how, in this kind of working environment, we can be happy at work?

A lot of the philosophical views on happiness concern being happy with where you are, which seems to contrast with the constant striving that characterises modern business. The Greek Stoic Epictetus said, 'Don't seek that all that comes about should come about as you wish, but wish that everything that comes about should come about just as it does and then you will have a calm and happy life.'

The eastern philosophies stress the importance of reflection. Buddha said, 'Meditation brings wisdom. Lack of meditation brings ignorance.'

In the work we do with companies, we find many workplaces in which people are very busy but often not that productive. They are overloaded with email, constantly interrupted and spend vast amounts of time in unproductive meetings. When we ask if they get time to reflect, they say, 'Where would we find the time?'

In her book *Radical Candour*, Kim Scott describes her time working at Twitter. She reports that Dick Costolo, CEO from 2010 to 2015, would schedule two hours' thinking time into his diary – every day. This was during the period of Twitter's most hectic growth, as it grew from thirty million active users to over 300 million.

This is backed up by research from Harvard Business School, which found that when people took fifteen minutes to reflect at the end of the day their productivity improved by an average 22.8 per cent. To produce these dramatic results, the participants simply spent that time writing in a journal to embed their learning from the day.

Frédéric Lenoir, in *Happiness: A Philosopher's Guide* (translated by Andrew Brown), describes two forms of reflection found in the literature. There is meditation – or mindfulness, in its modern secular form. Here you seek to still the mind and empty it of thoughts. And then there is reflection, where you take time out to think through how you are working – as in the Harvard study. You might go out to a café, you might record thoughts in a journal or you might just go for a walk in the park.

One UK school headteacher told me how she spends two hours on a Monday morning going for a walk in the woods with her dog. Crucially, she does this in her work time. 'It's the most productive time of my week, I get so many ideas.'

Jeena Cho, a lawyer who teaches others to practise mindfulness and meditation, describes the scientifically proven benefits: the practices reduce anxiety and implicit age and race bias, can prevent depression, improve cognition and help reduce distractions.

Lenoir argues that meditation and reflection are two different approaches and we need both. We need a time in our day when the brain is stilled. But we also need to take time in our day to step back and reflect.

Perhaps the ancients do still have wisdom for the modern world. If we can find time to meditate and reflect, we can both be less stressed and more effective at work. And if we can create happy workplaces, they will not only be better places for people to work but more effective too.

DEALING WITH LIFE'S LABYRINTH: THE ART OF SELF-REFLECTION

Kriti Jain

What does our typical day look like? I bet the first thing we all do after we wake up in the morning is to check our phones for the news, updates, and emails that we missed while we slept. And soon enough, we are on our way to the office – checking our calendars for the meetings, that never-ending to-do list and the social events scheduled for the day. Day after day, this cycle repeats and life moves on at a rapid pace.

A packed schedule does provide a sense of importance, purpose and self-worth. After all, being able to complain about 'being too busy', 'crazy schedules', 'always racing against time', 'feeling exhausted' and 'being in need of a holiday' does have a charm to it. Even though it might reflect poorly on one's time-management skills, people do find it cool to show off being tired and busy. Our human mind seems to conflate being busy with being important. Important people are busy. Busy people are important.

Take a careful look under the facade of busyness, however, and we can easily detect a life devoid of meaning, connection or contentment. Even though mankind is at its peak in terms of prosperity and scientific progress, issues of mental health such as depression and loneliness are at an all-time high. One can only wonder if it has something to do with mindless wandering across the various loops we have created for ourselves – the endless cycles in the arenas of home, office, social spaces and social media. We are constantly chasing – perhaps due to the fear of missing out.

You can add to this the issue of 'infoxication' – a portmanteau of 'information' and 'intoxication', signifying the overload of information – that has become a serious issue today. Our radios, music, and podcasts are on when we are driving, exercising, or even taking a casual walk. At home, discussions and debates are typically playing in the background as we prepare for dinner. There is constant bombardment of information. With this, our deep thinking is dulled and there is a constant feeling of 'being not enough' – others' lives seem to be fancier, prettier and happier.

In such a chaotic environment, there is an urgent need to diligently guard our time and our mind. One solution is to create deliberate pauses for self-reflection; a time where one is able to clear up all the cluttered writings on our mind's blank canvas in order to start painting on it all over again. Setting aside even as little as fifteen minutes every day with the goal of creating stability in the mind can help. *Bhagavad Gita*, the classical Indian scripture, has deep insights into how to do this. As an example, Arjun, the prince, asks his guide, Krishna, about the signs of intelligence and wisdom. To this, Krishna replies:

दुःखेष्वनुद्विग्नमनाः सुखेषु विगतस्पृहः ।

वीतरागभयक्रोधः स्थितधीर्मुनिरुच्यते ॥

Translation: *He whose mind is undisturbed in the midst of sorrows and amid pleasures is free from desire, from whom liking and fear and wrath have passed away, is the sage of settled understanding.*

These lines provide us with several ways to spend a quiet time of self-reflection. First, develop contentment with what has been. One easy technique is to generate gratitude for people and things around us. It is the nature of the human mind that negativity sticks. We are often critical of others – more focused on that one thing that they didn't do right while forgetting all the other things that they did right. We are less forgiving to others for their transgressions. To overcome such a bias, we need to provide ourselves with constant and often high doses of positivity. Consciously creating a habit of gratitude can go a long way.

Second, meditate on purpose and values. A practice well-known across cultures is to create awareness of our mortality. This is represented as a 'memento mori' in medieval Christianity or *maranasati* in Buddhism. A related technique could be to think about what kind of legacy one would like to leave behind. Recalling that our time on this planet is limited, we can focus on what's important and realign the lost focus. As Mark Twain said, 'The two most important days in your life are the day you are born and the day you find out why.' A sense of purpose creates determination and dedication.

Third, practise a healthy detachment from outcomes and consequences. This helps bring a sense of inner equilibrium, especially in times of crisis. One way to do so is to list all factors that could have contributed either to the success or failure of an event. That way, one understands the complexity and contingencies better. Such an exercise also provides a healthy learning mindset in accepting failures.

In all this, one thing to remember is that time is our most valuable resource. We can do clear cost-benefit calculations when it comes to money but it is difficult to quantify and measure time. Multiple things demand our time and multiple distractions give us the illusion of being busy. The one skill we need to master is to identify when to say 'yes' and when to say 'no'. Importantly, we always need to learn to say 'yes' to creating genuine time for ourselves. Creating pure, unadulterated space for oneself can help in freeing oneself from the unending cycle of identical days of mindless existence.

LEADERS WITH DECEPTIVELY SIMPLE ANSWERS

Gianpiero Petriglieri

For distressed people in troubled times, the least rational leaders make the most sense. This hundred-year-old theory harks back to the work of Sigmund Freud – and having to resort to it to explain a leader's rise is never good news.

After all, a decade after he cast light on the social forces that would sink Europe into the abyss of totalitarianism, an ailing Freud was forced to flee Vienna for London, where he could, as he put it, 'die in freedom'. It was 1938. Soon after, World War II broke out and hundreds of thousands began to die for it.

Although most people associate the Viennese psychologist with his controversial conjectures about the unconscious mind, sexuality, and neuroses, fewer know (or acknowledge) that he also put forward one of the most enduring and validated theories of leadership.

In the 1921 book *Group Psychology and the Analysis of the Ego*, Freud turned his attention to the influence of groups on individual behaviour. He did not regard groups kindly. As Freud saw it, groups amplify emotions and inhibit critical thinking.

When people come together in numbers, they are more likely to be swept up in a shared fear or to be enthused by a common faith than they are to engage in reasoned problem solving. For Freud, group membership creates a kind of love that makes people vulnerable and often spells trouble. Groups, he observed, are eager to follow not those who present the most accurate picture of reality, but those who most clearly reflect the group members' cherished ideals. And the more distressing the group's reality is, the more divorced from that reality those ideals become.

Freud's theory was both a challenge to so-called 'great man' theories of leadership and an explanation of their enduring appeal. Behind every great man, he argued, there is an anxious group craving clarity, deliverance, or revenge. What makes groups select leaders, in short, is not judgment but rather a force entirely opposed to judgment: a wish.

'It is impossible to grasp the nature of a group if the leader is disregarded,' he wrote, because it is through picking leaders that groups bring their nature to life. While groups might share a kind of love for an idealised leader, 'the leader himself need love no one else,' Freud warned. 'He may be of a masterful nature, absolutely narcissistic, self-confident and independent.' People will love such a leader all the same, so long as the group continues to cherish the ideal that the leader represents and so long as the leader can continue to credibly uphold that ideal.

But since reality can only be defied for so long, leaders who inspire the greatest enthusiasm by catering to powerful wishes also provoke the most disillusionment when those wishes do not materialise. And when that happens, groups hardly ever blame themselves for being irrationally hopeful. We blame the leader for not being good enough – or for not being good any longer.

Like all theories, Freud's does not apply universally. It suits groups under threat, where cohesion is neither assured by a shared enterprise nor ensured by trusted institutions. In other words, it suits the very circumstances many of us live in today. Even though the 'great man' theory of leadership has fallen into disrepute in academic circles, the wish for great leaders remains very much alive in both politics and business.

Contemporary social psychologists have found new evidence for Freud's insights. A growing amount of recent research shows that the more uncertainty we feel – especially about our identities, relationships and future – the more vulnerable we are to the reassuring appeal of leaders peddling the simplest and most dangerous of narratives: 'We are good and they are evil.' It is a 'we' that is defined sharply, superficially and narrowly; defined to build a wall between those who can claim it and everybody else. Narcissism and divisiveness, Freud understood, aren't flaws of a certain kind of leadership; they are what define it and make it attractive.

It's wishful thinking to retort, as some do, that this does not describe real leadership, and it's no more useful to analyse such leadership from a distance, as if only people with certain personalities or of a certain class become infatuated with leaders who look like they themselves wish to be.

Our own theories of leadership may also be made of private wishes. When writers praise gentle, thoughtful, inclusive and process-loving leaders, they are no more or less in denial of what 'real leadership' is than angry voters who admire a populist strongman or board members who select charismatic CEOs.

In the end, the 'soft leader' is just a 'great leader' in a different guise. Both are charismatic individuals with a vision and both influence others – something we continue to celebrate rather than regard with caution. We should not be surprised when aspiring leaders who appeal to our judgment rather than our wishes are seen not as sane and rational but rather as lacking leadership qualities.

Like romantic relationships, leadership might be always be made up of illusions, but that doesn't make it less consequential.

In picking leaders, groups might seem to lose their minds. It is more accurate to say that it is at that precise point that their true minds are revealed.

BECOMING A LEADER OF CHANGE

Anders Indset

A short introduction to beginning the journey

Define your style and focus on what you stand for (and what you love)

I am often asked what I see as being the greatest challenges. I do not like this question. I am not looking for hurdles, but for possibilities and opportunities. Instead of focusing on what separates us, the focus should be on what connects and unites us. We should focus on the possible. For starters you – as a leader – should define your style and outline a maximum of two or three values that define you and what you stand for. Stand up for something, something you are enthusiastic about. Carry this vision to the people with your full power. We need people with passionate, honest and positive visions. If you show spirit, employees and citizens will be more likely to forgive your mistakes.

Be self-critical

We are all shaped by our environment, origin and past. Nothing is more important than being self-critical; questioning our point of view and our opinions over and over again. 'Why do I see it this way?' 'On what assumptions are my opinions built?' We all have biases. Find them, take a different perspective and work out why you think the way that you do. Find people with different opinions and try to understand their point of view. Free yourself from dogmas and your own biases.

Respect people with less authority

I have met many people who earn far too much in relation to what they have achieved. The sad thing is that they often behave accordingly and take themselves way too seriously.

How do you deal with the young person at the check-in counter in the hotel or the waitress in the restaurant if something doesn't go your way? When you are standing in the priority line at the airport, you don't have to act like an asshole if you can't get straight through or if you find someone from economy in front of you. These character traits are often replicated in managers when dealing with their employees. My basic tenet is clear: I am not interested in your doctoral and professional degrees, titles and roles, annual income or ego. I am interested in how you deal with people with the least authority. I don't want to live in a world where 'being nice' is a sign of weakness, when that's exactly what good leadership should be about.

Be humble

It's all luck. Yes, there's certainly a lot of hard work involved, but at the end of the day your life is a cosmic lottery of coincidences; that you were born (at all), what you have experienced, how your body is put together and so on. A series of unbelievable coincidences, both small and large. Don't forget that when subject and ego take over – and when you think you are the one creative genius and believe you have mastery over something called free will. It is not so: life is a coincidence. Appreciate that and share that happiness with the people around you.

Do not focus on happiness

It's not about the pursuit of happiness. It's about being less unhappy. Happiness is a by-product. Keep yourself busy and aim to make other people happy and allow your happiness to find you. The Dalai Lama once said very aptly, 'If it were possible to become free of negative emotions by risk-free insertion of an electrode, I would be the first patient – without compromising intelligence and critical mind.' Technology makes many things possible, but we should be careful with it and ask ourselves what we really want.

The great 'American dream' does not work everywhere

Cartesian individualism, as practised in the USA, is not a universal model. We can only really enjoy lasting individual freedom if we invest in the common good. Many aphorisms, such as, 'A team is only as strong as its weakest link,' are repeated by experts. Even more important is the appreciation of normality. Create participatory cultures, promote togetherness and focus on your input. If you follow these steps, you will also end up with good output. An extraordinary year or an extraordinary life will happen by itself if you learn to appreciate the wonders of the ordinary.

Be a teacher – share your knowledge

Lifelong learning and curiosity are the keys to success. Being a teacher will not only increase knowledge within your company, but also allows you to learn yourself. Experience-based learning is the basis for lasting personal development and change.

Deep squats for the brain and thinking hours

Good physical health is essential to cope with stress and should be the focus for managers in the twenty-first century. However, don't forget to practise deep squats for the brain. At least one hour of thinking per week (or, better yet, every day) should be a fixture in your diary, a regular appointment, just like your visit to the gym. Due to the rapid development of technology we are turning more and more into digital reaction junkies. The only way to break out of that is to set aside thinking time. Stay healthy for your hundred-year journey – your hardware must work – but rediscover the art of thinking. The symbiosis of heart and mind is essential.

The project is the boss

The idea of the 'boss' has had its day. Management today is shifting to algorithms, technology and smart tools. The project is now in charge. We are only as successful as the project is performing. Leadership is not only at the top, it is everywhere in teams and companies today. We just have to free this leader.

Future leadership will be about shedding tears in moments of sadness, breaking into smiles and experiencing the joy of acquiring new knowledge or skills. It will be about the small and ordinary things that bring us to life.

It should be about the joy of tasting the fresh snow, the wonders of the polar clouds and the lights shining in the old wooden houses where families play a board game together.

It should be about remembering that the little things are actually the big things and make all the difference.

It should be about appreciating the ordinary and dealing with the people around you. In a world without a defined agenda or over-arching purpose, it is OK not to take yourself so seriously.

INTERVIEW WITH STEW FRIEDMAN

Four-way wins: total leadership as a way of living and leading a richer life

Philosophy@work: Stew, as a professor at the Wharton School and an expert in the field of organisational psychology you have created a method called 'total leadership' that allows leaders to connect their private to their professional life in a way that they can act authentically, wholly and innovatively. Can you explain the philosophy behind total leadership?

Stew Friedman: Total leadership is a holistic approach that aims to educate and shape leaders to live a richer life and perform better in all four domains in life: work, home, community and self. To reach an improved performance in all the domains in life, Total leadership focuses in particular on becoming authentic, whole and innovative. With these three principles, the total leadership method is unique because most approaches that aim at improving and educating leaders focus solely on professional skills. Different from that, Total Leadership views a leader and his/her complete life holistically and improves skills that are helpful in every domain in life – not just the work or professional aspect.

Philsosophy@work: Can you tell us a little bit more about combining work and life in this rather unique way?

Stew Friedman: Due to my field of research I always engaged a lot with themes like leadership and leadership development. When I wrote my dissertation I also did a large-scale study and worked with many companies and their talent management systems. After that I started even more research and landed my dream job at the Wharton School. Although I engaged with management and leadership every day I at first never really thought about a different approach – that took all the domains in life into consideration; seeing leadership holistically.

Suddenly, something outside the business world changed things for me when our first child was born and I became a father for the first time. While holding this practically perfect being one question arose in me, What must I now do to make our world a safe and nurturing one for him? Sharing my latest experience and discussing with students in my Wharton MBA class the question transformed into a more concrete one: What will you do, as a business professional, to weave the strands of work, family, community and self into the fabric of your own life? The answer to this question is the total leadership method that helps to weave all the strands in life together. Of course, the total leadership method needed some time to develop but the key idea arose within this time and due to the profound event of becoming a father.

Philosophy@work: How did the development of the total leadership method continue?

Stew Friedman: After the vision was clear, my career changed entirely. I like to think of it as embarking on a new journey. Total leadership really started growing at a time when I worked as the director of the Wharton leadership programmes. In this setting, I was trying to create a new model of business education for Wharton. The goal was to develop a model that encouraged students to question their perspectives about career success. Within this process we built our research on data we were generating through the Wharton Work/Life Integration Project, which was an initiative that gathered information from thousands of students and alumni. The data helped us focus on our plan, which was to explore the intersection of career and life interests. Within that research process the main ideas for the total leadership method became very clear.

To give my new ideas a try, I left academia and started working at the Ford Motor Company. The new CEO wanted to connect leadership development with the need to help employees find better ways of integrating work with the rest of their life. With my team we supported the company in the pursuit of this goal with our programmes. They were dedicated to learning leadership by doing it. 'Total leadership' became my shorthand for a new way to think about leadership, from the point of view of the whole person. We created something new: a programme that starts and ends with the person – not the business person, but the whole person. Since returning to Wharton in 2001, I've refined this programme while offering it in a variety of settings around the world. The point of total leadership is to create what I now call 'four-way wins'– better results at work, at home, in the community and for yourself.

Philosophy@work: What does it take to become a whole conscious person or leader?

Stew Friedman: If leaders and other people in the business world have a real hunger to focus on the things that really matter, the time has come to change the way we structure our working day. Between that already-structured day, with one thousand meetings or telephone conferences, it seems hard to remember what is important and how the different parts of life can actually work together and achieve more benefits for the working-space, the home, the community and the private self.

The four-way view is practised in small groups – two or three people – and challenges each and every one to look at their work and their life. They get a hundred points to allocate, according to how important each of the different parts of their life is. That is the first and simple step to start with.

In the second step the attendees estimate the amount of attention they give to the different parts of their lives in a typical week or a typical month. Due to this attribution, the proportion of their attention during their waking hours becomes clear. Afterwards, they are asked to rate how satisfied they are in each of the different domains or parts of their life, on a simple scale of one to ten.

Finally, the group members should evaluate how well they think they are performing in that part of their life, according to the expectations that people have of them. All of this takes only three minutes from the day. The method is a very fast way to see clearly and increase awareness for all the alternatives that could be used to structure a working day. It turns out that the things business-people miss in their working life are not far away or unattainable. It might be a little challenging to find those three minutes at first, but the quality of these well-spent three minutes is way higher than three hours of talking about a new project nobody actually cares about.

Philosophy@work: What are the biggest surprises that you experience from this approach?

Stew Friedman: In order to double the positive effects of the challenge, we ask the attendees to share their results with the other people in the group. The challenge tries to get people out of their comfort zone and maybe overcome fear by talking about the priorities in their lives, their attention-paying proportions and their performances, while the other people simply listen to them and respond with curiosity.

I have experienced many business-people going through this process and thinking that it is remarkable what happens. People from all different kinds of cultures – from investment banking to manufacturing companies to brand companies or the financial service – really enjoy having this conversation. It is liberating for them to realise that it turns out what you have just talked about is not something in which you are alone. Others have got the same problem and challenges. The same problem, in a sense – that there is a struggle with the challenge to bring all parts of life together in a way that makes sense. This method makes people accept themselves for who they are, and other people too. And all of this has an impact on our society as well.

Philosophy@work: How do you see the impact on society?

Stew Friedman: Society benefits from the way leaders come to a deeper appreciation of the consequences of their bad choices. They learn to create real change and change in a way that makes things better for all the different parts of their lives, including the stakeholders around them.

One of those parts is the community or society. Thinking deeply and measuring the impact of their current history can spread positive effects to all the different parts of life, even if this happens indirectly.

Imagine the following situation: you might make a change in your business, maybe through the way you change your schedule.

From now on you're more available to your children. That has an effect on the security level; on how your child shows up as an eight-year-old in her or his classroom. Your child may interact in a way that is more pro-social and empathetic with classmates. This leads to a change in the culture of that class or maybe the neighbourhood or the community. Directly or indirectly, that's an impact that you're having on the world.

People who deeply reflect on their decisions also escape the 'reaction' mode. An issue that everyone feels – but sometimes never even realises – is the pressure to be available twenty-four-seven. Our society puts a lot of trust into the technologies like AI or the blockchain and tries to keep up with the speed of change subconsciously. We can get a lot of knowledge about everything from everywhere (especially Wikipedia), but knowledge is not understanding. Within that ocean of information, we sometimes forget what is really important and – especially as a leader – one must row back and reinstall understanding in our fast working life. If we do that, we can build a whole society that is capable of keeping up with the developing technologies by improving individuals through total leadership.

PART II

THE ART OF LEADERSHIP

THE EVOLUTION OF LEADERSHIP – YESTERDAY, TODAY AND TOMORROW

Marshall Goldsmith

Think back on our history as human beings. Many of our current stereotypes of leadership come from a past that no longer exists. They come from a yesterday that is very disconnected from today and miles from the world of tomorrow. Yet the images of the past are reinforced in our contemporary literature, TV, movies, videogames and art and they can hinder our understanding of what great leadership should be today and what it will look like in the future.

Here's a brief journey through the various areas of leadership in our recent history:

The cave people – leadership through physical strength

Thousands of years ago, our ancestors lived in a brutal and harsh world. Small clans grouped together in caves to protect themselves from the elements. Leaders were usually strong, young men and ruled through physical strength.

The land-owners – leadership through control

As we evolved, humans began to gather and store crops. Ownership and control of the land became the key to power. Leaders were not necessarily physically the strongest, they were the people who controlled the land. Control of resources became the key to power.

Royalty – leadership through family

For much of the last two thousand years, the source of most leadership has been the family. Kings and queens ruled with no need to justify their power, since they declared their legitimacy came from God. Anyone who criticised or challenged royalty was to be imprisoned or executed.

The church – leadership through religion

Historically, the church provided spiritual leadership for the mass of people and supported royal families, whose number also provided its key leaders. The church had the ability to determine what was right or wrong and criticism of its doctrine was not tolerated. Critics were referred to as heretics and would be excommunicated, tortured or put to death.

The military – leadership through power

While the church provided the moral case for royalty, the military provided the power needed to keep the members of the ruling class on their thrones. In the world of monarchs and absolute rulers, the strongest army won. Military leaders were often, but not always, related to ruling families. Sometimes generals worked their way up the hierarchy and were rewarded for their loyalty, bravery, intelligence and competence.

The university – leadership through education

Until very recent times, the best formal education was largely reserved for the elite. Liberal education separated the elite from the masses and, along with the church and the military, reinforced the status quo of the country.

The master – leadership though skill

As the merchant class began to rise, a new type of leader emerged, the master. The master was typically an expert in a certain trade who taught his skills to a younger apprentice. The apprentice practised the craft, and eventually became the master to a new apprentice.

The politician – leadership through support

Eventually, the subjects of royalty rebelled. In early democracies, power and control were maintained in the hands of an elite group. Only in recent years, and in a few countries, has democracy evolved to a level of true representation of the people. Politicians, like kings and queens, have historically been more focused on maintaining power than on building collaborative relationships.

The owner – leadership through control of the corporation

With the advent of capitalism came the rise in company and resource ownership. While these early entrepreneurs may not always have been descended from royalty, they were able to acquire wealth and pass it on to their families. Since they owned the controlling interest in terms of stocks, they maintained ultimate decision-making power.

The manager – leadership through promotion

As organisations grew and the families of founders became less focused on the operational aspects of leading their companies, a new class emerged – professional managers. The key role of these workers was to protect and grow the assets of the owners. These managers typically worked their way up through the company and were rewarded by promotion for their effort, achievement and loyalty.

Common characteristics of leadership in the past

As we look at leadership in the past we can see that leaders historically had the following common characteristics:

- *Leadership was local.* From the tiny world of the cave, to the village, the city and the nation, the history of leadership has almost all been domestic.

- *Leaders managed uniformity.* Throughout history, almost all leaders have been men who represented the ruling class of their countries. Women were not considered for most leadership roles – or even many salaried roles. Leaders were also of the same race as their subjects, set the religion and were brought up in the same culture.

- *Leaders managed slow rates of change.* Throughout most of history, leaders managed technology that did not change at all – or changed very slowly. Masters could prosper for generations without being concerned about the impact of new technology.

- *Leaders knew all the answers and did not encourage differing opinions.* Religious leaders, masters, academics and generals were said to have the right answer. Followers who disagreed with authority were often punished severely by being fired, excommunicated, ostracised or even killed.

- *Leadership was top-down.* Most leadership involved having immediate control over direct reports – as opposed to team-building or building peer relationships. Being able to influence colleagues without direct line authority was not a skill that was required for success.

- *Leaders were bosses.* From monarchs to generals and managers, leaders had one important quality in common: they had clear power over the people whom they led. They could easily punish those who did not demonstrate loyalty. Once they acquired power, they did whatever was necessary to maintain their position. One definition of 'boss', as a noun, is 'a person who makes decisions, exercises authority and dominates'. Another definition, as a verb, is 'to order about' or 'to be master over'. The leader of the past was clearly the boss!

These characteristics of leaders may (or may not) have been effective in the past. In practical terms, it doesn't matter. These characteristics will not work for the most important leaders of the future.

The one, over-arching theme that emerges from studying leaders of the past, is that, in some very important way, leaders were supposed to be superior to the people they were leading. Monarchs were said to have been endowed with the divine right to rule, clergy were closer to God, masters were more skilled, academics had more knowledge, generals had more experience, owners had more wealth, politicians had more support and cave leaders had more strength.

Almost all movies, videos, TV shows and games reinforce the concept that great leaders are, in some way, superior to the people that they lead. Looking at the history of leadership it is very easy to understand why 'servant leadership' is such a recent concept!

As the world and its people are evolving, so is leadership. The leader of the future will have qualities that are clearly different from the leader of the past and many of the characteristics of yesterday's leader will not work for tomorrow's leaders.

The leader of the future

Accenture invited me to partner with them in a two-year research project around the turn of the century that compared the qualities of leaders of the past with those that would be required of leaders in the future.* Instead of interviewing current CEOs and leaders,

---

* The result of this project was the book *Global Leadership: The Next Generation*, which I co-authored with Cathy Greenberg, Alastair Robertson and Maya Hu-Chan. Valuable contributions to the research were made by Warren Bennis and John O'Neil.

who would not be leading the organisations of the future, we interviewed two hundred future CEOs from around the world. Common qualities were flagged up as being likely to become important. Looking back on this study years later, I find that the direction of the predictions from these potential leaders were amazingly accurate. If anything, the degree of change, the speed of change in the importance of new leadership qualities may have been understated.

Combining this research with all that I've learned since the study's completion, I can share seven key trends that have emerged and will dramatically impact the leader of the future. I can explain why the changing world calls for an end to old assumptions about leadership and show how a new model is emerging to fit today's world.

From thinking locally to thinking globally

Globalisation is a trend that will continue to have a major impact on the leaders of the future. Even twenty years ago, leaders in some huge companies could focus on their own countries or, at most, their own regions. Those days are rapidly screeching to a halt! The trend toward globally connected markets and globally integrated organisations is going to become even stronger in the future.

From requiring uniformity to seeking diversity

In the past, seeking diversity was not even on the radar for most leaders. In fact, they usually required uniformity in the workforce and actively eliminated the possibility of diversity. As globalisation continues to be important, leaders will need to appreciate and strive for diversity in new and different ways. They will have to appreciate not only economic and legal differences, but also the social and behavioural differences that are part of working around the world. The most effective leaders of the future will understand that developing an understanding of other people and other cultures is not just an obligation, it is a requirement. Even better, it is an opportunity!

From understanding a single technology to becoming tech-savvy

In the past, the core technology of organisations changed very slowly or, in many cases, not at all. Leaders of the past could understand their company's core technology, develop enough expertise to direct their people and stay as current as they needed without a huge effort. That is not the case with the rapid pace of technological change today. This does not mean that every future leader will be a gifted technician or a computer programmer, but it does mean that leaders should understand how the intelligent use of new technology can help their organisations; that they should recruit, develop and maintain a network of technically current people; know how to make and manage investments in new technology and be positive role models in leading the use of new technology.

From 'leader as knower' to 'leader as learner'

In the past, leaders generally knew more about what they were doing than the people they led. That is why 'masters' were called 'masters' and 'apprentices' were called 'apprentices'. In the future, the most important leaders will manage a workforce who know far more about what they are doing in the new world of global organisations, diverse stakeholders and rapidly changing technology. The higher the leader moves up the organisational chain of command, the more this is true.

From eliminating challenge to encouraging constructive dialogue

Leaders of the past went out of their way not only to discourage challenge, but to *eliminate* it altogether. Providing negative feedback to landowners could lead workers to starvation and providing negative feedback to royalty could lead to execution. In a world where leaders knew more than their followers, the drawbacks of leading by intimidation were not nearly as great as they are today. Today, leaders who cut off the flow of constructive dialogue run the risk of becoming obsolete in a very short period of time.

From top of the hierarchy to alliances and teams

Leadership has traditionally been thought of as a top-down, hierarchical process. In the world of the past, with leaders controlling knowledge and subordinates doing what they were told, this model seemed to make sense. It is becoming increasingly hard to fix such roles and in industries as diverse as energy, telecommunications and pharmaceuticals, the same organisation may be your customer, supplier, partner *and* your competitor. In this new world, building positive, long-term, win-win relationships with many different types of stakeholders is critical.

From leader as boss to leader as facilitator

As we consider the trends listed above, it becomes clear that the leader of the future needs very different skills and qualities than the leader of the past. The leader as boss told people what to do and how to do it. In the old world, for all of the reasons that we discussed, this was understandable. The leader of the future will not have all the answers. The leader of the future is not only learning as opposed to knowing – the leader of the future is a facilitator who is helping everyone on the team learn.

One of, if not *the*, greatest leader I have ever met is Frances Hesselbein. Frances retired after serving for fourteen years as the CEO of the Girl Scouts of America. Management guru Peter Drucker said that Frances was the most effective executive that he had ever met – and Peter Drucker never made remarks like this casually. Frances did an amazing job of changing an organisation that was mired in the past. As the CEO of the Girl Scouts, she developed a wonderful doctrine, 'Tradition with a future!' At the same time, she never demeaned the past – in fact, she celebrated its positive aspects. On the other hand, she did not live in the past. She realised that, in her organisation, the leader of the future would have to be very different than the leader of the past.

As a CEO, Frances was remarkably ahead of her time. She coined the phrase 'circular leadership' to describe her style and the style that she wanted to promote in all her leaders. She envisioned herself as a person in the centre of circular relationships, not a boss sitting on top of a hierarchy.

Frances saw herself as a servant leader who facilitated the success of her team – not a 'boss' who was there to tell people what to do and how to do it. She was constantly learning and helping others learn. She encouraged constructive disagreement. She did an amazing job of building alliances inside and outside the organisation.

As you think about your role as the leader of the future, remember the 'Frances doctrine' – tradition with a future. Whatever you have done in the past – or other leaders have done in the past – is over. Recognise that the leaders you have known in the past have done right. Appreciate what you can learn from their mistakes. But focus on the future! By understanding the past, you can see why leaders ended up being the way they were and you can also see how leadership needs to change in order for organisations to thrive in the new world – a world where leaders do not strive to be superior to the people they lead; a world where leaders strive to develop people who will become, in many ways, superior to the leader!

*

Reflection questions

1. Think about your leadership journey, as a leader or as one being led, which qualities and characteristics do you find most valuable in leaders – those of the leaders of the past or those of the leaders of tomorrow?

2. Who do you think is a good role model for tomorrow's leaders? What qualities do they exude?

3. How can you enhance your own leader of the future qualities?

SUPERBOSS LEADERSHIP: A NEW MODEL FOR THE TWENTY-FIRST CENTURY

Sydney Finkelstein

Is there anyone out there not concerned with talent? Time and again, in survey after survey, when CEOs and other senior executives are asked what keeps them up at night, the quest for world-class talent keeps coming up.

For example, PwC's seventeenth annual global CEO survey in 2013 found that an incredible 93 per cent of surveyed CEOs were changing, or planned to change, their talent strategies. At the same time, there was significant dissatisfaction with HR; only one-third of surveyed CEOs said that HR was well prepared to meet this challenge.

Surely it's time to consider some new ideas. The good news is that, if we know where to look, there are some truly remarkable examples of genius HR practices at work from which we can learn. Ten years ago I set out to find these 'superbosses', study what they did that was different from so many other leaders and decode their methods so that any leader, any manager, any boss, can get better at the one essential task they all share: developing world-class talent that can adapt and adjust, learn to get better at whatever they do, and in the final analysis, create value for themselves and their organisations.

I compiled, dissected, and analysed stories about the lives and careers of eighteen primary superbosses in fields as diverse as casual dining (Norman Brinker), hospitals (Tommy Frist), comic books (Stan Lee), non-profit endowment investment (David Swensen), filmmaking (Roger Corman), hedge funds (Julian Robertson), newspapers (Gene Roberts), and special effects (George Lucas), among others.

Looking for recurring themes and patterns, I discovered that superbosses differ considerably in their interpersonal styles, but that the ways in which they identify, motivate, coach and leverage others are remarkably consistent, highly unconventional, and unmistakably powerful. Superbosses aren't like most bosses; they follow a playbook all their own. Superbosses are super-motivators. They help other people accomplish more than they ever thought possible. Superbosses create attachments to their people that engender tremendous loyalty and effort. It's almost like a Stockholm syndrome of leadership: Employees push themselves to their limits for their superbosses but, rather than resent the superboss for it, they feel even greater loyalty. They'll do anything to keep from disappointing their superboss and they yearn to please them not just because they've completely bought into the boss's vision, but also because they want to feel that their boss was correct in selecting them for the job.

So how do superbosses do it? The first thing to know is that all superbosses drive their people exceptionally hard.

'Everybody knew that Bill demanded results,' said Ronald Blankenship, president and CEO of the Verde Group and long-time associate of superboss Bill Sanders, 'and if you were going to work with him, you need to be prepared to make that the primary focus in your life.'

Comedian Andy Samberg remembers that after working for superboss Lorne Michaels at *Saturday Night Live*, acting in movies was a cakewalk. 'The pressure doesn't really seem that high. You've dealt with this thing that's *SNL*, which is just this crazy, intense, beautiful pressure cooker.'

In setting ever-higher expectations, superbosses aren't bound by last year's figures or by a sense of what normal performance might look like for an employee in a given position. They're certainly not bound by what employees conceive to be their natural limitations. Superbosses want to see how far people can go. They treat staff like Olympic athletes, pushing them to the limit and beyond. As Lee Clow, chairman of TBWA\Media Arts Lab, put it, co-founder Jay Chiat was 'always demanding of everyone to do something better than they very often knew or thought they could or were capable of'.

Isn't all this hard-charging, whip-cracking pressure ultimately counterproductive? Some employees at superboss-led companies do drop out, but those that remain respond to the constant intensity by developing an even deeper emotional bond with the superboss. Even though superbosses keep the pressure up, they also inspire performance, emboldening employees to push themselves. Superbosses get that individuals – even the most driven and talented – accomplish so much more when high expectations come with a sense of possibility. They understand that people will work their hardest to become bigger, better, tougher, more resourceful and more creative when they see they can be these things themselves. And they sense that it is their paramount job as leaders to inject a strong and unforgettable sense of possibility in their workforce.

It's hard to go back to being ordinary

Superbosses are geniuses at motivation. Unlike some bosses, they don't want eighty per cent of the attention and dedication of their people. They want a hundred per cent. And they get a hundred per cent. People know when they're working for a special boss – someone who is changing the rules, is unafraid to take risks, deeply cares about achieving a higher objective, and invites employees to be a part of it. When a boss like that is giving orders or, as is more often the case, pushing and inspiring their employee in a powerful way, workers don't perceive the pressure to perform as being tedious or unwelcome. They perceive it as part of a gigantic, unbelievably important and exciting mission. They thrive on this pressure. And, just like their boss, they lose themselves in the mission.

It is the superboss's combination of lofty expectations and aspirations, then, that enables the exceptional people under their wings to do impossible things. An upward spiral of performance is engendered among the protégés of superbosses: as they become accustomed to surviving and thriving in an intense environment, their ambitions only increase. They become so addicted to success that they seek out ever more challenging assignments. And they feel so good about meeting or exceeding the superboss's expectations that they want to do it again and again. They yearn to be even closer to the superboss, their inspiration, their energy, and they will do whatever it takes to stay in their orbit. It's a cyclone of pressure, success, acknowledgment, rising confidence and even more success that makes the protégé, the superboss, and the superboss's organisation utterly unstoppable. An employee of Jay Chiat summed it up, 'He left something in people that makes it hard for you to go back to being ordinary. Once you feel it, you can't change it.'

It's one thing to motivate your people to do great things, it's quite another to unleash their potential for innovation. Yet when you look closely at what superbosses actually do, a clear pattern emerges from which every other leader, manager and employee can learn.

There are three distinct kinds of action superbosses take to nurture openness and innovation in their people: first, superbosses encourage risk-taking and rule-breaking. Kyle Craig, former chairman and CEO of Steak and Ale, remembered that his superboss, Norman Brinker, 'would challenge you. He would say, "What do you think you could do there? What is working? Go try something." It was very empowering because it gave you a licence to say, "We can do some things differently!"'

The second way superbosses nurture openness is by removing anxieties that get in the way of people doing new things. If you analyse why individuals in your workplace just don't seem to come up with anything new, I bet you'll find that fear of failure plays an outsized role. This isn't such an irrational fear, either – in many companies, failure is a dirty word. Mess up and you get labelled as unreliable, incompetent or worse. Superbosses, of course, don't think about failure the way most people do. Rather, they are masters at reframing failure as an opportunity in disguise. By implication, they don't fear failure but instead view it as just a step you sometimes end up taking on the way to success.

Superbosses blast away at fear by creating work environments where creativity and innovation can thrive. According to Steve Alburty, Jay Chiat's ad shop was, 'The most unique work experience of our lives because there was such a sense of creativity and personal freedom.'

Legendary film producer Roger Corman was known for letting his actors do their own thing when they were in front of the camera. Recalling Corman's logic, one actor mused, 'I don't recall him ever telling me how a line should be read or telling actors I was working with what our motivation was.'

Without a boss breathing down their necks at every turn, employees feel as if they have implicit permission to take chances and express themselves in their work. Their superboss trusts them – that's precisely why they hired them. Compare that to many offices today, where employees send emails to colleagues at all hours of the day and night because they don't feel confident to make a decision on their own.

Another way superbosses help protégés overcome their reluctance to innovate is by creating new opportunities for them. Hedge fund impresario Julian Robertson, for one, would sit in the middle of his company's large workroom and loudly debate ideas his analysts presented. Not every analyst who volunteered an idea got a pat on the back; when Robertson thought an idea was dumb, he would say so, 'You say this company has got some great product and I just called so-and-so and he said the product is just terrible.' Employees understood that unfettered debate was simply Robertson's style, that he deeply appreciated new ideas and that they didn't need to fear pushback. Robertson's office became what so many offices today aren't: a safe space for fresh thinking and experimentation.

The show must change

The third way superbosses nurture openness and innovation is by encouraging their employees or associates to never, ever rest on their laurels. 'To be and stay a great musician,' Miles Davis used to teach, 'you've got to always be open to what's new, what's happening at the moment. You have to be able to absorb it if you're going to continue to grow and communicate your music.'

Time and again I found that superbosses were consummate cool hunters – always on the prowl for the next great product idea, the next great trend, the next great person to hire. Speaking of *Saturday Night Live*, comedian and *SNL* alum Conan O'Brien once said, 'You always get the sense that the show is almost like a shark that's constantly on a mission to find what's new, what's hot, what are people into now? And chomp its teeth into it.'

The image of a shark always on the hunt is apt for every superboss I studied. They all had an inexhaustible drive to improve, something that was in part a reflection of competitive pressures. As chef Alice Waters told me, she perceives the constant need to change as 'just kind of a compulsion, an obsession, and I don't know where it comes from. It's just pushing me'. David Murphy, who worked for Jay Chiat from 1975 to 1980, noted, 'Jay's middle name was innovation. He had a singular vision that it was totally acceptable to risk; playing it safe was just not acceptable.'

A superboss's cool hunting can take any number of forms. Norman Brinker was good at anticipating emerging restaurant industry trends because he was constantly probing the minds of consumers. Not content to peruse the usual market research reports, Brinker would spend hours in his restaurants, talking to customers and staff, developing a reputation in the industry for his approachability and willingness to learn.

Employees of superbosses get swept up in a whirlwind of constant innovation. The result is not merely great wealth and influence for the superboss; it's a lifetime of career success for those lucky enough to become their protégés.

The apprenticeship model

So much of the way people learn in the workplace today – from 360-degree performance evaluations to mentoring and coaching – has become bureaucratised and impersonal. Most competent bosses generally don't prioritise immersive learning experiences. Aiming for greater certainty and clarity in their organisations, they promulgate rules and establish bureaucracies that distance them from employees. They also choreograph their days to assure that work gets done, leaving very little unstructured time for instructing or coaching. They certainly don't use the word 'apprentice' very much. The very concept seems quaint, the product of a bygone age. Superbosses, by contrast, embrace the apprenticeship model wholeheartedly as a way of doing business. When they hire, they know they are giving an employee a chance to learn a craft at their feet. Staying in the trenches with protégés and serving as something akin to a player-coach, superbosses use this informal manner of instruction not only to convey knowledge but to also exert a powerful, almost parental influence on their protégés.

The most basic and critical set of practices underlying the apprenticeship model concerns simply being with employees; getting to know them and letting them in. You can't develop a personal approach to training staff if you aren't there in person (or, if necessary, via communications technology), day in and day out. Yet most bosses don't do this – in fact, they don't even come close. The CEOs appearing on the hit television show *Undercover Boss* are, sadly, not all that unusual. Imagine having to resort to impersonating low-level employees to find out what's really going on in your own company. These clueless, distanced bosses are the complete antithesis of the superboss. They focus on getting closer to the customer, while superbosses are very much focused on getting closer to their employees or team members.

HCA Healthcare co-founder and superboss Tommy Frist, who was also a pilot, would sometimes fly his protégés to events in other cities, letting them sit in the co-pilot's seat and talking business with them. Similarly, world-renowned conductor Jorma Panula would spend all day with his students and then he would invite them to a restaurant to talk even more.

In the corporate world, employees who seek to speak with their bosses normally attempt to book time. They might send an email to an assistant and the resulting meeting would occur outside of the actual work being done. Such practices seem to bring bosses and employees closer together but in reality they distance and control the degree of contact bosses have with staff. While today's hyper-scheduled executives obviously need to control their time, we often forget about what we lose when we run from event to event – the casual, ongoing contact in the moment that is essential for learning, serendipity and building meaningful relationships.

Teachers

Protégés of all superbosses related similar powerful, career-shaping lessons they learned during the course of informal, apprentice-style interactions. Superbosses deliver multiple lessons at once. First, they teach technical nuances about their business – insights employees can't get anywhere else, as well as memorable reminders of the fundamentals that protégés are already expected to know. If you want to learn the finer points of running a newspaper, who better to teach you than Gene Roberts? If you want to learn the secrets of starting a successful restaurant chain, who better than Norman Brinker?

Just as valuable is a second layer of lessons, the make-or-break advice superbosses impart on how to run businesses and lead organisations. Billionaire entrepreneur and designer Tory Burch credits Ralph Lauren with teaching her 'the importance of having a complete vision for a company, from product to marketing to store visuals'. Alice Waters taught Gayle Ortiz, now chef and owner of Gayle's Bakery in San Francisco, how to 'pay attention to detail and demand perfection' in all aspects of a restaurant's operation, a lesson that became the 'main focus of the way that I looked at business'.

Finally, on a day-to-day basis, superbosses also customise their general teaching style to fit the individual. 'He didn't react the same way to everyone,' saxophonist Bill Evans said of Miles Davis. 'Everyone was different and personal to him and that is one of the things that he was able to do… get to know each person and what each person needed. Some people he would be harder on than others. He was interesting in that way.'

Of Julian Robertson, Chase Coleman said, 'He was very good at understanding some combination of what motivated people and how to extract maximum performance out of people. For some people, that was encouraging and, for other people, it was making them feel less comfortable.'

The cohort effect

At a glance, it may seem hard to appreciate how special superboss workplaces are. Many workplaces have at least some degree of team spirit, right? Colleagues celebrate one another's birthdays. They throw parties. They participate in fantasy football leagues. They connect on social media. And when challenges arise, they help one another out to get the job done.

Here's the difference: the teams that superbosses assemble aren't just pretty good – they are exceptional. Even at the best workplaces, where employees might refer to their team as a surrogate family, it's rare for employees to go so far as to describe their teams as 'cults'. When I talked to protégés of superbosses, however, that term came up over and over. Designer Joseph Abboud described working for Ralph Lauren as being 'very much like a cult. You wanted to be part of it. Ralph was our hero. We believed the myth; we dressed the myth. We were the legions.'

You might think creating such a profound experience would be hard for superbosses, requiring some sort of special energy, devotion, and commitment – not to mention resources. Doesn't it take millions of dollars to create team-building retreats and pay for intensive coaching? In reality, crafting a 'cult' experience isn't that hard. As Abboud's language suggests, strong bonds between teammates arise as a happy side effect of key elements of the superboss playbook. First and foremost, Abboud identifies the distinctive vision of his superboss (Lauren's 'myth') as the cornerstone of the cultish identity. In agreeing to go all-in with a unique vision, protégés naturally feel different from those who don't get the vision or are unlucky enough to work for a leader without any kind of vision.

Superbosses also find creative ways to publicise the unique skills and qualities of their protégés. For example, artists who drew comic books used to be anonymous. Marvel Comics impresario and writer Stan Lee introduced a credits page, giving his artists 'brands' for the first time. The credits might read something like, 'Written with passion by Stan Lee, drawn with Pride by Jack Kirby. Inked with Perfection by Joe Sinnott. And lettered with a Scratchy Pen by Artie Simek.' Lee also talked up his staff in his monthly newsletter, the *Bullpen Bulletin*. These shoutouts often shaped the careers of people in his department. For instance, Stan Lee proclaimed Jack Kirby, a mid-career artist at the time, the 'king of comics', a moniker that has stuck to this day. Of course, many would argue that Kirby would have been the king of comics regardless of what Lee thought. But certainly Kirby's coronation helped him secure his stature in the public eye.

The 2-C principle

Saturday Night Live is an institution built on comedy talent, but the way the show is structured offers a key lesson on how superboss teams work. The building blocks of each episode are skits created by cast members and writers; they cannot succeed without a significant degree of collaboration. Many collaborate selflessly – in some cases helping to refine skits that others are credited with writing. But if all you ever did was collaborate, you wouldn't succeed at *SNL*. That's because each week the cast produces two to three hours' worth of material that must fit into a ninety-minute time slot. This limitation creates a sense of competition – it is the definition of competition. To make it on the show, in other words, you've also got to compete.

Superbosses encourage teamwork, then, but they also deliberately encourage sharp competition among their intensely unified teams. This combustible mixture of collaboration and competition – what I call the '2-C principle' – dramatically boosts the performance of individual team members.

One reason healthy, balanced competition is so valuable for organisations is that it generates a 'cohort effect' when it comes to talent: the more you help people become better, the more they help one another get better. As Paul McCartney said of John Lennon in the days of writing in the Beatles, 'If I did something good, he'd want to do something better. It's just the way we worked.' Healthy competition also drives excellence in so-called technology clusters or geographic hubs such as Silicon Valley, where a critical mass of companies exist side by side and talent pushes more talent, causing new ideas to percolate.

By mobilising both 'Cs', superbosses create their own talent hubs, marked by intellectual and social fermentation. Some protégés, like visual effects expert and director Mark Dippé, explicitly compare their experience to attending a competitive graduate school. Dippé said that working at *Star Wars* creator George Lucas's Industrial Light & Magic was 'the best film school for me'. Both consciously and unconsciously, superbosses create a kind of cauldron in which ideas collide, prompting new creations. This cauldron in turn becomes an engine, powering exceptional performance. The cohort effect enables superbosses to take all the techniques they use to motivate individuals and turbocharge them. It's a powerful formula: individual employees can grow beyond their wildest dreams; teams and organisations can add value that far exceeds the sum of their parts.

Conclusion

Superbosses do something that every leader needs to do: they help other people accomplish more than they ever thought possible. This gets me back to one of the best definitions of leadership I ever heard: leaders are people who create other leaders. In a world of constant change, driven by globalisation, technology and economic and geopolitical shocks that seem to happen on a regular basis, the need for world-class leadership has never been greater. The best news of all is that the superboss playbook can be learned and disseminated by any individual leader and in any organisation, as long as they are willing to invest the time and energy to make it happen.

IF YOU WANT TO BE A GOOD LEADER, YOU HAD BETTER UNDERSTAND PHILOSOPHY

Santiago Iñiguez de Onzoño

I believe that management is philosophy in action and that every management theory has a philosophical background. I also believe that every manager has a view of the world, consciously or inadvertently, explicit or emergent, that conforms to a certain sort of philosophy. Interestingly, even affirming the contrary is in itself a philosophical proposition.

The same is applicable to theories of leadership: they can be ascribed to some philosophical movement or trend. In this regard, modern theories of leadership owe a lot to Friedrich Nietzsche, a German philosopher of the nineteenth century, famous for his affirmation, 'God is dead', whose contributions have been both influential and controversial. Nietzsche distinguishes between two types of morality: the 'master morality' and the 'slave morality'. The first is applicable to the leaders of society, who create their own values for themselves. The 'slave morality' is applicable to the herd and, according to its standards, the behaviour of masters is accounted as evil. But masters, maintains Nietzsche, stand 'beyond good and evil'. They are subject to their own principles, different to the norms enacted for the herd that favour mediocrity and prevent the development of higher level persons: the true leaders.

Curiously, a passage from one of Nietzsche's books could have been extracted from the management literature on modern leadership of the 1980s:

> To give style to one's character – a great and rare art! He practises it who surveys all that his nature presents in strength and weakness and then moulds it to an artistic plan until everything appears as art and reason, and even the weakness delight the eye ... it will be the strong, imperious natures which experience their subtlest joy in exercising such a control, in such a constraint and perfecting under their own law.*

Nietzsche's theory reminds me of some characters in novels and movies from that same decade. The two most remembered icons are probably Gordon Gecko, the protagonist of *Wall Street*, preacher of the 'Greed is good' maxim – a part of the Reaganite credo of the time – and Sherman McCoy, the doomed executive of *The Bonfire of Vanities*, described in the novel as a financial whizz-kid, a 'master of the universe'. Both characters feel, using that Nietzschean expression, 'beyond good and evil' and not subject to the standards that affect the rest of mortals. Another passage from Nietzsche's work is appropriate to describe their attitude to life:

> For believe me! The secret of realising the greatest fruitfulness and the greatest enjoyment of existence is to live dangerously! Build your cities on the slopes of the

---

* Friedrich Nietzsche, *Die fröhliche wissenschaft* (*The Gay Science*), quoted in R. J. Hollingdale, *Nietzsche: The Man and His Philosophy*, (Cambridge, UK: Cambridge University Press, 1999), 143

Vesuvius! Send your ships out into uncharted seas! Live in conflict with your equals and with yourselves! Be robbers and ravagers as long as you cannot be rulers or owners, you men of knowledge! The time will soon be past when you could be content to live concealed in the woods like timid deer!*

Both modern stories end similarly. Gecko and McCoy are caught, punished, and consequently lose their 'superman' status. We witness a moralistic finale, something that does not necessarily happen in real life.

In the past two decades, business schools have witnessed the flourishing of postmodern theories of leadership that demonise Gecko and McCoy's attitudes and propose new, renovated archetypes of business leaders. This has happened at the time of the renaissance of business ethics, concomitant with some widely publicised business scandals. Indeed, today it is not possible to understand business leadership without referring to corporate responsibility, deontology or sustainability, at least conceptually.

---

*   Ibid., 144

A CEO PHILOSOPHY IN THREE QUOTES

Karl Moore

Since 2012, I have been teaching 'CEO Insights' for the McGill University MBA. Each year I teach with a current or recent CEO. Co-teachers have included Paul Tellier, former CEO of CN and Bombardier; Dick Evans, former CEO of Alcan; Zoe Yujnovich, former CEO of IOC and now chair and EVP of Shell Australia and, currently, Emma Griffin, a former senior executive who is now very active on boards. Indeed, all my co-teachers are very active on boards. They were – and continue to be – very experienced senior executives with ongoing involvement in today's business world.

We ask each CEO to bring three quotes to class that help people understand them better and that reflect their view of leadership and organisations. In our experience, the vast majority of CEOs and other accomplished leaders have a philosophy which they find helpful to communicate to the people they lead. Part of the rationale of the CEO Insights class is to help participants to further refine their leadership/management philosophy.

In the reflection paper, the capstone assignment for the class, we ask participants to discuss three quotes that encapsulate their own personal leadership philosophy (inspired by our twenty-four guest CEOs and their three quotes). There is rarely any overlap between the quotes of our CEOs and the students – a testament to the multifaceted, unique ways there are of managing organisations.

Adopting an approach used at McGill for our International Masters in Practising Management and International Masters for Health Leadership, participants in the CEO Insights class write a reflection journal. After each class, students write a page or two around that class that are then included in their journal and, although the work is not graded, I ask to look at them to encourage ongoing progress during the semester, rather than leave it to the end of the semester when their memories might fail them.

We also expect an overall class summary of two or three pages in which they reflect on the readings and class sessions and how they would be useful in their past, current or future career.

Generally, we have two CEOs per three-hour class. After an hour or so of conversation with the CEO (no PowerPoints allowed) the students form groups of three to discuss their key takeaways. After ten minutes or so I then lead (perhaps too strong a word – a good session is one in which I don't say a word) whole class reflections, where they share comments from their discussion in their small groups. Often one or more of the three quotes will be part of the group reflections.

What often strikes the students is the passion that the CEOs put into talking about their three quotes. These quotes matter to them and they say that they often share them with people in their organisations. It is a way of sharing their worldview, key lessons, key aspects of the organisational culture – in a word, their philosophy.

Today we are blessed with an abundance of resources and information from the business world, the cultural scene and political leaders. It's all at our fingertips in the form of memoirs, blog posts, news articles, and press releases. I believe, though, that there is a unique viewpoint and nuance that can be gained by having leaders encapsulate their philosophy in three soundbites.

Sheila Fraser, the former Canadian auditor general, gave us two quotes. Sheila was a formidable auditor general who stood up to more than one of Canada's prime ministers and has a reputation for fearlessly telling it like it is. Her staff reports needed to be very thorough; they had to check all the facts and be strictly neutral – her quote, 'If something is worth doing, it's worth doing well,' rang true. She was also beloved by her staff and hence came one of her other quotes: 'Treat others as you would like to be treated.' This too rang true after she told us, at some length, how we should treat staff who work for and with us.

The president of one Canada's largest financial firms, whose CEO is worth almost $2 billion, gave these three quotes:

> *When two businessmen always agree, one of them is unnecessary.*
> William Wrigley Jr. (of the chewing gum manufacturer)

Our guest CEO maintains that two analysts should contradict each other, to foster healthy debate and to encourage progress; he expects this within his organisation.

> *The toughest thing about success is that you have to keep being a success.*
>
> Irving Berlin, composer

A wry reflection on the continued pressure that comes from success, it is hard to keep hitting the ball out of the park!

And finally a quote from the CEO himself:

> *Hire character, train skill.*

He added that one ought to show vulnerability and humbleness – this is probably because he's in an industry that has to deal with big egos.

A few of our CEOs have bought quotes that they have come up with themselves over the years that really, truly, capture a key lesson they have learned. All the CEOs spoke with emotion when giving their quotes; clearly, these words meant something to them. Those they have thought of themselves were generally delivered with the most emotion and, hence, I took them to have most meaning.

One of the most storied CEOs, Mike Roach, CEO of CGI, one of the world's largest IT outsourcing companies, had three quotes of his own that have been central to CGI's business philosophy. At CGI, founder and executive chairman Serge Godin and Mike take key roles in their leadership training programme for senior people. In their sessions, they clearly express in very understandable terms what they believe has made CGI the global giant it is today. Coming from the executive chairman and CEO these are powerful sessions.

One billionaire who ran the giant firm founded by his father shared how this one wealthy family managed to stay wealthy: 'We work hard to make our money; we need to spend it wisely.' This philosophy was in contrast to some investment bankers he knew who made a great deal of money (from doing M&A with his firm) but spent it, he felt, rather unwisely. Another piece of advice he had was 'to treat everyone with respect and to listen more than you speak'.

One MBA student wrote, 'You could tell that he lives these principles from the way he greeted each of us as we walked into the room and the way he looked us right in the eyes when answering our questions. When he answered my question, looking at me all the while, it made me feel like what I'd said was important and he was giving the answer the weight it deserved.'

Bertrand Cesvet, CEO of creative firm Sid Lee, spoke about the importance of being yourself and not being afraid to stand out from the crowd. He went on to argue that we spend our youth doing everything we can to fit in. Bertrand even sees the desire to get into management consulting as representing every MBA student's desire to fit in. But ultimately, Bertrand said, 'It is the things that make us different that give us real value, at work and in every sphere of life.'

Marc Parent, the CEO of CAE, a global firm with a staff of eight-thousand-plus and a strong share in the aircraft simulation for pilot training market, told us one of his favourite quotes, 'Success blinds you to the need to change.' He added, 'You should never get so good or powerful or confident that you forget to be humble and adapt to your changing environment.' Given that they have the highest share of any company globally in their market this clearly was an important bit of business philosophy for CAE.

Not Plato or Aristotle perhaps, but nevertheless, our CEO guests succinctly expressed central parts of their business philosophy in a down-to-earth way that we could grasp. We took away a sense of the core ways they wanted the people in their organisations to view the world and how to they wanted them to do business. Philosophy in practice.

STRATEGIES TO BUILD A COLLABORATIVE CULTURE

Erica Dhawan

As the first 'mash up between Disney and Marvel Comics', the animated movie *Big Hero 6* required a combination of emotion and adventure. Its production was 'uniquely challenging', said co-director Chris Williams – requiring, for starters, the building of a supercomputer system that ultimately became the seventy-fifth largest in the world. Robust technology in place, the final cut boasts a level of detail unknown in animated film in 2015, including an urban setting, San Fransokyo, replete with 83,000 buildings and 260,000 trees. And, of course, there's the film's emotional core: a cuddly robot, Baymax, who walks like a penguin.

Big Hero 6 was awarded an Academy Award for best animated feature in 2015. Supercomputers aside, what did Williams consider most crucial to his team? Collaboration. But he acknowledges the challenges. 'In some ways, [collaboration] fights human nature,' he told an audience at the Academy of Motion Picture Arts and Sciences. 'We all want to be told, all the time, that … every thought we have is gold. But if that's all you ever get, the story's not going to get any better.'

It's one of the greatest challenges to any business; one I'm asked about most often. How to establish a collaborative environment? After all, as Williams says, it just might be that unexpected, outside input that shifts an idea from the everyday to the extraordinary. While *Big Hero 6* proves that there are exceptional rewards for those who master the art of sharing ideas, in reality it's often necessary to start with the basics – simply learning how to get along. Indeed, this is the heart of collaboration and, without this skill set – which can be learned – achieving true teamwork across an organisation is complicated, if not impossible. Here are some essential guidelines to improving communication among employees and teams.

Speaking their position

'When I was working at Citigroup we used to say that the traders were "speaking their position",' says Leah Johnson, a communications strategist who spent years in companies like Citigroup and S&P. 'For example, if you're holding a lot of a certain financial instrument that you want to sell, you're going to talk it up. That's what teams or groups within organisations do.'

Understanding the other person's position is the key to better communication. When working with another department, consider its end goal, the shared goal that drives tasks and motivations. It might not be the same one that drives you. In fact, it probably isn't.

'It's not rocket science – traders want to do right by their clients. Public relations is looking for a good story to feed the media. Investor relations is looking to engage the analysts that interpret their business,' says Johnson. These are three equally viable and equally necessary – if very different – motivators.

Here's a big-screen example. In making *Big Hero 6*, the character development team spent weeks inspecting how each lead player would sit down at a table. Meanwhile, the special effects team looked for every opportunity to blow things up. The point? We can't all be alike and we shouldn't try.

Goals affect communication styles

It's not only crucial to understand what people communicate but how they do it.

'Different communication styles are often mandated by the nature of what you do,' explains Johnson. After all, each team serves a specific set of people and follows a precise set of rules. These, says Johnson, 'dictate their roles; what they feel they are safeguarding; what they feel they are advancing and what their priorities are. And that very often dictates how they can communicate internally.'

For example, IR (investor relations) tends to be proprietary about the intel it handles. And that's really not surprising, when you consider the importance of keeping financial messaging on target – not to mention the rules and regulations that govern IR activities. Alternatively, PR executives seem to operate at consistently breakneck speed, needing everything now. They don't do this for the fun of it, but because they are at the beck and call of journalists on deadline. Without understanding each team's specific inspiration, these vastly different styles of communication can be alienating – a reason for employees to escape to their individual silos and create a sense of disengagement among colleagues.

Don't fear cultural differences

Differing teams aren't the same as opposing teams; save the battle between accounting and marketing for the summer softball league. Perhaps you think other departments move too slowly? Or too fast? Don't expect others to operate by the same rules that govern your actions – even if your colleagues live in the same town and shop at the same grocery store.

'When we are sitting in the same room, sharing geography, we tend to assume we share the same way of operating' said Johnson. In fact, 'the way you see the world is totally different from the way other people see the world. You have certain pressures, certain issues that others don't have.' Try to observe, not judge. And when you understand the other person's issues, you'll know better how to work with them.

Even when the other team is across the ocean and the physical distance is greater, the approach is the same – it's merely another opportunity for understanding. Johnson describes a common challenge in her business experiences in Japan. 'If I ask my Japanese colleagues to do something,' she says, 'they may not be willing at first blush to say no to me.' It turns out that the Japanese believe turning down a request causes them to lose face and they will rarely say 'no'. But they may not follow through. Understanding this, Johnson usually follows up with appropriate decision-makers after a request is made (especially when a request has been made in front of a group).

Change through determining culture and incentives

Knowledge is the foundation of change. To achieve effective transformation, you first need to understand the thoughts, ideas and biases that drive your team or business. Ultimately, this information will reveal the issues, attitudes and processes that need tweaking – and it can inform managers how best to manifest change.

When a company is experiencing divisiveness among teams, you can't simply initiate 'a lot of training sessions on talking to each other,' says Johnson. The effort will come off like window-dressing; employees will probably just zone out and chalk it up as another wasted hour 'doing the values thing'. To forge better relationships, you first have to understand each team's culture and know what drives its members. Next, ask (and be ready to answer) the crucial questions: 'What's the point of change?' 'What modifications do you want to make?' 'Why?' And, importantly, 'What's in it for employees?' Any less, says Johnson, is like 'driving long distances without a GPS'.

Finally, understand the incentives to change – and discuss these incentives with employees. Some departments may be more difficult to convince than others. For example, why would the top money-making department feel the need to do anything differently? Understand team members' thoughts and concerns. Be ready to address them from the start. And for those who simply refuse to budge? Perhaps share the wisdom of Benjamin Franklin, who once said, 'When you're finished changing, you're finished.'

THE PHILOSOPHY OF THE HIDDEN CHAMPIONS

Hermann Simon

Who are the hidden champions?

In 1987 the famous Harvard professor Theodore ('Ted') Levitt invited me to a conversation in Düsseldorf. Interested in the topic of international competitiveness, he had made the term 'globalisation' popular through a seminal article in the *Harvard Business Review*. That day he asked me a simple question: 'Why is Germany so successful in exports?'

Germany had become the world's export leader for the first time in 1986 and held that spot until China surpassed it in 2009. Since then, German and US exports have been virtually equal, although Germany is only one quarter the size of the US in terms of population and gross domestic product.

Levitt's question gnawed at me. Why is Germany so successful in exports? I thought first of large companies – Volkswagen, Bayer, Siemens, Bosch, and the like were all very strong exporters at the time. But this couldn't be the explanation, because the USA, Japan, and even France had more Fortune Global 500 companies than Germany.

Little by little, I found out that there are a lot of medium-sized world market leaders in Germany that nobody knows. Buried deep below the headlines of spectacular business successes and breakthroughs lay a largely ignored source not only of exports, but of management wisdom. I began to research these special companies and named them 'Hidden Champions' for the first time in a 1990 article. Five years later, Harvard Business School Press published my first *Hidden Champions* book. Several editions followed and the books have been translated into twenty-five languages. In China alone, more than one million copies have been sold.

I define a hidden champion by three criteria:

1. It is one of the top three in its world market, or No. 1 on its continent.

2. It has less than $5 billion in revenue.

3. It is hardly known to the general public.

I have discovered three thousand hidden champions around the world. About 40 per cent of them are in Germany; this category of companies seems unique to German-speaking countries, but hardly exists elsewhere (Germany, Austria, and Switzerland have about sixteen hidden champions per million population. All other countries have only 1–3 per million).

The more I dug into the hidden champions, the more fascinated I became. A whole category of truly global competitors had remained under a layer of seeming invisibility, even secrecy. Few practitioners, journalists, and academics know the names of these companies or are aware of the products and services they offer, let alone the way they conduct their business in Globalia (the term I coined to describe the globalised world). Many of them enjoy world market shares of over 50 per cent, numbers that few giant multinationals can match. And this hasn't changed much since Levitt posed his question.

I did numerous surveys on the hidden champions and undertook hundreds of visits to their sites, where I was impressed, especially by personal encounters with their founders, owners, and CEOs. If I had to choose one common root of the success of the hidden champions, it would be their leaders. At first glance, they are as diverse as people in general, but as I explored further I could distil several common traits which deserve to be called 'philosophical'. Their leadership and the cultures they create are very different from large corporations. Many of these traits have their own roots in the work of famous philosophers, both eastern and western.

Willpower

Having an idea and realising it are two different things. If your idea or vision is to become the global market leader – the best in your market worldwide – you have a long and torturous road ahead of you. Hidden champions are proof that you have a chance to reach that goal if you possess the combination of outstanding willpower and relentless ambition.

The definition of 'will' or 'willpower' leads us to the philosophers Arthur Schopenhauer (1788–1860) and Friedrich Nietzsche (1844–1900). Schopenhauer says, 'A man can do what he wants, but not want what he wants.' In Nietzsche's philosophy, the 'will to power' is a central concept, understood as an irrational force that can be channelled to different ends. The 'will to power' is not an independent work by Friedrich Nietzsche, but a thought which he presents in *Die Fröhliche Wissenschaft* (*The Gay Science*) and the subsequent work *Also Sprach Zarathustra* (*Thus Spoke Zarathustra*) and which is mentioned in all his subsequent books. This concept hardly ever appears in the management literature, however.

One exception is the work of Marvin Bower, the co-founder of McKinsey, who published books with the titles *The Will to Manage* and *The Will to Lead*.

I found that willpower, combined with the relentless ambition to become the global market leader, are defining characteristics of the leaders of hidden champions. These traits forge a profound unity of person and purpose. The person and the company are indivisible.

'His person and his company have always been one entity,' is a common description of the late Hans Riegel of the German firm Haribo, world-market leader in fruit gums. Heinz-Horst Deichmann, who founded Germany's eponymous European market leader for shoes, said, 'I savoured the smell of leather from my infancy. I love people and I love shoes.' Jake Burton, the American founder of Burton Snowboards, advised, 'Live your work.' These remarks reminded me of a finding about artists and scientists. In their collection of twelve case studies of famous creative people, authors Doris B. Wallace and Howard E. Gruber concluded, '[f]or many creative people the life is the work. They integrate rather than separate their personal life and their work.'

As genuine people who identify completely with their companies, the leaders of the hidden champions have charisma and persuasive power. Their attitude toward work implies that money is not their primary driving force. Motivation derives primarily from these leaders' identification and satisfaction with their work. Economic success is secondary. Their willpower and their absolute commitment and responsibility give such leaders tremendous credibility. They have no reservations about their work and assume full responsibility. True leadership can never be play-acted; it must reside in the leader's core.

Focus

If you have the willpower to strive to become the best and the leader in your market, how do you pursue this goal? The answer is clear and simple. You will succeed only if you focus on the one thing you want to achieve. Only focus leads to world-class. The literature on this subject is overwhelming and ranges from philosophical to trivial sources.

Peter Drucker labels this trait 'single-mindedness'. He knew the physicist Buckminster Fuller and the communication expert Marshall McLuhan personally, and said they 'exemplify to me the importance of being single-minded. The Fullers and the McLuhans carry out a "mission"; the rest of us have interests. Whenever anything is being accomplished, it is being done by a monomaniac with a mission.' Bill Gates, the founder of Microsoft, echoes this, saying that '[m]y success is that I have focused in on a few things'. These quotes fully capture the essence of hidden champion leaders: they are monomaniacs with a mission.

Manfred Bogdahn, the founder of Flexi, says, 'We only focus on one thing, but we do it better than anyone else.' Flexi is the market leader in retractable dog leashes, with a global share of 70 per cent. Beware of encountering these monomaniacs as competitors! I have met them. They may be no smarter than you or I, but they are more obsessed with their ideas. Their absolute focus on their missions makes them unbeatable.

Self-reliance

Wilhelm Tell, the Swiss national hero, says in Friedrich von Schiller's eponymous play, 'The strong one is most powerful alone.' In the essay 'Self-Reliance', American philosopher Ralph Waldo Emerson recommends that all individuals 'avoid conformity and false consistency and instead follow their own instincts and ideas'.

Many modern management fashions reject the relevance of self-reliance by insisting that managers seek their salvation outside the company. Two such popular tactics are outsourcing and strategic alliances. Outsourcing delegates to others everything that those others can produce more cheaply. Strategic alliances create the hope – often in vain – that cooperation with other companies makes one stronger.

The actions of hidden champions follow the classic tenets of Tell and Emerson rather than management fashions. They rely on their own strengths and prefer to go it alone. Two cases illustrate this 'antiquated' attitude. Wanzl, Germany's global leader in airport luggage carts, says, 'We produce all parts ourselves, based on the quality standards we define.' You will find Wanzl carts in airports all over the world, even in Tokyo-Narita airport, in Beijing, and in Shanghai.

Faber-Castell, the global leader in pencils, based in Germany, states, 'We grow our own wood in our own plantations.' When I challenged the late Count Faber-Castell by suggesting he ought to purchase his wood on the market instead, he responded, 'Yes, when I took over from my father in 1978 we actually bought the wood. But I found that we never got the same consistent quality year after year. Therefore, I decided to grow our own wood.' Today, Faber-Castell runs its own plantation of a hundred square kilometers in Brazil, where they grow the wood to make 2.3 billion pencils per year.

Many hidden champions even build the machines they use to make their end products. When I asked for an explanation, they said, 'In order to achieve the superiority and uniqueness of our end product, we have to go several steps deeper in our value chain. There we create the unique processes, machines and features which lead to the superiority in the end product.' This reveals a much more general and deeper lesson: you can never buy the qualities of being unique and superior on the market; you can only create it internally. Self-reliance may sound old-fashioned, but it is one foundation of the hidden champion success.

Fearlessness

Fear is a recurring theme among philosophers, with Søren Kierkegaard's *Fear and Trembling* perhaps the most prominent work. Nietzsche and Spinoza have also written about fear. Last but not least, Sigmund Freud wrote a lot about fear and anxiety. Fear protects us against all kinds of dangers, but it also constrains us.

The opposite of fear is courage, a trait often ascribed to entrepreneurs. Berthold Leibinger, who led TRUMPF to world market leadership in laser machines, regards the 'courage to take a risk' as the most important entrepreneurial quality. However, I would prefer to call the hidden champions' entrepreneurs 'fearless' rather than 'courageous'. They are not people who jump from the sky. Rather, they appear to have understood and embraced the Chinese philosophy that 'ignorance of your freedom is your captivity'. The hidden champion leaders do not share the same inhibitions and fears as other people, so they can deploy their skills more effectively. It is impressive to see how many of these leaders have conquered the world's markets without higher education, foreign experience or language skills.

Interestingly, I see these traits again today in Chinese entrepreneurs who have set out to turn their companies into hidden champions. They may lack foreign experience and speak only rudimentary English, but they are fearless. Nowhere else in the world do I encounter more entrepreneurs who raise their hands when I ask, 'Who wants to become a hidden champion?'

Innovation

'Not to innovate is to die,' writes Christopher Freeman, the doyen of innovation theorists. Few would argue this point. However, when we talk of innovation, we typically think of radically new products and processes. Breakthrough innovators such as Apple and Google attract attention and become media darlings. But breakthrough innovations are rare in the real world. Berthold Leibinger of TRUMPF observes real breakthroughs only once every fifteen years in his high-tech laser sector.

Hidden champions rely on continuous improvement rather than on groundbreaking innovation. Wanzl says that their history 'is a story of continual innovations', referring precisely to the goal of ongoing improvement. Breakthrough innovations, whether in shopping or baggage carts, remain the exception.

Sennheiser, one of the global market leaders in microphones and headphones, states, 'Evolution, not revolution, has made the company strong.' Swarovski, the global market leader for cut crystal, still propagates the slogan of its founder, 'Constantly improving what is already good'. For 120 years, the maxim of Miele, global market leader in premium washing machines, has been 'Forever better'. This simple slogan expresses the determination to deliver the absolute top product in every market in the world. In a single year, the global leader in chainsaws, Stihl, introduced forty-two innovations, albeit none spectacular.

Hidden champions' superiority is often based on doing many small things better than their competitors. Their products and services are closer to perfection, the result of a never-ending series of improvements, rather than single breakthrough innovations. All this is similar to the Japanese method of 'kaizen', which is often labelled 'the philosophy of continuous improvement'.

Levitt also described this tenet, 'Sustained success is largely a matter of focusing regularly on the right things and making a lot of uncelebrated improvements every day.' The gradual innovation can also be seen as a realisation of Immanuel Kant's 'middle way' between breakthroughs and zero innovation.

What is the deeper meaning behind this innovation philosophy? With gradual steps, even someone who is not an Einstein or a Steve Jobs can become world-class. The hidden champions have proven this a thousand times over by doing something a little better every day.

Polarity

There is simply no mathematical optimisation that can be applied to regulate such stark polarities as centralisation versus decentralisation or customer orientation versus technology orientation. Contradictions or polarities are typical of the hidden champions and arise in many forms. They have learned that it is better to permit flowing relationships or grey areas between these polarities and to allow for different courses of action, depending on the situation. This thinking has deep philosophical roots too.

In western culture, we tend to distinguish right from wrong, true from false, black from white. By contrast, eastern cultures consider the world as flowing, without strictly defined boundaries. Where people from the west see contradictions, people from the east see complementary elements. The philosopher Edward de Bono speaks of a western 'stone culture' and an eastern 'water culture' in this context. The philosopher Nicholas of Cusa (1401–64) saw in all things *coincidentia oppositorum* ('opposites coincide').

Authors Paul R. Lawrence and Jay W. Lorsch have addressed such contradictions in relation to centralisation and decentralisation in organizations. The physician Barry Johnson deals with similar issues in his book *Polarity Management*. Gore, the hidden champion best known for Gore-Tex products, includes specific polarities in its company philosophy. The principle of 'freedom' applies to the extent that each employee has the freedom to do what they consider right. The freedom is, however, restricted by the 'waterline' principle. As soon as a decision could hole the corporate ship below the waterline, a colleague must be consulted to share the responsibility for the decision. While this freedom principle encourages all employees to make use of their full potential, the waterline principle is intended to guarantee that the company does not suffer any serious damage.

One may interpret the strategy and leadership of the hidden champions as contradictory in many aspects. Yet these contradictions, alongside the capacity to handle them, together conform to Johnson's proposals for the solution of 'unsolvable problems'. The study conducted by Lawrence and Lorsch points in the same direction. The most successful organisations were those that displayed a high level of integration (centralisation) as well as a high level of differentiation (decentralisation).

Inspiration

Artists may acquire global fame as individuals. But in an economic enterprise, nobody can single-handedly create a world-market leader. They always need cooperation and support from others. Augustine of Hippo, bishop and philosopher, formulated the challenge, 'What you want to ignite in others, must first burn inside yourself.' The fire that burns in a leader alone is insufficient; they must ignite it in others – usually in many others.

According to leadership expert Warren Bennis, we still don't know why people follow certain leaders and don't follow others. A key capacity of the leaders of hidden champions is the ability to inspire others with enthusiasm for the company's mission and to encourage them to deliver the best performance they can. I can only say that they are very effective and successful in this respect. Maybe the strongest proof is the extremely low employee turnover rate of 2.7 per cent per year. (The annual average for most countries lies between 10 and 20 per cent.) This cannot be attributed to superficial attributes such as style or communication, because many hidden champion leaders are not great communicators in the usual sense.

I believe that the qualities discussed above – willpower, ambition, unity of person and purpose, focus, self-reliance, fearlessness and continual innovation – play a crucial role in the ability to ignite the fire in others.

The last building block is that of continuity. The leaders of hidden champions stay at the helm for twenty years on average. In most large corporations, the leaders' average tenure is six years. That says everything about continuity and long-term orientation.

Summary

Hidden champions apply their own philosophy to strategy and leadership. They neither believe in nor follow many of the modern management fashions. Most of their practices can be traced back to prominent philosophers. Hidden champion leaders understand and live their wisdom. They go their own ways. In essence, their only secret formula for success boils down to common sense – so simple, yet so difficult to achieve. This is the ultimate lesson of the hidden champion philosophy.

INTERVIEW WITH MEGAN REITZ

'I and thou' – interaction in the workspace and relational leadership

Philosophy@work: Megan, as a facilitator, executive coach and researcher you mostly focused on the way people encounter one another in organisational systems and you became an expert in this field. Encountering one another can be anything – seeing each other, speaking to one another or learning from each other. You claim that the way we communicate with one another in the workspace is a highly complex and dynamic process that shouldn't be underestimated. Therefore, you developed a concept called 'relational leadership'. Could you explain this concept and why the complexity in our dialogue is so important?

Megan Reitz: The concept of relational leadership includes both of the things you just mentioned: speaking to one another and encountering one another in the workspace. The underlying potential of these phenomena lies beyond regular notions of communication and encounter. Different from a common conversation, real dialogue is about two individuals opening up and the new mutual shared understanding that is created through the dialogue. Likewise, leadership is also a lot more than a hierarchical position. Leadership is about real dialogue that leads to connection and flow within the organisation. Unfortunately, it is often the case that people in senior roles don't realise how complex and dynamic communication and leadership actually are. This unawareness leads to a loss of the great potential that a group of people could embrace if dialogue and leadership were mindfully practised. Often leaders tend to underestimate and accidently silence people around them who actually influence and create the culture within the organisation.

Since dialogue and leadership both are mostly much more complex processes than we think, I created the concept of relational leadership. It clarifies that leadership must be observed from a specific point of view: the relational one. Leadership is relational and not hierarchical. This means that the process of leadership can only occur in relation and is more complex than having a single leader and a follower.

Leadership doesn't have a clear definition and, therefore, we can recognise leadership in ourselves and others for many different reasons. It is possible to feel led by someone in some ways but not in every way. Everything depends on the context, the actual moment and the dialogue. From this perspective, leadership is similar to a relationship that is also more dimensional and includes many factors that can be combined in many different ways.

Therefore, the term 'relational leadership' probably describes the general term 'leadership' in a closer way if you consider all the great potential that is behind it.

Unfortunately, traditional leadership development approaches underestimate this complexity mostly because of a more simplistic understanding. With the concept of relational leadership, leaders are aware of the fact that there is a highly complex relation between them and their employees that has the potential to go the way everybody within the organisation strives for. This relation includes all of the things you mentioned in your question – seeing each other, communicating and also learning from each other depends on the relation that is created by the leader. The quality of the seeing, communicating or learning, of course, depends on the quality of the relationship but it's also the other way around, because the relationship is built upon the experiences we shared while seeing, communicating or learning. If leadership is considered relational and dialogue created in a relation improving way, the leader can create a positive working environment in which everybody actively participates.

Philosopy@work: That means if we are aware of the underlying complexity of our actions we can create a positive working environment. This sounds wonderful because it's what so many leaders set as their goal but not everybody seems to successfully fulfil that goal. But isn't it still a quite rare situation in which everybody fully participates and connects with each other?

Megan Reitz: Of course, the quality of the relationship and dialogue grows or shrinks gradually and there can be different states in which a working environment can be considered as positive. It doesn't always have to be the ultimate connection or 'flow', as I like to call it, but I think that the concept of relational leadership always aims for the best possible version of dialogue and relation. Whether the dialogue is an OK one, a good one or a perfect one also depends on the participants in this dialogue, the situation and the day but, if leadership is considered in the relational way and therefore practised openly and mindfully, a positive environment will arise.

There can even be a state that is a great example for the ultimate version of dialogue and leadership. I like to describe it as 'resonance', 'connection' or 'flow'. Throughout my career I have experienced this state a few times and immediately became very interested in this kind of experience. At some point I called it 'empathic resonance' but even with a title it is still very difficult to describe what exactly is meant by this phenomenon. There is a way to describe empathic resonance but it is always in the presentational form or – to it put another way – by going into poetry or metaphor. The best description of my experience I call empathic resonance was given by the philosopher Martin Buber, especially within his work *I and Thou*. When I first read this work I was really fascinated by the way Buber described the encounter in a unique way and felt like his thoughts perfectly described the experience that I made with empathic resonance. To create an understanding for the term 'empathic resonance', and also Buber's work, I would like to give a short introduction to his theory in *I and Thou*.

His best known/most-famous philosophical work, *I and Thou* distinguishes between two word pairs that name two basic modes of existence: 'I-thou' and 'I-it'. The I-thou relation is the pure encounter of one unique entity with another in such a way that the other is known without being seen universally. The I-it relation is driven by categories of 'same' and 'different' and gives a universal definition. An I-it relation experiences a thing – fixed in space and time – while the I-thou relation participates in the dynamic, living process of an 'other'.

Furthermore, Buber explains that the self becomes either more fragmentary or more unified through its relationships with others. This also means that a human being becomes whole only through a relation to another self. The formation of the 'I' in the I-thou relation takes place in a dialogical relationship in which each partner is active and passive and both are accepted as a whole being. Only this kind of a relationship makes it possible to experience the other truly as an 'other' and only in this encounter can the 'I' develop as a whole being.

The way Buber engages with the themes around the quality of encounter, genuine dialogue and seeing one another made him extremely important for my work. His theory and especially the I-thou relation refers to the way in which humans are intertwined and interconnected with one another and also the way we participate constantly in one another's worlds.

While getting to know Buber's wonderful work, I found answers for the experience of empathic resonance because his poetical description of the I-thou relation gave me a feeling of him describing the same phenomenon. The I-thou relation reminded me of the experiences of resonance, connection and flow.

Philosophy@work: The I-thou relation is probably not the first thing a leader has on their mind when engaging in a new project but it sounds like this would actually be a good move, if leadership should be considered as relational. How applicable is the existence of the I-thou relation to the relation between a leader and an employee?

Megan Reitz: The I-thou relation is perfectly applicable to the relation between a leader and an employee. In fact, the I-thou relation was a very profound finding in the discovery of relational leadership and is therefore a very important part of it. 'I' and 'thou' actually bear all the great potential that relational leadership aims to embrace because the ground rules for a successful encounter and dialogue are defined by fully understanding the interaction between them.

A conversation between you and me or a leader and an employee can go any which way but if the conversation is understood in terms of the 'I' and 'thou' it is automatically clear that both of the partners are active and passive at the same time and need to see each other as a whole human being to become a whole human being. Furthermore, I and thou remind of the fact that all people are interconnected and participate constantly in each other's worlds.

I think that this understanding of human interaction is helpful in every encounter – also outside the workspace – but it is especially helpful in context of the leader-employee relationship. It's because the classic construct of leadership is an issue. Normally, the understanding of a leader will always be connected to authority, power and difference. Furthermore, the working environment is one of hierarchy and labels which makes it even harder for people to trust the leader and mentally disconnect leadership from authority, power and difference.

Of course, these three notions stand in the way of what the I-thou relation aims for. Perceiving one another as whole human beings and engaging in successful dialogue can arise on a basis of the I-thou relation, but not on the notions of authority, power and difference.

Philosophy@work: How can relational leadership and the underlying I-thou relation be successfully taught to leaders who want to change their working environment to a more positive, dynamic one?

Megan Reitz: Mindfulness is the most important practice when it comes to a pursuit of a change towards positivity, real dialogue and flow. After I discovered the interesting coherences of Martin Buber's I-thou relation and leadership I always worked on a programme for the concept of relational leadership that would make it possible for leaders to see everyone as a human being, base the dialogue on that relation and therefore create a positive working environment. Just the understanding of what is meant by the I-thou relation and relational leadership won't make leaders immediately act in a different way.

Becoming mindful is not easy and needs hard work and dedication. But aiming for more mindfulness is absolutely worth it. Within my research I found out that sustained practise of mindfulness leads to statistically significant improvements in resilience, adaptability, emotional regulation, empathy and focus. There is also evidence that more mindful people are also less prone to cognitive biases in their decision making. Mindfulness is a skill that can be trained and its improvement brings along a variety of positive skills. Of course, the mind can be trained just like the body. And when the mind gets trained it affects the entire way someone perceives the world and therefore the way someone acts. That's why the thinking needs to be changed first in order to change actions.

Changing thinking is what mindfulness is all about. I think that the best way to become more mindful is to engage in self-reflection. The goal of self-reflection for leaders contains being conscious about themselves and their actions. The best way to reach this goal is to actively engage in self-reflection in an indirect way. Buber's work and the concept of relational leadership are topics that feel uncooperative and maybe also un-workplace-like. The key to integrate these topics anyway is to speak the language of the people a leader is working with. A conversation that should result in a realisation about mindfulness starts with some general questions like:

What is your life like at the moment?

What is your experience of life?

What challenges do you face?

To be even more specific a question like this would be helpful: what would you love to be doing better in your organisation?

Questions like these are especially helpful when it comes to the realisation of possible improvements and/or weaknesses. The self-reflection makes people not only realise their weaknesses, it also makes them come up with ideas that could be improved in order to overhaul these weaknesses. Throughout my career I collected a bunch of traits that many leaders in the twenty-first century considered crucial: resilience, collaboration and leading in complexity.

When they come up with capacities that would decrease the impact of weaknesses and improve the working of the leader and the team, the next step is to consider how these capacities can be developed.

Philosophy@work: That seems like the leader somehow usually has an intuition that already bears good ideas for improvement of the working environment, but self-reflection needs to be encouraged in order to get to those ideas. This is a completely different approach than planning a regular meeting on a topic like 'mindfulness', but I guess that many companies organise meetings like this. What do you think about planned mindfulness?

Megan Reitz: Unfortunately, the typical way for an organisational system to teach mindfulness is exactly this way. Most organisations have a business case for themes like 'reduction of stress and anxiety' or 'increasing focus and awareness'. Mostly, these business cases fail because there is a difference between forcing people to reduce stress in a certain amount of time once a week and integrating a way stress can be reduced constantly. It is the same thing when it comes to mindfulness. Mindfulness cannot be taught in forty-five minutes during a mindfulness workshop. Openings like, 'Let's talk about mindfulness,' are not going to start an open discussion about mindfulness.

The best basis for all of these aims, like reduction of stress or increasing of mindfulness, is what the I-thou relation and relational leadership teaches us: there should be an open dialogue in our organisations, from a moral, ethical and human perspective. With an open dialogue like this, stress would be reduced constantly and mindfulness would be an essential part of the working environment.

Philosophy@work: I see. Mindfulness cannot be forced – it must be implemented in the whole structure to succeed. But training to get mindfulness into the organisation is the perfect way to create a positive working environment.

Megan, for the last question I want to ask you about the consequences that arise if a leader doesn't engage in mindfulness. You wrote a book on 'speaking up' – a concept or practice which should be possible if the working environment is positive. Could you give an insight to the concept of speaking up and its relation to mindfulness?

Megan Reitz: When it comes to speaking up we especially have to consider the fact that the employee is not entirely responsible for speaking up. Although the majority of management writing suggests that the individual should be brave and courageous in speaking up, it is a shared responsibility to involve the great ideas of the employees into the working process. Of course, the employee has to be brave for speaking up but also the leader has to listen up and skilfully invite others to speak. The possibility to speak up relies on the shared responsibility of both things: bravery and active listening.

Not only poor listening skills hinder people from speaking up. It is also the concept of power that can scare people in a way that they have a hard time speaking up. Within business settings, no one talks about 'power' and the influence of it. Somehow, we all wish that power away because it influences the way we behave in an organisation. The underestimation of power causes worries about whistle-blowing, promotion or the possibility of losing jobs. The two most common reasons why people stay quiet is because they are worried about being perceived negatively and also worried about being rejected. Humans are social animals and, therefore, anything that inhibits that or threatens belonging is something that will silence ourselves.

Another reason for people staying silent is something I discovered in research and named 'titles' or 'labels'. As human beings we tend to label each other within milliseconds, taking into account gender, age and ethnicity and also a variety of other things, like appearance or attractiveness.

On top of that, inside organisations we have all the labels like 'director' or 'chief executive'. In fact, all of these labels come together to affect whether we feel like we have the status and authority to say something and whether other people have the status and authority to be listened to. It turns out that the labels and the titles that we give to one another affect the dynamics of the whole system in an organisation. Of course, that means if we want to change the way people speak up we have to be aware of the labels and titles we give each other and how they affect the dynamics in the whole system.

The relation between speaking up and mindfulness is similar to the relation between encounter, dialogue and mindfulness. If a leader wants to listen carefully and invite others to speak up, mindfulness must be practised and be implemented in the organisation. With practise of mindfulness, genuine dialogue and the idea of the I-thou relation and relational leadership, people will be able to speak up and connect to each other so that the working environment becomes positive and everything flows.

PART III

COPING WITH THE FORCES OF CHANGE AND EXPONENTIAL TECHNOLOGIES

KARL POPPER'S EPISTEMOLOGY AND THE DESIGN OF BUSINESS STRATEGIES

Anil K. Gupta and Haiyan Wang

Karl Popper, the Austrian-British epistemologist, is widely regarded as one of the twentieth century's greatest philosophers of science. Outside of Popper's massive impact on the design of scientific research, we argue here that his arguments also have potent implications for the design of business strategies.

In *The Logic of Scientific Discovery*, one of his seminal books, Popper argued that – even though the goal of scientific research is to discover the truth – strictly speaking, this goal can never be achieved. Whatever we believe to be true is nothing but a conjecture, waiting to be falsified. Consider, for example, the question, 'What colours do swans come in?' After looking at many swans, a scientist may conclude, 'All swans are white.' Logically, however, this conclusion would be wrong. The only thing that the scientist can really say is, 'I have not yet seen a swan that is other than white.' Thus, the statement, 'All swans are white,' is merely a hypothesis, i.e. a conjecture.

Importantly, Popper further argued that it is futile to try and test if any hypothesis is true. No matter how many more observations keep yielding only white swans, we'll never know if there may exist non-white swans. Thus, hypotheses can only be falsified. The moment one observes one black swan, the original hypothesis is proven to be false. The new hypothesis might now be, 'All swans come in one of two colours – white or black.' This hypothesis too can never be proved. It can only be falsified. Maybe there exist green swans that nobody has seen yet. In short, scientists should focus on attempts to falsify hypotheses rather than on trying to prove them. That is the only way to advance knowledge.

Popper logic and business strategies

In the light of Popper's advocacy of falsification, the primary focus of business strategies should be to upend accepted industry wisdom rather than follow the current rules of the game. Rules are analogous to theoretical hypotheses that merely represent the best knowledge of the time. As an example, prior to Tesla Motors, electric vehicles were regarded as low-powered, short-distance vehicles most appropriate in niche areas, such as golf carts or passenger transporters inside airport terminals. Elon Musk's strategy with Tesla has been to develop electric cars that could take on Porsche in terms of power while also going farther on one charge than a gasoline-driven car on a full tank.

As another example, take the mobile phone industry. Prior to Apple's launch of the iPhone, virtually the entire industry – including leading players such as Nokia, Samsung, and RIM (parent of BlackBerry) – thought of mobile phones as mainly voice telephony devices that could perform one or two other functions, such as email. In contrast, Steve Jobs and his team conceived of the iPhone as an internet-connected, small PC that – by the way – could also do voice calls.

Secondly, upending the widely popular 'five forces' framework of US academic Michael Porter, business leaders need to think of companies not being at the mercy of industry structure but as potentially capable of altering the industry structure themselves.

Forces such as buyer power, supplier power and the height of entry barriers are not simply exogenous variables. They are open also to proactive actions by individual companies.

In Popper's terminology, this is like falsifying current conjectures. Take Apple Watch, which was launched in 2015. Within a mere three years, it became the biggest-selling watch globally. A five-forces analysis in 2014 might have suggested that the watch industry was mature, dominated by major Swiss and Japanese companies, and with extremely high barriers to entry. Yet, this seeming lock-in by existing players was not much of a barrier for Apple.

As another example, look at Gatorade's 1965 entry into the beverages business. Given the dominance of Coca-Cola and Pepsi, a five-forces analysis would not have predicted successful entry or scaling up by a small start-up. Yet, Gatorade did enter and did scale up until the best option for one of the incumbents was to buy the company rather than try to kill it. Under Armour provides a similar example. The athletic apparel industry is dominated by Nike and Adidas. Yet, Under Armour came from literally nowhere to become a successful third major brand in the industry.

In sum, like Popper's favourite scientists, business leaders need to think of themselves first and foremost as explorers or rule-makers rather than as merely exploiters or rule-takers. There is no logical basis for them to treat current best practices as the ultimate truth. Their primary goal should be to invent the next practice which falsifies our existing notions of what is current best practice.

ORGANISING FOR UNCERTAINTY: CHINESE 'RULES OF THUMB'

Mark J. Greeven

> *The blowing of the wind is never the same, but it gives*
> *everything something of its own. All will get its own*
> *place. But who is the one blowing the wind?*

> *Zhuangzi*, Chapter Two

A contemporary of Aristotle, Zhuang Zhou (known as Zhuangzi) (c. 360 bc) was a true independent thinker from ancient China. He lived during the Warring States period (c. 475–250 bc), a period of unrest in ancient China between competing warlords.

This was also an era of bureaucratic and military reforms; a time of searching for novel social and political models, innovations in technology and sophisticated arithmetic. It was not unlike the era in which Aristotle developed his thoughts among the competing city states of ancient Greece. And, come to think of it, the Warring States are not that different from the twenty-first century – with turbulent politics, changes in society, technological breakthroughs, hyper-competition and, unfortunately, still warfare.

It should come as no surprise that in such times of widespread uncertainty, a multitude of great thinkers emerged in China, later known as the Hundred Schools of Thought. Laozi's *Dao De Jing*, the *I Ching* (or the *Book of Changes*, as it is popularly known), Confucius' *Analects* and Sun Zi's *The Art of War* were among the many emerging philosophies.

Zhuangzi, however, stands out with his collection of eponymously titled fables and allegories, renowned for their wordplay and use of parables to convey messages. *Zhuangzi* was– along with the *Dao De Jing* – one of the two foundational texts of Daoism. If *Dao De Jing* is a song, then *Zhuangzi* is a symphony (Schipper, 2007); a symphony of disparate thoughts that have inspired writers, leaders and thinkers for more than two thousand years.

Interestingly, classical Chinese philosophy has recently made a comeback in modern China. We now often hear references to the classics in interviews with entrepreneurs and we can observe a revival of interest in Chinese business leaders. In fact – modern China's central government's relative stability notwithstanding – there is no place in the world more dynamic and turbulent than China. Decades of reform, decentralised implementation of policy, drastic changes in consumer behaviour with the rapid emergence of a middle-class, competition in private markets and the embrace of new, digital, technologies are sources for turbulence.

According to the 2017 Global Entrepreneurship Monitor report, entrepreneurs rate China's internal market dynamics as, on average, 40 per cent higher than global or regional averages. As I was told during an interview in Hangzhou, 'You ask me how I perceive the changes in the business context? For me, change is the essence of doing business in China. I have never known any different. Of course, I can try to ignore or hide from change, but it will catch up anyhow. I'd rather be flexible and embrace such changes and exploit the opportunities they may reveal.'

What guiding principles can we derive from the contemplations of *Zhuangzi* for organising for uncertainty in modern times? In itself this question would be a misreading of *Zhuangzi*, as there is no belief in 'rules' or 'prescriptions'. At the risk of being ridiculed by Daoist scholars, however, we can fairly safely derive some heuristics, or rules of thumb. I am, after all, just a business thinker looking for guidance in how to organise people to thrive on – and not fear – uncertainty in business. Four such rules stand out and are reflected in today's business world in China and may prove relevant elsewhere as well.

Uncertainty is natural ➜ 'no such thing as an established enterprise'

Everything is in perspective ➜ 'fight your subconscious biases to find a perspective'

Rules are unnatural ➜ 'design for an emergent organisation'

Boundaries do not exist ➜ 'we all live in ecosystems'

The first rule of thumb: uncertainty is natural

One of the fundamental thoughts in *Zhuangzi* is that uncertainty is natural. Through the various fables it becomes clear that we cannot distinguish between what is known and what is not known and that nothing is certain universally. The emphasis, therefore, is less on who a person is but more on the knowledge a person has: What do I know and how do I know that?

In philosophical terms, Chinese schools of thought focus on epistemology rather than ontology. The big divide with western schools of thought comes with the focus on correlational logic, i.e. that two things are related but we do not know what causes the other. This stands in contrast to looking for causal explanations.

The natural tendency is, then, to treat phenomena and behaviour as correlational and holistic. This forms the basis for accepting that uncertainty is natural and change is continuous.

Today we look at China as an economic powerhouse with hero entrepreneurs like Jack Ma, Ren Zhengfei and Zhang Ruimin. But, not long ago, private entrepreneurs in China were seen as the signs of unwanted capitalism. Huawei and Haier, Lenovo and Wahaha were established in times when even the legal status of ownership was ambiguous, let alone the wider rules of the business game.

Former president Deng Xiaoping's endorsement of private enterprise in 1992 and the promulgated retreat of the state in the early 2000s introduced market competition. But it hasn't been a smooth ride: continuous reforms and regulatory changes have kept enterprises mostly in the dark. For instance, new IPO filings have been stopped for periods of three to fourteen months on eight occasions in the last two decades. Each stoppage heralded a cold winter for investors. Today, however, entrepreneurship and innovation are celebrated again.

For Chinese enterprises there is no doubt that the current prosperous situation will not continue indefinitely. In fact, Ren Zhengfei, the founder of Huawei, famously said, 'There is no such thing as an established enterprise.' Considering that Huawei is one of the world's largest and most innovative companies, it is surprising to hear that they are not resting on their laurels.

Another iconic enterprise, Haier, established by Zhang Ruimin, works on the same premise. Since the late 1990s, the company has been experimenting with new ways of organising – reducing bureaucracy and increasing entrepreneurship within Haier.

Even in the internet industry, already flatly organised, we see widespread changes to organisational structures. The most recent example is Tencent, who have scrapped three business divisions, Mobile Internet Group (MIG), Online Media Group (OMG), and Social Network Group (SNG). They have also integrated cloud and content into two new divisions. This is Tencent's third large-scale reorganisation in its twenty-year history.

Uncertainty is natural: 'There is no such thing as an established enterprise.' Perhaps we should redefine the success of a company to include adaptability and innovativeness and drop revenues and market share. Innovation cannot only be focused on products and technology but must be about reinventing the organisation itself.

The second rule of thumb: everything in perspective

> *Once, Zhuang Zhou dreamed he was a butterfly, a butterfly flitting and fluttering about, happy with himself and doing as he pleased. He didn't know that he was Zhuang Zhou. Suddenly he woke up and there he was, solid and unmistakable, Zhuang Zhou. But he didn't know if he was Zhuang Zhou who had dreamed he was a butterfly or a butterfly dreaming that he was Zhuang Zhou. Between Zhuang Zhou and the butterfly there must be some distinction! This is called the Transformation of Things.*
>
> Zhuangzi, Chapter Two

Nothing is what it seems. A fundamental thought in *Zhuangzi* is that everyone and everything has its own perspective. It would be futile to try to agree on one perspective, as even a bystander or a neutral observer would bring their own view. It becomes clear from *Zhuangzi* that we should instead fight our subconscious biases and not only try to change perspectives but also learn how to take a perspective on things.

Chinese business leaders are adept in taking perspective and challenging assumptions. For instance, Uber underestimated local competitor DiDi Chuxing and misunderstood the local game in China; here, it was never about taxis but about mobile payments. Uber was de facto competing with Alibaba and Tencent, who had much deeper pockets, and better user-facing technology. Take Amazon, which is operating in China but just does not do as well as local competitors such as JD.com because they do not understand the Chinese consumer well enough.

A similar thing happened when eBay entered the Chinese market. At the time it had global revenues of more than two billion dollars. As a young, domestic entity, Alibaba's consumer platform Taobao was taking on a huge rival while also fending off many similar small competitors. Key factors in its success included using the apparent weakness of being a small Chinese company as a strength by emphasising Chinese culture, choosing kung fu names for moderators, developing a chat-based customer service and a user-driven merchant review system. Jack Ma had turned the disadvantages of being small, new and Chinese into distinct advantages, besting eBay in China.

Everything is in perspective. This translates into 'Fight your subconscious biases to find a perspective'. There is nothing wrong with following a deliberate strategy or copying best practice, as long as your company proactively challenges assumptions and takes in new information while implementing its processes. A diversity of perspectives, employed by a diverse organisation, is necessary and will allow you to fight subconscious biases in your organisation.

The third rule of thumb: rules are unnatural

> *Follow the spontaneous movement of things and cherish*
> *no personal preference. Then the world will see order.*
>
> *Zhuangzi*, Chapter Seven

Zhuangzi dedicated multiple chapters to his criticism of the dogma of the Confucian way of life. In particular, he was strongly against fixed rules and universal morality. His thinking is unique, in that he had no political affiliations nor was he endorsed by political or military leaders. His critiques of Confucian society and historical figures are humorous and at times ironic.

In fact, *Zhuangzi* does not read as a book. There is no particular sequence and it is not intended to be read as a guide or treatise. There is no developed argument but merely a collection of fables and allegories. However, read together – in whatever order you please – it provides an anti-conformist and highly independent way of thinking.

Eliminating rules does not mean promoting chaos. In fact, Chinese companies have adopted organisational approaches that keep rules and bureaucracy to a minimum but provide sufficient guidance. Two approaches stand out and provide excellent references for organising for uncertainty: internal competitive markets and de-organising.

The first approach – internal competitive markets – refers to a practice that many Chinese firms have adopted. Companies such as Ele.me, the location-based service provider; DJI, world-leading consumer drone manufacturer; Xiaomi, the smart-home ecosystem, Tencent, Haier and DiDI all have a product development process based on competing projects. When they come up with any concept for a product or service, the companies organise competing project teams that, in parallel, develop similar and often competing products. The company chooses the best option and the other project teams are dissolved.

It is not just companies with resource slack but also those resource-bound ventures, like Ele.me, DJI and DiDi Chuxing, who have taken this approach.

While at first sight this method appears to lead to a waste of resources, being ineffective and the opposite of lean, in fact, internal market competition has driven innovation and new product development more than most other approaches.

The second approach is de-organisation. Companies such as Haier and Xiaomi are continuously reorganising into platforms on which internal and/or external autonomous teams and ventures can flourish. Xiaomi's organisational model is driven by projects. Over forty of its products are not organised in strategic business units and have not become part of the organisational hierarchy. Each new product is treated as a project that can be achieved by mobilising resources inside and outside Xiaomi.

As another example, Haier has been experimenting in reducing hierarchy and increasing autonomy with self-organising teams. Through measures such as disintermediation and the elimination of internal communication barriers, Haier has decreased staff numbers by 45 per cent but has created more than 1.6 million job opportunities.

Rules are unnatural. This translates into 'design for an emergent organisation'. Perhaps we should not use strategic business units as the dominant organisational structure or as a way of running management governance. Moreover, Chinese organisations show that entrepreneurial motivation and dedication in relatively simple organisational structures may provide enough guidance. Using the principle of 'figure it out' and tinkering with solutions can form heuristics better suited to a changing context. We are moving from deliberate organisation design to designing heuristics for an emergent organisation.

The fourth rule of thumb: boundaries do not exist

> *How much more should people focus on what connects*
> *and what provides the fundamentals for all change.*
>
> *Zhuangzi*, Chapter Six

Zhuangzi does not separate life from nature. On the contrary, building connections with nature is one of the fundamental thoughts in *Zhuangzi*.

Chinese entrepreneurs traditionally have been strong networkers and orientated to personal relations. Chinese companies are not afraid to enter into unusual partnerships to leverage opportunities and create innovations across industry boundaries. For instance, we can find this mindset in Ping An, one of the largest Chinese financial groups.

Ping An incubated two companies, fuelled by external investors, which became small ecosystems themselves: Ping An Good Doctor and Ping An Lufax. Ping An Good Doctor has, in turn, developed many partnerships with care providers but also with real estate developers to find ways into communities. Lufax, a unicorn-valued fintech start-up, signed agreements with Ele.me and Durex recently.

Similarly, Alibaba and its peers Baidu, Tencent and Xiaomi (popularly termed BATX in China) have no respect for boundaries. While the roots of BATX are in search technology, e-commerce, social communication and software, these technology giants are now active in more than twenty sectors. BATX has gained hundreds of millions of users in international markets, with footholds in American, European and Asian markets, more than 150 direct overseas investments and acquisitions and rapidly developing pioneering payment, cloud and communication technology services. Alibaba and Tencent's advances in mobile technology are world-leading. Baidu's ambition for driverless cars beats Tesla's. Xiaomi's internet-of-things network, with more than three hundred million connected devices, has made many traditional appliance and electronics manufacturers reconsider their business approaches. BATX have created business ecosystems rather than corporations, with connections reaching out everywhere like tentacles.

Boundaries do not exist. This translates into, 'We all live in ecosystems'. Perhaps we should focus on building business ecosystems rather than hierarchies – firms – as the alternative to markets. Organisational rules and structure cannot be independent from the context. It is not possible to make the context less complex. Therefore, organisations should rather match the complexity of context and give new meaning to a boundary-less organisation.

Warring States thought experiment

Chinese business leaders do not believe in their enterprises being 'established'. Rather, the sense of threat and urgency is omnipresent in Chinese business leaders' minds. Secondly, fighting their subconscious biases allows business leaders to find new possibilities in existing opportunities and threats. Third, it is difficult to enforce rules in a turbulent environment. Chinese organisations are in a continuous state of emergence, driven by a strong sense of entrepreneurialism. Lastly, Chinese businesses are characterised by a strong sense of being embedded, with deep interconnections across technologies, sectors and geography itself.

Of course, everything is contextual and the rules of thumb may not be readily transferrable to other countries. What I propose is to conjure up the Warring States period and adopt Zhuangzi's rules of thumb. It could be a great thought experiment for global leaders facing uncertainty. Moreover, it will allow those leaders to fight their subconscious biases – the old tropes, such as 'Headquarters knows best' and 'Legacy thinking'. Implemented well, Zhuangzi's rules of thumb can lead to important competitive advantages in turbulent times. Like Chinese business leaders, you can adopt heuristic organisational principles to embrace rather than eschew uncertainty.

WHAT'S YOUR RECURSIVE QUESTION?

Hal Gregersen

A great business leader I know recently came up with an insightful observation: 'When we see the point of our work as all about arriving at smart answers,' he noted, 'too often we mistake an answer for an ending point to an effort. We celebrate arriving at a point from which we need go no further.' He proposed an interesting alternative. 'What if, instead, we valued the answers we arrive at mainly because of all the new and better questions they led us to? Put another way, what if, instead of seeing questions as the keys that unlock answers, we saw answers as stepping stones to next questions?'

That was Ed Catmull, the long-time leader of Pixar and, since its merger with Disney, also Disney Animation Studios. He wrote these lines as part of a brilliant foreword he contributed to my book, *Questions Are the Answer* – not reiterating anything that I had thought to put into the text, but expressing his own thoughts on the topic. In other words, he was doing exactly what he was describing. Usually, when someone offers to write a foreword, the publisher of the book sends the text along when it's finished, and the foreword ends up praising whatever that person thinks is most interesting to take away from it. In Ed's case, instead of highlighting some conclusion I had come to, he used the book as a springboard to ask his own next round of questions.

What has been especially interesting to me is how right he is. Since the book came out, I keep finding that the most valuable conversations I have are not ones where I repeat what I've already written or read, but where those of us in the conversation push the topic forward with new questions that intrigue us.

This is the first insight I wanted to share. And I would ask you, what if you saw your latest project not as a culmination of your most recent phase of work, but as a door-opener to the next phase – as a stepping stone to your next great question? Would that change what you did in connection with the project? Would you seek out different venues to talk about it? Would you say different things?

And this brings me to another, more philosophical point Ed Catmull has made in subsequent conversation. When I talk about the quality of a great question, I like to use the word 'catalytic' – meaning that it knocks down a barrier to thinking and sends creative energy down a more productive pathway. Ed prefers another description: he says great questions are 'recursive'. With his background in computer science, he's referring to the sense in which mathematicians and programmers use the term. As opposed to an explicit formula, a recursive formula involves getting to the next term in a sequence by cycling back to immediately preceding terms and repeating an operation on them. Metaphorically, a great question can do the same thing: it doesn't solve a problem once and for all, but continues to engage solving energies and push refined answers forward.

To take this into managerial territory, here is what a recursive question does. It recognises that organisations exist and must endure in highly dynamic markets. The idea that an enterprise could solve a problem once and for all – just about any problem

– seems absurd when the underlying conditions that led to that solution keep changing. But a great question can endure and can keep being asked in light of new conditions.

For those of us who study and work with organisations and their leaders, this suggests some useful considerations: is the work we are doing equipping them with recursive questions? Does our advice try to give cut-and-dried answers or does it have enough juice to allow managers to address generation after generation of a problem? Do our findings halt their progress by claiming to be the last word on the subject – or propel it by suggesting there will never be a last word?

And what about you: is your own work driven by a recursive question? If so, I would love to know: what is it?

ON THE NOBILITY OF GUIDING GOLIATH

Scott D. Anthony

I'm often asked why Innosight, the consulting firm at which I am a partner, primarily works with big, established companies. It is a natural enough question.

After all, Innosight was founded by Clayton Christensen, the Harvard Business School professor who brought the term 'disruptive innovation' to the business lexicon. That heritage would seem to point our hundred-person team towards insurgents seeking to overturn the natural order. Look, however, at the names of companies on the 'client impact' tab on Innosight's website. The first six companies you see are Bayer (founded in 1863), Aetna (1853), Kennametal (1938), Walgreens (1901), Citi (1812), Medtronic (1949). The average age of these six companies at the time of writing in 2021? One hundred and thirty-five years. Medtronic is the group's whippersnapper at a sprightly seventy-two!

A cynic might answer the 'why' question by channelling the line ascribed to prolific US criminal Willie Sutton. When asked why he robbed banks, Sutton responded, 'That's where the money is.' Big companies are natural consulting clients because they have sufficient funds to pay for consulting services. Because helping large companies innovate and grow is essentially unsolvable, the cynic would argue, you can provide endless service that appears valuable, but at best simply exposes other problems to solve.

I have some empathy for this view. Indeed, I remember a massive division in a massive company that asked us to help them develop a process and structure for innovation about a dozen years ago. We created a detailed process manual, helped to stand up a team and helped that team explore a range of new opportunities. About ten months later, the CEO was fired and the team disbanded. A couple years later, the new management team called and asked us to... help them develop a process and structure for innovation (we sent them the output from the past project and declined the work).

While the cynic finds the desire to earn a quick buck lies behind our strategic direction, a critic might note that our effort to help established companies harms the greater good. The critic would note that yesterday's companies should fail in the face of disruptive change. Efforts to prop them up only impedes economic progress and productivity. As such, the critic would say Innosight's focus on helping large, established companies to innovate and grow, ironically, serves as a barrier to innovation achieving its natural and full impact.

An alternative view, and the view to which our team ascribes, is that helping large companies innovate and grow is a worthwhile task. That as much as the parables make a hero out of giant-slayer David, guiding Goliath can be a noble endeavour.

This argument has three components. First, those hailing the power of creative destruction fail to properly account for its transaction costs. Second, unleashing innovation inside large organisations creates powerful amplifying effects that have the potential to do good for society. And third, there are some opportunities that simply wouldn't be realised without the focus and attention of large, established incumbents.

Creative destruction's transaction tax

The phrase 'creative destruction' is generally attributed to the economist Joseph Schumpeter, who used the phrase in his 1942 landmark, *Capitalism, Socialism and Democracy*. In that book, Schumpeter challenged an orthodoxy that traced back to the idea of the 'invisible hand' that Adam Smith introduced in *The Wealth of Nations* in 1776. For the next 150 years, economists had focused on how capitalism administered markets. Schumpeter disagreed, noting that the essence of capitalism was how it created new structures and destroyed old ones.

The business press often glorifies the Davids that drive this process. Stories involving plucky underdogs taking down the establishment are persistently popular. Indeed, nature shows us that, in the right circumstances, creative destruction can help to improve an ecosystem's health. The US Department of Agriculture will often allow forest fires started by lightning in controlled areas. Those fires can transform growth-constraining tangled brush and deadwood into fertile soil. Similarly, when a large, poorly run incumbent fails, employees are free to work in more hospitable environments and customers can choose more efficient, effective offerings.

Replacing deadwood with fertile soil is one thing. Razing the ground is another. The entrepreneurial hero stories often fail to mention creative destruction's transaction tax. Many large companies are the anchor for the employees in their community. While top executives might be able to move to another location, the rank and file often finds it much harder to move. What about the work-in-process solutions, the accumulated know-how? Sometimes, of course, another company can acquire a patent portfolio, but often generations of carefully built knowledge are simply lost.

Consider, for example, Rochester, New York. The US Bureau of Labour Statistics report that the area's workforce peaked in July 1997 at about 580,000 people, of which about 560,000 were employed. Rochester was home base for two imaging giants, Xerox and Kodak. Kodak, of course, went bankrupt in 2012. Xerox managed to survive the onslaught of disruptive change, but only through radically restructuring its core business, and decreasing its 91,000-person workforce by 40 per cent. In January 2018, Rochester's workforce had declined to 520,000 (even though the area's population had increased in the same time period) and total employment was down to 490,000.

A 2017 study of US Census microdata by economists from Stanford, MIT and Northwestern found that, contrary to the theory that creative destruction leads to economic vibrancy, bankruptcy leads to significant and persistent decreases in employment among surrounding businesses. 'Overall, these results indicate that liquidation adversely affects the local economy through spillovers,' they wrote. 'As such, our results are inconsistent with the "creative destruction" argument, which posits that forcing the liquidation of distressed firms will help revitalise the local area and induce entry by freeing up resources for healthy firms to use. Under creative destruction, we would expect higher employment following liquidation, or at least higher entry into the area. Yet, neither is supported by the data.'

Kodak is a particularly painful story of opportunity lost. A persistent myth has emerged that Kodak was simply blind to the changes that ultimately would lead to its downfall. Not true. Steve Sasson worked for Kodak in 1975 when he created the first prototype of a digital camera. He told the *New York Times* in 2008 that management's response to the potentially disruptive innovation was, 'That's cute – but don't tell anyone about it.' A clever line, but not a completely accurate one. In fact, Kodak invested heavily in the technology and ultimately created a viable line of digital cameras. What really did for Kodak was the merging of cameras and mobile phones, alongside the move from printing pictures to sharing them online.

Here again, they almost got it right. In 2001 Kodak purchased OFoto, one of the early photo-sharing sites. In a parallel universe, Kodak encourage people to not just share photos, but also news and personal updates, in essence creating Facebook or Instagram well before Mark Zuckerberg and Kevin Systrom founded their respective companies. In this universe, Kodak didn't make the transition. Perhaps controversies about the civic responsibility of social networks would look very different if leading networks were run by managers who had honed their craft over decades versus entrepreneurs learning on the fly. We will now, of course, never know.

Amplifying impact

In 2010, Christensen addressed the eight-hundred-odd graduates of the Harvard Business School. A survivor of cancer, a heart attack, a stroke, and type 1 diabetes, he used the speech to describe how to use the models he taught students to inform personal decisions. The speech became one of the most reprinted articles in the history of the *Harvard Business Review*, and the backbone of a 2012 book by Christensen and two co-authors, *How Will You Measure Your Life?*

One memorable portion of the speech discussed the nobility of management. Christensen described a thought experiment he did back when he was a CEO about the impact he had on his people.

In my mind's eye I saw one of my managers leave for work one morning with a relatively strong level of self-esteem. Then I pictured her driving home to her family ten hours later, feeling unappreciated, frustrated, under-utilised, and demeaned. I imagined how profoundly her lowered self-esteem affected the way she interacted with her children. The vision in my mind then fast-forwarded to another day, when she drove home with greater self-esteem – feeling that she had learned a lot, been recognised for achieving valuable things and played a significant role in the success of some important initiatives. I then imagined how positively that affected her as a spouse and a parent. My conclusion: management is the most noble of professions if it's practised well. No other occupation offers as many ways to help others learn and grow, take responsibility and be recognised for achievement and contribute to the success of a team.

I am the father of four young children. They serve as a persistent reminder that humans enter the world as naturally creative, curious creatures. Then we send our children to school, where they learn there is a right answer and a wrong answer. They go to work at organisations where they learn there is a way to do things and a way not to do things. Gallup famously reports that 85 per cent of employees are either not engaged or are actively disengaged at work. I believe at least one reason for that depressing statistic is that we shackle and constrain naturally creative and curious individuals.

Unleashing, harnessing, and amplifying those latent characteristics provides clear business benefits. A study by Bain shows that innovative firms have significantly higher shareholder returns than their less innovative peers. Research by Adobe shows that companies that foster creativity and question the status quo are 3.5 times more likely to outperform peers in revenue growth. Google found that teams that report high degrees of what Harvard professor Amy Edmondson dubbed 'psychological safety' exceeded their revenue targets by close to 20 per cent.

Tapping into shackled creativity and curiosity also has the potential to dramatically raise employee engagement. Go back to Christensen's thought experiment. Imagine a world where people are free to explore, experiment and learn – and are therefore more engaged and more fulfilled in their jobs. It is hard to imagine that leads to them being worse spouses, parents, and members of their community. It is easy to imagine that leads to them being better spouses, parents and members of their community. The second-order effects of helping large companies realise their full innovation potential have the potential to be massive.

Unique opportunities

When I moved to Singapore in 2010, my intent was not to expand our consulting presence to Southeast Asia (which is what I ended up doing). Rather, my intent was to leave consulting behind. You see, in 2007 Innosight set up a sister organisation called Innosight Ventures to incubate and invest in start-up companies. What better way to have impact, I thought, than to create, seed and shape insurgents?

A paired set of experiences in October 2010 showed me that I had framed the problem incorrectly. That, in fact, the best way to have impact is to empower forward-thinking companies to navigate disruptive change. The first experience was a pitch from a start-up called Plunify. The details of the company don't matter. The important thing is that it was the first time that we were pitched not with a business plan but with a business. What is the difference? A business plan is facts and figures; slides and spreadsheets. A business has a functioning website, real customers and revenues. The two kids behind Plunify had built this business using nothing more than their credit cards.

A few weeks after the Plunify pitch I found myself in the dusty town of Durgapur in north-east India to see a project that one of our consulting teams was doing with Medtronic. India should have been one of Medtronic's leading markets. After all, Medtronic's flagship product is a pacemaker, a device that regulates the flow of electricity to the heart, and India has more heart disease than any country in the world. Yet, Medtronic's sales in the country were miniscule.

It was easy to understand why. Many people pay for healthcare out of their own pocket, which means they can't afford a thousand-dollar pacemaker. Even worse, primary care doesn't work that well in India and many customers who desperately need a pacemaker don't even know it. Our consulting team cracked the problem, not by inventing technology but by creating a new business model called 'Healthy Heart for All'. The model featured three key components: direct-to-consumer advertising to raise awareness of the disease, rural diagnostic camps to rapidly identify patients and the world's first loan programme for implantable devices. Eight years later, more than 100,000 patients have been screened and more than 15,000 have received potentially life-saving therapies.

I reflected on the two experiences. When people in big companies first hear the story of Plunify, the first reaction typically is despondency. What hope does a big company have if creating a company is costless? Here's the rub. Yes, it never has been easier to start a company. But that means it also has never been easier to copy one. The second a start-up company gets a whiff of success, the race is on and they have to fight against hordes of me-too copycats. Sure, every once and a while an Airbnb or Gojek emerges from this process, but, make no mistake, the start-up world is brutally difficult. In contrast, I could tell you every single detail of what Medtronic did and the odds are high that you couldn't do anything about it. You don't have patented technology. You don't have access to doctors in India. You might not have a balance sheet to cover the loans. There are literally three companies in the world that could do what Medtronic did.

I described Healthy Heart for All in a 2012 *Harvard Business Review* article titled 'The New Corporate Garage,' describing a pattern of 'corporate catalysts' combining assets of scale and entrepreneurial energy to unleash massive impact on often overlooked markets.

Venture capital generally flows to very narrow segments of the global economy. All too frequently, bright young talents are sucked into what might be called the advertising-narcissism complex, where they create ever-more addictive ways for us to feel worse about ourselves and ever-more effective ways to try to sell us things we fundamentally don't want and need.

We can, and should, do better. The world has big problems. We have to figure out how to feed more than 7.5 billion people. We have to deal with changing climates. We have to bring education and healthcare to hundreds of millions of people who desperately need it. We have to grapple with the ethical issues of artificial intelligence (AI) and the employment concerns raised by AI and robotics. There is no doubt that entrepreneurs have a part to play in developing solutions to these and related problems. Big companies have a unique and vital role to play as well.

My October 2010 experiences serve as the equivalent of my origin story. It was the moment where it became clear to me that the best place in the world to have impact is, in fact, inside large organisations that have, through their histories, developed unique, difficult-to-replicate assets.

Let's be realistic. The titles of critical innovation books highlight the difficulty of the problem. In the 1980s, long-time McKinsey director (and, from 2005–12, Innosight advisor) Dick Foster wrote *Innovation: The Attacker's Advantage*. In the 1990s, Innosight co-founder Christensen described *The Innovator's Dilemma*. Note how the titles get more ominous as the years go on. A few years ago, Dave Ulmer drew on his experience at several large companies (including Innosight clients) to describe *The Innovator's Extinction*, which carried the subtitle 'How best intentions and natural selection will drive your company into the grave'. Ouch.

Plenty of large companies are dysfunctional beyond belief. Some employ legitimately bad people who take advantage of their power to do bad things. They can drive you crazy with their inane bureaucracy, power struggles and ineptitude. But that does not change the fact that large organisations can be tremendous forces for good.

Working for the establishment need not be dismissed as working for 'the man'; it need not be selling out; it need not be crass commercialism. Guiding Goliath can be a noble, purpose-driven task.

THE FOURTH INDUSTRIAL REVOLUTION WILL CHANGE BUSINESS, WORK AND THE PLANET: BRACE FOR IMPACT?

Mark Esposito

The long path towards sustainable development and continued economic growth is obscure and opaque, as the global economy is currently consuming natural resources one and a half times faster than the planet can cope with each year. Other statistics are even more dire. According to the Global e-Sustainability Initiative, for every 1 per cent of growth in global GDP, CO_2 emissions and resource consumption also grow by another 0.5 per cent and 0.4 per cent respectively. Eventually, if this status quo persists, it is predicted that current production practices will cease to create GDP growth and instead turn into a loss valued at $4.5 trillion by 2030 (Lacy and Rutqvist, 2015).

The DRIVE framework

DRIVE is:

- Demographic and social changes

- Resource scarcity

- Inequalities

- Volatility, scale and complexity

- Enterprising dynamics

The DRIVE framework, of present author and Terence Tse (2017), can be used to observe the megatrends that have contributed to the degradation of the planet and the well-being of its inhabitants.

On a global level, several issues in demographic and social trends have persisted in the long term, including poverty and over-population. The United Nations' 2017 revised population assessment (Department of Economic and Social Affairs, population division) projects a 48 per cent growth in human population by 2100, while resource scarcity continues to plague us.

Inequality also continues to grow. In 2017, 82 per cent of all wealth created globally went to the top 1 per cent, while the bottom half received nothing (Pimentel, Aymar and Lawson, 2018).

Volatility, scale, and complexity can take any form: natural disasters, technological revolutions and trade wars, for example.

The fifth megatrend, enterprising dynamics, which can be briefly defined as competitive pressure that gives rise to new business models and disruptive innovation, points to recent momentum from movements like systems thinking and the circular economy as well as the advanced technologies of the fourth industrial revolution. These may comprise a possible solution to the problems of unsustainable resource consumption and emissions. For the purposes of this article, the 'fourth industrial revolution' can be defined as a new technological era in which the digital, physical and biological converge.

Additional encouragement for solutions to our resource and social imparity conundrums can be found in the leadership at the UN, who have created impetus for change through the establishment of the 2030 Agenda for Sustainability Development. Among other things, the ensuing sustainability development goals (SDGs) target sustainable production and growth, resilient infrastructure, innovation and productive employment. Given the proper amount of investment, capital and political will, the advantageous synergies behind the technological capabilities of the fourth industrial revolution can accelerate achievement of SDGs and begin changing the current course towards potentially irreversible resource depletion and social disparity.

The fourth industrial revolution

Why does the fourth industrial revolution (4IR) give us hope? Technology has always been a driving force behind exponential growth and development to create human progress. The first industrial revolution, in the late eighteenth century, created great economic expansion through the development of steam power and manufacturing mechanisation, while the second industrial revolution (the technological revolution) transformed communication and transportation through steel technology, railroads and electricity. The third industrial revolution – also known as the digital revolution – took us from analogue devices to the digital technology that we take for granted today; the internet, microprocessors and mobile communication.

Since the advancement of the digital revolution, the 4IR has emerged as a second manufacturing revolution. Emergent technologies, including artificial intelligence (AI), advanced robotics, genome editing, enterprise wearables, 3D printing and the internet of things (IoT) will permanently transform global production systems.

We have already seen how AI and IoT have influenced stalwart industries such as getting taxis and e-commerce. If properly placed within the context and framework of the UN's SDGs, we can see that the 4IR will and should accelerate achieving those goals. While this article offers a discussion of these technologies, the emphasis is on the value creation along the production chain – not just for firms and industries, but also social development – the SDGs.

This article begins with a survey of the key technologies behind 4IR, followed by specific examples of 4IR tech and innovation across various industries. It concludes with observations of the impact of 4IR on SDGs and the greater good, the social changes involved and a discussion of the role of firms and governments.

4IR in action

Some of the greatest emerging technologies of 4IR are IoT, AI, advanced robotics, enterprise wearables, and 3D printing (World Economic Forum, WEF, 2017). Taken together, these five technologies combine to impact global production from the bottom up. While the technology of IoT is simple to understand, the power behind it is that it allows for real-time asset management via smart products and services when combined with AI.

Through machine learning, patterns in data can be identified and analysed quickly for insights that companies can use to make actionable business decisions. Presently, 70 per cent of such data collected goes unused due to lack of AI implementation (WEF, 2017).

With AI and IoT, producers can establish business processes across silos and suppliers to achieve supply chain optimisation, quality management and predictive maintenance. According to Deloitte (Schatsky, Kumar and Bumb, 2017), machine learning makes operational predictions with greater accuracy and twenty times faster than conventional business intelligence tools. Other applications of AI for IoT include speech recognition and voice recognition to eliminate human review. The broad benefits of AI and IoT together are clear: businesses can mitigate risk, reduce downtime, improve operational efficiency and innovate existing products and services.

With about 1.8 million robots in operation today (WEF, 2017), advanced robotics and automation have distinctly altered the value chain, with labour cost savings anywhere between 18 and 33 per cent and estimated productivity increases of about 30 per cent. Robotics are predominantly used for handling items – including packaging, picking and placing. In automotive production, robotic welding is a large application, while assembly has become an important application in electronics and electrical industries, where precision quality and accuracy with small components is central to production.

All told, the economic benefits of advanced robotics will be valued between \$600 billion and \$1.2 trillion by 2025 ('Robot revolution', 2015), with new capabilities still being captured today, leading to additional decreases in costs. For instance, machine learning can be used to improve iterative manufacturing processes. The advantages of robotics are especially significant for enabling a just in time (JIT) model to produce only on-demand and for smaller, localised factories that need to scale.

Enterprise wearables (which include augmented reality, AR, and virtual reality, VR) offer excellent opportunities for quality improvement through increased capabilities such as remote verification, live instruction and automatic mistake-proofing. Company pilots of wearable technology have shown up to 25 per cent improvement in operator productivity and significantly reduced training time (WEF, 2017).

The health implications are also clear: the ability to track health and fitness (with the help of IoT) will cut down on safety issues and reduce insurance premiums. VR and AR can also be used as part of the process of design methodology and design for manufacturability by making real-time adjustments possible.

Although enterprise wearables show promise, they are less tested and have more caveats than the other 4IR technologies. As an example, hardware design for wearables can change quickly as prices drop, creating a risk of unsupported models being phased out too quickly or losing their practical application.

The last technology to be discussed is 3D printing, which has been a game-changer for custom medical devices such as dental implants and hearing aids. 3D bioprinting (the layering of living cells to create tissue or organs) is also on the horizon.

In the factory environment, 3D printing is creating enormous value as a complementary process for industries that require components in small quantities but with high levels of customisation, such as healthcare, aerospace, and defence. While 3D printing will never replace factory manufacturing, it changes the way industrial engineers work with product design – from rapid prototyping to scaled production – and how they can integrate practices inherent to the circular economy, such as achieving zero-waste and material reuse. SDG value creation through 3D printing is especially notable, for 3D printing can help create a more innovative, inclusive and sustainable factory environment while reducing dependency on virgin materials.

While these five technologies are applicable to any enterprise scenario, there are many other technologies, innovations and approaches that can be methodically applied to any industry, as the following examples will demonstrate.

Uncovering SDG value creation

Beyond the five key technologies driving 4IR and identified by the WEF, we can also look at more specific uses, additional technologies and specialised innovations that continue to drive value creation and SDG potential.

For instance, the automotive industry is over a century old, but new developments are unending. There is strong potential for SDG value creation in automotive manufacturing with such processes as short-loop recycling and advancements in bio-based plastics and composites. (Short loops refer to recycling processes that remain in the automotive sector for remanufacture.) Currently, short loops are set up to recycle raw materials such as steel, coppers, textiles and plastics, thereby leveraging geo-proximity for local jobs and reduction in transport costs and collaborative partnerships between original equipment manufacturers (OEMs) and suppliers.

Short loops enable OEMs to reduce the amount of energy required to transport materials and keep materials in use for longer. For some heavier metal and plastic components, reuse can be supplemented with environmentally sustainable engineering-grade biopolymers and lighter, natural, fibre-reinforced plastics derived from plant feedstock can replace them altogether.

4IR also has potential for creating transformative change in textiles, apparel and footwear. Dormant SDG value creation includes using fibres from non-edible parts of plants, like the leaves of pineapple trees and the husks of coconuts. Though we cannot derive nutritional value from such plants, they are high in cellulose, a property that makes them strong and durable. Moreover, these source materials are often farm residuals not of crop value.

Other renewable and biodegradable alternatives to cotton and petroleum-based textiles include flax and hemp, which can be either woven into a fabric or incorporated into cotton as a textile blend. Cotton crops themselves can be gene-edited to become more resilient in the face of soil erosion, water scarcity and overuse of chemicals.

Gene-editing also represents a massive SDG opportunity in the food and beverage industry. It allows agriculture companies to select certain mutations for multiple types of crops to become more disease-, pest- and drought-resistant, thus making gene-editing an essential technology to help address food security amid population growth and increasing extreme weather events.

In the field of microelectronics, semiconductor and microchip fabrication has traditionally been energy- and resource-intensive.

But application of 4IR technologies like cloud computing, machine learning, IoT and cobotics (collaborative robots that work alongside humans) have enabled more vertical and horizontal integration in the manufacturing process. This leads to increased levels of operational accuracy, thus enabling closed material loops and circular economy business models. In sum, the 4IR factory of the future will reduce supply-chain risk and reduce the use of virgin materials.

Factory future

The earliest factory floors, of the nineteenth century, neglected the well-being of their line workers and were severe environmental pollutants. The factory floors of the 4IR represent tremendous new opportunities for value creation: more automation, modularity, flexibility and connectivity, along with a greater collaborative environment between workers and machines. This will create an immediate impact. Digital factory processes that use IoT and AI can improve resource efficiency, reduce waste, increase yields and cut down on unplanned maintenance, while also collecting data and analytics that will allow producers to discover more sources of value on the shop floor.

According to the Smart Manufacturing Leadership Coalition, the factory of the future will be characterised by efficiency gains and cost reduction estimates of up to 30 per cent, 20–30 per cent lower carrying costs, 25 per cent reduction in consumer packaging costs, 25 per cent drop in health and safety incidents, a 40 per cent reduction in water usage and 20–30 per cent reduction in energy use ('Economic Benefits', 2016).

Moreover, developing new and innovative products and services will also be faster in the 4IR. Digital techniques like 3D printing make it possible to speed up the iterative processes of product development, thus reducing costs and making it possible to reconfigure quickly to adapt products to changing market preferences.

Firms that have not yet investigated 4IR technologies need to be aware that they will eventually become ubiquitous and business decisions will have to be made quickly to avoid being left behind. Specific indicators – affordability, connectability, a growing demand for customisable products and the switch from capital expenditures to external servicers – are signals that adoption rates will only to continue to accelerate.

A.T. Kearney (as cited in WEF, 2017) estimates the cost of smart devices has fallen 50–70 per cent, while 40 per cent of production assets are connected. Twenty-five per cent of traditional capex products are now fulfilled by service-based expense spending and one out of every four products produced now require some form of customisation.

Other data points on the adoption rate of 4IR technologies also indicate growth. Fifty billion smart objects are expected to be deployed by 2020 (DHL and Cisco, 2015), while 75 per cent of all enterprises have already either deployed, piloted or researched IoT applications (IDG Enterprise Marketing, 2016).

In 2015, advanced robotics was a $35-billion market worldwide, while AI hit $8 billion, 3D printing reached $5.2 billion and enterprise wearables approached its first billion, with a projected market value of $5 billion in 2020 (World Economic Forum, 2017). These revenue numbers are an indication of 4IR adoption rates suggesting that, as affordability, technological readiness, customisation and ubiquitous connectivity rises, these advancements will only become more pervasive and universally present. The message of these trends is clear: anyone on the sidelines must get aboard, or risk becoming obsolete.

The role of producers and governments

Having discussed the five primary convergent technologies of 4IR which demonstrate the value to firms and industry, let us now shift to the larger perspective: value creation beyond the factory floor to SDGs and the further reaches of society.

While there has been much contention over issues of wealth distribution and inclusive economic growth, the opportunity for sustainable growth, innovation and healthy employment cannot be ignored. According to the Centre for Climate Change, Economics and Policy and the Grantham Research Institute on Climate Change and the Environment (Boyd, Stern and Ward, 2015), 4IR technologies could reduce net CO_2 emissions by 26.3 billion metric tons within ten years. By the year 2025, that amount would be the equivalent of 8.5 per cent of total global emissions.

Automation has already spared workers the dirtiest and most dangerous jobs and robotics will continue to free individuals from low-skill, low-value work. Ideally, workers can then focus on higher-value tasks and get training for the connected economy. Such improvements and higher skillsets would translate into more empowered workers, better wages and better working conditions.

Though each technological revolution has always brought with it some form of gain, whether it be productivity gains or job creation, there have always been costs associated with industrial revolutions. Historically, inequalities tend to persist and countries do not uniformly capture the value made available by new technologies.

4IR may be no different but liabilities can be mitigated by staying vigilant; be aware of the risks involved and make business decisions that keep economies headed toward growth while conserving resources. If we know, for instance, that labour-intensive work is to be overtaken by automation and robotics, then the human workforce must learn new skills or face unemployment. To avoid this scenario, firms and governments must take a lead in preparing local communities to adjust and also provide training to help workers move into new roles as technologists, repairmen and other highly specialised positions. Companies can offer tuition reimbursements and training programmes while governments can offer funding and tax incentives to help with adapting to change and encourage growth in 4IR technology. These endeavours will necessarily be part of a smooth transition if companies are to remain competitive as well as maintain a mutually beneficial relationship with their workforce.

In addition to retraining the human workforce, there are other hurdles to overcome if we are to capture the value locked within the 4IR and achieve SDGs. Currently, we lack industry standards, infrastructure support, good cyber security and regulations on IP infringement – particularly with regard to 3D printing (WEF, 2017). Having appropriate regulations in place will safeguard the economic and societal benefits that we aspire to gain from these new technologies.

Much of this responsibility will fall to governments, who are also in the unique position of having the authority to do more. In addition to creating the necessary regulations to accelerate SDGs and the development of 4IR, governments can also commit financial resources into job programmes, new public-private partnerships and product knowledge repositories to help producers and entrepreneurs master new technology (WEF, 2017). Finally, given that natural resources and free markets are not exclusive to any one country, policymakers must work towards inclusive economic growth and make multilateral choices.

The barriers are not insurmountable and the promise of value creation in SDGs and 4IR outweigh the short-term challenges. And, truthfully, moving into a 4IR world is not purely an altruistic endeavour. Firms must move quickly if they are to get ahead of their competitors. They must be fearless and willing to upgrade, invest and tackle new ideas. They must collaborate and create new partnerships. We live in exciting times. Here at the forefront of the fourth industrial revolution, we are in a position to shape the factory of the future and, with it, the future of business, work and the planet.

INTERVIEW WITH CAROLINE WEBB

The role of perception

Philosophy@Work: Caroline, your work and research revolves around perception and intention and the power we have over both when setting our minds to the task. Your methods as a coach are founded in scientific research from behavioural sciences and you draw on personal and professional experiences regarding the workings of perception. What role does perception play at work and in our lives more broadly?

Caroline Webb: What we perceive – that is, what we're conscious of seeing, hearing and feeling – makes up the reality we live in, both at work or beyond. And we tend to believe that our perceptions give us an objectively true and complete picture of reality.

And yet, research is pretty clear that this is not the case. It turns out that we only consciously notice part of what's happening to us and around us at any given time. In each second of the day, we subconsciously block out much of what's around us as if it were irrelevant spam. This phenomenon is what behavioural scientists refer to as 'selective attention' and it's a very well-established finding.

So, why do we filter out so much information? The answer lies in how our brain works. Our conscious mind is capable of great feats, but we only have the ability to consciously process a small proportion of the trillions of bits of data around us at any given time. If we were not able to block out most of that information, our brains would crash like overloaded computers. So, our brain filters out whatever seems unimportant or off-topic, so that we can devote our limited conscious attention to things that feel more relevant. This is mostly useful. We don't want to be distracted by the contours of every object in our field of vision, or by the timbre of each sound that's in earshot; we need to ignore most of that to focus on the person we're supposed to be talking to or the document we're supposed to be reading.

But our brain uses a fairly crude rule of thumb to determine what's important enough for us to notice: we tend to pay attention to things that confirm or resonate with whatever is already top of mind for us. So, if we have a particular aim as we go into a conversation, we'll see things that might help or hinder us in meeting that goal – and we're capable of missing anything else. This aspect of selective attention is known as 'inattentional blindness.'

If we have certain expectations of a person or a situation, we'll tend to see evidence that confirms we're right to have those expectations – and we'll tend to be blind to signals that contradict our ingoing assumptions, a phenomenon scientists refer to as 'confirmation bias'. And the effects can be very subtle. Studies have found that merely being in a bad mood leads us to perceive people, objects and situations in a more negative way.

All of this can leave us missing a lot of unexpected or interesting things that are actually worth noticing. We're all experiencing an incomplete, subjective slice of reality, where our starting point plays an enormous role in shaping what appears to happen around us.

Go into a meeting expecting it to be awful and you'll notice every frown and sigh; go in with a goal to find ways to collaborate and you're more likely to spot the moment where an opportunity for cooperation arises. Read a benign email in a bad mood, and you may mistakenly interpret it as being annoying or ill-judged. Reread it in a better mood, and you'll notice that it was more nuanced or generous than you'd first thought, perhaps noticing words or phrases that you missed completely the first time around.

All of which to say, modern science suggests that Kant was absolutely right when he wrote in 1781 that, 'We can cognise of things a priori only what we ourselves have put into them.' He was pushing us to ask ourselves, 'How do I know that I am perceiving this thing that I think I'm perceiving?'

Philosophy@Work: How does our perception of the world affect our actions and our outlook on the world?

Caroline Webb: Given the path dependence of our perceptions – where our initial state of mind goes on to shape what we see and hear – it's not hard to imagine how it's possible to fall into a vicious circle with people or projects in the workplace. For example, if we've had a negative experience with a colleague in the past, we'll likely have pessimistic expectations of their behaviour the next time we encounter them.

Those expectations will shape our perceptions in that next conversation, making it more likely we hear what they're saying as being wrong-headed or annoying – while perhaps missing an interesting insight they share or signs of warmth they're showing us. Over time, our negative perceptions can become steadily reinforced, and this inevitably skews our own behaviour towards them. We might become less helpful, more guarded, less friendly. All of which makes it still less likely that we'll see anything conciliatory in their behaviour in future. One small niggle can evolve into a weirdly tense working relationship.

None of this is to say that you can assert, 'Everything is awesome,' and have it be so. But there's no doubt that choosing to look for the good in a meeting, a person or a situation, makes it more likely that you will perceive it.

On the other hand, if you're working with a colleague you like and respect, you're less likely to see the flaws in any ideas they share with you, because you're likely to filter out anything that contradicts your positive expectations. So, once again, it's important to be aware of your ingoing assumptions, to check your perceptions and ask yourself whether you're wearing rose-tinted spectacles as you pore over a proposal together.

If people were more aware of the fact that their starting point has the potential to drive a vicious or virtuous circle in perception, I think we would all be a little more deliberate in deciding what aims, assumptions and attitude we wanted to have top of mind.

Philosophy@Work: What role does learning play in how we greet the world and interact with others?

Caroline Webb: Obviously, there's a good reason that our past experience shapes our expectations. If we didn't learn to spot patterns in the world around us, we'd be as unformed as a newborn baby each day. If someone has hurt us in the past, it's right that we're wary when we encounter them again. We just want to make sure we're not missing opportunities to make a better connection or to build more trust – and that can be a risk if we rely only on past observations.

Philosophy@Work: You argue that much of our more problematic behaviour and perception is the result of a fight/flight/freeze reaction to threats. How does this mechanism work? How can it be that we feel threatened in a stable work environment?

Caroline Webb: Our brain is constantly scanning the environment around us for potential threats to defend us against. By 'threat', I don't mean just physical threats. Our brain is exquisitely sensitive to anything that threatens our sense of self-worth or social standing. So, a threat might be as minor as being left off an important email chain, or being talked down to in a meeting.

And when our brain spots something that could be a threat of this sort, it mounts a defensive 'fight, flight or freeze' response. In the workplace this can, on the surface, look quite mild – perhaps a snappish comment or someone going silent in a meeting. But underneath the surface, a lot is going on. Physically, our body is readying us for battle. Our heart rate might rise and our breathing might become shallower. Our sight becomes more tunnel-visioned, making our perceptions starker and less nuanced. Meanwhile, there's reduced activity in the prefrontal cortex, the part of the brain responsible for sophisticated thinking. This impairs our ability to weigh things up wisely, to think ahead and exercise self-control. We're more likely to see a situation in black-and-white terms and to say or do something we'll regret.

So, when we're stressed, we're less perceptive than when we're at our best and even more likely to miss signals that are important.

Philosophy@Work: How do we circumvent this reaction?

Caroline Webb: You want to reduce the sense of threat as far as possible, to take your brain off the defensive. There are ways of doing that centre on taking back a degree of control in the situation. For example, research has found that noticing and acknowledging what's going on and labelling your emotions – 'I'm feeling uptight' – reduces the state of alert in people's brains. So does distance. You can't always go for a walk in the middle of a difficult situation, but you can ask yourself, 'When I look back in a year's time, how will I be glad I handled this?' or, 'If this were happening to someone else, what would I advise them to do?' There are plenty of other techniques too, but labelling and distancing can be done very quickly, in the heat of the moment, which is why they're often the ones I reach for.

Philosophy@Work: I am curious: How did you come across Immanuel Kant's theory of perception and why did this eighteenth-century philosopher speak to you? In other words: what were the circumstances for you to be open to perceiving his ideas? After all, you study the modern-day natural sciences in order to grasp how our brain works and how we can work our brain – and Kant is neither modern nor a scientist.

Caroline Webb: I began studying economics when I was sixteen, with a highly unconventional teacher who took us well beyond the formal syllabus, encouraging us to think critically about human topics from a number of different perspectives – including political, psychological, and philosophical. Through him I learned that economics had been born as the field of 'worldly philosophy', a broad discipline seeking to illuminate the ways that people make practical and financial choices. And though economics drifted a long way from that human-centered starting point in the second half of the last century, I never lost my interest in a more multidisciplinary approach to thinking about human behaviour.

More specifically, when I became interested in the topic of selective attention, I was surprised that it was not more widely discussed, given that the research on the topic dates back to the late 1960s. I discussed this with someone with a background in philosophy, and she recommended I read Kant to get a truer historical perspective on how long the concept had been around! I'm very grateful that she did.

Philosophy@Work: Is perception an inherent action that simply is, or can we learn how to do it differently?

Caroline Webb: At its root, perception is, of course, an instinctive process. Perceptual filtering happens below the level of our consciousness – and that's by design. After all, this filtering process is supposed to lighten the load on our conscious brain. But it takes very little to redirect that precious stock of conscious attention. We merely have to ask ourselves, 'What would I like to look out for?' to find our attention redirected in the following seconds and minutes. That's encouraging. Of course, the tricky thing is to train yourself to ask the question that sets clearer intentions for your attention. But like any personal change, this just takes practice.

Philosophy@Work: What methods have you found to work well for perception-setting?

Caroline Webb: To have a good chance of adopting any new habit, you need to make the first step feel clear and easy to take. So, I don't suggest people meditate on their intentions for half an hour each morning. I give people a few simple questions to experiment with using before important interactions or situations, to help them find a workable intention-setting routine that they can remember in the middle of a busy day. I suggest that they try some or all of the following questions.

- What's my real aim – what really matters most here?

- What attitude do I most want to project at this moment?

- What negative assumptions do I have – and what would a more positive assumption be?

Or even more simply: Where do I want to put my attention? What do I want to notice?

I've found that alliteration makes it easy to recall a kind of checklist – aim, attitude, assumptions, attention – for setting deliberate intentions before an important interaction or difficult task. But frankly, you only need one question to get you on the right track. So, when people are starting out with this, I suggest they pick just one question to practise and keep close to hand – perhaps writing it at the front of their notebook or putting it in a calendar entry, until it becomes natural to think of it when needed.

I would add that I find the last question a useful reset for times when I'm feeling cranky or worn down. If you push yourself to notice three good things in the next few minutes, you'll put those good things top of mind. And then, however small those good things are, the functioning of the brain's selective attention rules mean that you're more likely to go on to see more good things thereafter. That is a pretty quick, yet powerful, intervention in the process of navigating the world.

Philosophy@Work: How much time is needed to set one's intentions and perception for the day?

Caroline Webb: Some people build these questions into their morning routine as they plan the most important tasks or interactions of the day and they'll take perhaps ten to fifteen minutes to reflect. But these sorts of questions can make a difference even if you spend only ten to fifteen *seconds* thinking of any of them before you go into a meeting or a presentation. And, frankly, in the middle of a conversation that's not going as well as you would hope, you can take a second to say to yourself, 'OK, what really matters most right now?' to stop yourself getting into a negative spiral and redirect your attention in a fruitful way.

Philosophy@Work: Would you say your work [both in research and as a coach] has resulted in philosophical experiences and could you give an example?

Caroline Webb: I believe my understanding of selective attention has made me humbler and wiser over the years, because it tells me that I don't ever have the full picture, however sure I am of my perspective.

So, when I'm disagreeing with someone, it's just a little easier to imagine that perhaps I am missing something. And that makes it easier to say something conciliatory, like, 'But tell me, how do you see it?'

I've learned that, while everyone's perspective is biased by their perceptual filters, we can usually get to a fuller understanding by comparing notes. And it makes me less willing to argue about small stuff where it's practically impossible to be sure who saw it correctly.

Meanwhile, when I encounter things that I find upsetting or annoying, I recognise that it's going to affect everything I then perceive. So, I've become better at checking in with myself before I act on that biased perspective. One time, I remember missing a whole paragraph of apology in someone's email, because I was so annoyed at something they'd previously done. My knowledge of selective attention allowed me to pause halfway through writing an angry reply and to come back to their message when I was in a better mood – when, of course, I realised that I had misinterpreted it. I've found these sorts of small self-corrections add up to a more contented way of living life, at work and beyond.

Philosophy@Work: Would you say that a philosophical, humanistic approach to facts and figures has aided your work and personal development?

Caroline Webb: Absolutely – in fact, I would say the interplay between analytical and humanistic approaches has defined me as a professional. Taking a rigorous, science-based approach to behavioural change has allowed me to coach sceptical leaders and managers who have tended to think that people's 'issues' and 'personal growth' are rather woolly topics. And it goes the other way too; I've found that it's powerful to bring a sense of meaning, empathy and humanity into organisations and teams where there's been a high degree of conflict in the past.

Philosophy@Work: Free will versus determinism – where would you position yourself and why?

Caroline Webb: I am not an expert in metaphysics, so I will talk about this question in the context of everyday life. We have all heard of motivational speakers who argue that we have complete control over the quality of our lives, 'Just believe and you'll achieve.' Whenever I run into someone who says things like this, I think immediately about kids born in war zones or people who've lost their jobs in a recession. Of course there are aspects of their lives that they can't control. Of course there's plenty in our own lives that we do not control. In the purest sense, we do not have unfettered free will; we are constrained by our environment.

And then, regarding what happens inside our own heads, it is also true that much of what we do from day to day is run on autopilot – that is, it's handled by our brain's automatic system, which means that it's happening instinctively and below the level of our consciousness.

But I have always been interested in our capacity to shape our experience of life, whatever our current situation. And the science of selective attention is one of the areas of research that tells me there's quite a lot of room to shape the way we experience our lives, even when we've been dealt a rough hand. In other words, I do think that free will exists – that we can play our part in skewing the odds. That's why I call myself a 'realistic optimist' – I'm conscious of our limitations but hopeful about our chances of making things better, if we choose to do so.

PART IV

PHILOSOPHY APPLIED AND IN ACTION

WHEN WORK MEETS PHILOSOPHY: A TEMPLATE FOR WISE LEADERSHIP FROM PLATO'S *REPUBLIC* AND *SYMPOSIUM*

Dorie Clark

Plato was crystal clear in his worldview: philosopher-kings should reign supreme. Business was necessary but, at best, it was a distraction from what really mattered – the quest for wisdom. At worst, when it led to an excessive focus on wealth, it could be a pathway to immorality.

In *The Republic*, his treatise on the ideal society, Socrates (who serves as Plato's ideological stand-in) asks, 'Isn't virtue in tension with wealth, as though each were lying in the scale of a balance, always inclining in opposite directions?' The rapacious pursuit of wealth, then, is anathema to Plato's vision for a just society. But, of course, that's not how business has to be.

Today, business plays an ever-greater role in public life – shaping the political discourse (immigration, globalisation, etc.); spurring social change (smartphones, the internet) and creating a sense of personal meaning (as seen in the ubiquitous American introductory greeting, 'What do you do?').

What might it look like for a contemporary business leader to embrace Plato's ideas about wise leadership? *The Republic*, coupled with Plato's portrayal of Socrates as the ultimate role model in *The Symposium*, provides a clue. Here are three principles to guide aspiring philosopher-business leaders.

Care more for others than for your own financial interest

Plato wasn't opposed to money, per se. But an excessive focus on wealth can obviously lead to bad outcomes (just ask Wells Fargo or Volkswagen). Said Socrates, 'Isn't it the case that the doctor, insofar as he is a doctor, considers or commands not the doctor's advantage, but that of the sick man? For the doctor in the precise sense was agreed to be ruler of bodies and not a money-maker.' In other words, a doctor who cares more about money than helping others isn't a doctor at all: he's a businessman without morals. There's nothing wrong with charging for your services – but making money always has to be understood within the context of doing what's right by your clients and your employees.

Ask, don't tell

It's easy for leaders to slip into a didactic, 'Do what I say', mode. It's certainly faster to just tell people what to do. But that trains employees not to think and instead wait for orders – instructions whose rationale they may not even understand.

Instead, Socrates famously leads his companions to understanding through a detailed series of questions, forcing them to reflect on their beliefs and previous statements. 'It looks, Socrates, as if I didn't know what I was talking about when I said that,' his friend Agathon is forced to declare upon Socrates' cross-examination of his views on love.

When someone comes to their own conclusions, learning is far more likely to stick. As scholar Allan Bloom notes, 'The Platonic dialogues do not present a doctrine; they prepare the way for philosophising. They are intended to perform the function of a living teacher who makes his students think.' Today's best managers, then, can become coaches who help their employees develop critical thinking skills and learn to make smart decisions on their own.

Show that you're still learning

Many leaders, feeling the weight of their position, try to justify their status by pretending they have it all figured out. Of course, that breeds a sense of false certainty that can lead to bad decisions. Socrates, on the other hand, took pains to show that he was still a learner, just as much as the people he was coaching, because he knew the quest for wisdom is never-ending. In *The Symposium*, he credits his entire understanding of love to a mentor of his, a woman named Diotima.

Scholars say that Diotima is almost certainly fictional – but what concerns us here isn't her historical existence, but how Socrates, in a room full of colleagues, described their relationship. He made it clear that he originally had an erroneous view of love and that – just as he had questioned his compatriots – she had led him to the truth in similar fashion. Rather than simply presenting his knowledge as a fait accompli, Socrates instead made himself relatable by showing others his journey and modelling the way in which transformation is possible. Instead of covering up his past mistakes, he proclaimed them, demonstrating that if he could grasp the truth, others could do the same.

Let's be clear: Plato wasn't interested in writing management advice. He was far more concerned with how political leaders might create a just society. But times have changed, and business plays a much more central role in our society than it used to. Plato didn't love the world of business, but he respected those who sought to improve themselves and embrace wisdom. We may not be philosopher-kings, but we can heed his advice to become better and more just leaders.

EDUCATION AT THE HEART OF THE ORGANISATION

Robin Weninger

Making education the centre of attention is one of the key factors that will help organisations overcome twenty-first-century challenges. One could even argue that, if education becomes a fundamental component of the organisational design, it has the potential to tackle all future organisational challenges.

Unfortunately, education in organisations is quite often planned and rolled out when it's already too late or, in the words of management guru Peter Drucker, 'When a subject becomes totally obsolete we make it a required course.'

To harvest the benefits of education, tap into the potentials and create new opportunities, organisations must address the essential challenge of becoming an 'infinite organisation'.

Becoming an infinite organisation is not a process but a mindset. A mindset to build for future generations by taking all stakeholders into account. Building an infinite organisation is an ongoing journey without a defined start or end. It is a way rather than a finite goal. It's a constant flow in a highly complex environment in which new pieces are added and edited regularly.

The infinite organisation is interconnected and interdependent and, when coordinated and led for a common purpose, there are very few limits to what can be achieved.

The infinite organisation

The economy has changed and so have organisational requirements. One example of this is the role of the manager. People responsible for controlling, overseeing and administering individuals in an organisation have historically been of great importance. Today, however, more and more of these activities are being overtaken by technological innovation. New organisational designs, as well as decentralised structures and the removal of hierarchies, have undermined typical manager roles within the organisation and the related tasks. This has led and leads to:

1. The transition of structures from rigid and hierarchical to being fluid.

2. The constant reorganisation of work from manual to technology-driven on all levels.

3. The replacement of closed, linear thinking and politics by creativity and co-opetition (a portmanteau of 'collaboration' and 'healthy competition')

Technology is already proving to be much more efficient in the vast majority of management tasks, ranging from small things like planning a schedule to more advanced tasks like the optimisation of production lines. Technology is getting better every single day and at the same time easier to implement. Alongside this process of replacement, the prestige-driven role of the manager is dying, leaving organisations with people in their workforce who have nothing left to do. In other words, management is still very much alive, but the traditional role of the manager is dying.

What might sound dark to many senior executives today is, however, a great chance for organisations and managers alike to tap into unused potential and create new opportunities by mastering the essential challenges of:

1. Turning managers and administrators into leaders.

2. Turning information processors into problem-solvers.

3. Moving from authority and power to strength.

4. Moving from fragmented information to unification and interdependency.

The infinite organisation tackles these challenges by empowering the people within the company through education. The infinite organisation then drives the change internally and creates impactful spillover effects through the exploration of the unknowns. The infinite organisation is, therefore, constantly engaging and empowering their people to be learners and teachers.

In the following section, I want to shed light on how infinite organisations can make education a fundamental part of the operating model by taking the individual into account.

Learning to learn

What might sound strange is that one of the biggest challenges in education is the actual skill of learning in itself. A root problem in educational systems is that many people never really learn how to learn effectively and efficiently. Most educational models are built on finite and absolute structures in which memorising information, often for one test, is the sole purpose, in comparison to developing a deeper understanding of the subject matter.

People lack fundamental skills in some of the most important capacities in learning: critical thinking, problem solving, creativity and collaboration. Educational programmes are set up to gather knowledge as in comparison to seeking wisdom. Additionally, due to format and presentation, people are quickly bored in today's educational programmes, as they do not spark curiosity and/or trigger emotions and sensory experiences.

Without initial curiosity and interest, the learning process is interrupted and disrupted and the initial learning experience will most likely also end up being the end of the learning process altogether.

One very important reason for the relevance of curiosity and intrinsic motivation is the so-called 'learning plateau' that every learner will experience on various stages. The learning plateau is a long, flat stretch in the learning curve in which almost no progress in learning is experienced and/or recorded.

The learning plateau is best described as a love–hate paradox for learners. During this phase, the learning progress is almost non-existent but the adaptation of 'the learned', however, is strengthened. The learning plateau is essential for learning but at the same time introduces an unbelievably exhausting challenge for the learner (e.g. loss of attention or lack of motivation) in continuing and not becoming frustrated. Having the fundamental skills of learning in place can be essential during learning plateau struggles. In other words, interesting content that sparks curiosity makes the learner interested in the learning process during tough times on the learning plateau. Through being interested the learner will be 'interesting' and will, therefore, build relationships with others through collaboration and co-creation and – although it feels stagnant – continue to grow during this phase.

Given that there is no one-size-fits-all solution, the infinite organisation tackles the challenges of the learning process by implementing mechanisms to allow each individual to strengthen their ability to learn through the definition of an individual learning proposition (ILP). The ILP has three dimensions:

1. Instilling fundamental skills that supplement learning; e.g. critical thinking skills, problem-solving skills, creativity and collaboration.

2. Aligning content according to the individual's learning style and offering multi-dimensional access to content.

3. Providing learning environments and tools.

Instilling fundamental skills to supplement learning is often not addressed at all and only reflected in standalone (often short-term) programmes. These skills, however, require consistency in training and should be part of lifelong learning and all educational programmes.

Therefore, each and every educational activity should always include skill-based elements that foster the fundamental skills of learning. But also, outside dedicated educational activities, learning skills must be trained and fostered within the organisation based on the individual's learning proposition – an activity that can and should be facilitated by leaders on a daily basis. While entry-level staff probably require mentoring, an experienced team member might be better off with being set a challenging task that requires new solutions. This is also the reason why the focus must lie on an individual's learning proposition and not just a generalised learning proposition.

Educational activities are often designed to address only elements of one or two learning styles (e.g. presentations and readings) without tapping into other learning styles (e.g. audio or haptic) and preparing the content in different formats. For example, people who struggle with learning by reading will have a hard time in a textbook-only format. One thing to highlight here is that even a learner from textbooks benefits from other learning styles. The ILP of each and every learner should include elements from all/different learning styles. This is significant, as most people learn best when they experience content in an assortment of ways and can engage with the material on various fronts.

A similar approach should be chosen in the design of learning environments and the use of tools. Similar to different learning styles, everybody prefers different setups for learning. Making use of a variety of setups and tools can be helpful in designing great learning environments and offer choice to the learner to change and adapt accordingly. Choosing and creating the right environments for learning should receive proper attention and not be seen as a task of simply getting a room.

An important aspect of the learning environment is to not limit this dimension to a physical space but also have an extended perspective in virtual environments and use technology (e.g. digital campus, wikis and knowledge hubs). The infinite organisation seeks to support the learning process to all ends, respects the individuality of learning itself and creates a holistic environment for learning.

Establishing knowledge playgrounds
Knowledge playgrounds act as an open environment to create initial sparks for learners to leave their comfort zone and look at things from a different perspective. It's a playground that offers a safe space for exploration and experimentation that is open for everyone.

Establishing such a playground to gather inspiration is more of a cultural response than an operational one. It's certainly great if an organisation provides high-quality learning experiences and offerings, but it has almost no impact if learners can't make use of the offerings due to cultural limitations (e.g. in organisations where learning is seen as a 'waste of time' or where work schedules are fully packed without any room for learning).

Time and social pressure are two very big cultural challenges, especially when it comes to exploring something not immediately related to the existing job of the learner. How can you make progress if someone who is taking a course during work hours is seen by colleagues as the 'lazy guy that is "learning" and not working'?

Another cultural challenge to face is the outcome-driven focus of educational activities. Compared with absolute knowledge and output through rigid goals, the playground focuses on inputs and delivers in the long-term without predictable outcomes; learners grow with every experience in the playground. The impact of the playground can therefore only be evaluated in retrospect, if at all, as many long-term outcomes cannot be easily traced back to the playground. Planning, modelling and predicting the actual outcome of learning experiments is almost impossible. This makes it hard for many learners to justify why, for example, a course on game design might be a good idea, even if they are working in the legal department.

It is not suggested that people spend all their time on the playground, but it is exactly this stimulation that is often needed to encourage the development of ideas to overcome existing challenges in the organisation. It is, therefore, an investment in trusting progress through learning that is the very fundamental key for striving to build such a playground. It is a symbiosis of the market and working environment. In operations (the market) there is little room for failures and the pressure is high, while the training field offers a playground in which chaos and screw-ups are a part of the journey and the everyday experience. The infinite learning organisation therefore continuously works towards more chaos *and* more stability as a part of the learning environment.

Embracing in-depth learning

Learning something new and applying that knowledge does not always go smoothly. Especially in the early stages of learning, mistakes will happen and this might be seen as a 'learning failure' within the organisation. However, this is not true. New knowledge needs to be strengthened through in-depth understanding and reasoning before you can begin to see its positive effects. It is like driving a car: people who have recently obtained their licence are more likely to drive poorly and will be stressed in many situations by comparison to someone who has been driving for twenty years. Training, understanding and reasoning are fundamental processes in finding plausible explanations and making use of new knowledge to create impact.

A major challenge for many learners is to overcome emotional barriers to making use of their new skills. Being willing to prove yourself – or someone else – wrong is often a much harder challenge than the acquisition of a skill itself. The infinite organisation must build the capacity to reduce emotional barriers to employees applying new knowledge and skills. This is achieved by embracing in-depth learning through multiple learning cycles in an open and trusted environment. In the infinite learning organisation, time is given for change to happen. Drops in performance due to the change in progress applied through new knowledge is not seen as a critical risk but rather as a temporary effect that will be overcome in the learning process itself. In fact, organisations which embrace learning are also much better at 'change' in general.

Understanding and reasoning are important cultural pillars of the infinite organisation and can be seen as an active process that is required throughout the organisation via active dialogues, interdisciplinary collaboration and outcome-driven co-creation. By fostering these cultural pillars throughout the organisation, the infinite organisation avoids spontaneous decision making based on superficial knowledge and insights without reflection.

Embracing teaching

Not only is teaching a great way to strengthen the learning itself (in fact, it's the best validator for in-depth understanding), but it is also a catalyst for scaling knowledge in the organisation in terms of sparking new inputs. Embracing teaching capacities within the workforce of an organisation has multiple benefits.

First of all, knowledge can be better shared throughout the organisation. Instead of sourcing only external trainers, the organisation can make use of their own teachers. In addition to their availability, a major advantage is the fact that the internal trainer knows more about organisational structures and can tailor the content even better to the learner's needs, adapting according to their individual learning style. This needs to be carefully monitored to avoid 'getting stuck' and to make sure that enough external input is delivered. A healthy mix of internal and external teaching capacities – in which the goal of the external resource is to enable and qualify for internalisation – has proven to be successful. Building up internal teaching capacity also enables the organisation to offer more learning opportunities without formalising those opportunities (e.g. undefined training on the job).

All this leads to a positive impact on the learning culture itself, as education becomes visible in multiple shapes and sizes within the organisation and underlines its importance. Education within an infinite organisation can only reach its full potential if teaching is embraced.

Mastering the rhetoric of teaching by practising logical arguments and employing a structured approach to sharing knowledge (the logos), tapping into the emotions and connecting with the audience (the pathos) and building up and practising the ways of establishing authority to address the audience (the ethos) are all crucial skills necessary to grow as a teacher and also to manifest knowledge. In this way, further wisdom can be gained. The art of teaching is therefore also a skill that must be learned.

Learners who master the art of discourse and have the capacity to empower and activate people within the organisation will be the ultimate drivers for change and fundamentally shape the infinite organisation.

THE JOY OF STRUGGLE

Liz Wiseman

Is it possible that, in the name of advancement and process, our lives have become too easy? In his autobiography, the nineteenth-century philosophy John Stuart Mill asks, 'Suppose that all your objects in life were realised; that all the changes in institutions and opinions, which you are looking forward to, could be completely effected at this very instant; would this be a great joy and happiness to you?'

Is the aim of human progress – for which men and women have struggled mightily – to alleviate struggle? Or is well-being, and the very notion of progress, fundamentally dependent on continued struggle?

The notion of human progress was introduced in the early nineteenth century by philosophers of the Enlightenment, who defined progress as intellectual advancement and asserted that the human condition has improved over the course of history and would continue to improve. Some time in the twentieth century, economists joined the conversation and began to equate progress with a growth in gross domestic product (GDP). Their premise was that more goods and services per capita equalled progress.

They asserted that higher incomes would ease lives, make people more comfortable, provide them with additional options and satisfy desires for amusement, prestige, and pleasure.

Following suit, the industrialists built tools to remove physical labour and automate repetitive, manual work. Workers became detached from the outcome of their labour and susceptible to disengagement and passivity.

In the late twentieth century, as the industrial age gave way to the information age, the technologists joined the race, building tools to manage information and automate quotidian knowledge work, eliminating mental drudgery and speeding work cycles. The dawn of the twenty-first century brought the rise of data analytics, AI and machine learning, with its potential to rival or replace human insight.

Somewhere along the way, the notion of human progress and intellectual advancement became less about well-being and more about efficiency and simplicity. Perhaps it was just assumed that greater efficiency would lead to greater well-being. While the advantages of large-scale production, increased connectivity, access to education and the life-saving advancements of biotechnology are undeniable, does all of this ease and convenience pose a threat to human development?

What are the hidden dangers of collectively hitting the button marked 'Easy'? In seeking ease of use and the comforts of automation, we might be robbing ourselves of the joy that comes from struggle – not just the satisfaction of, for example, straining our muscles and breaking a sweat doing our own garden work, but also the satisfaction that comes from wrestling a tough mental challenge down to the mat.

Numerous studies have shown the importance of the relationship between job satisfaction (the positive emotional state resulting from the appraisal of one's own job) and the level of challenge in one's work. While there are many variables, empirical evidence suggests only one clear attribute of the work itself that consistently influences job satisfaction: the cognitive challenge. In addition, employees who are satisfied with their jobs tend to perform better, withdraw less and lead happier and healthier lives.

In my research, which investigated how people of varying experience levels approach work, my research team and I surveyed approximately one thousand people from across a variety of industries, asking them to indicate the current level of challenge in their jobs and their current level of satisfaction. We found a correlation between 'challenge level' at work and 'satisfaction level' at work. In other words, as the challenge level goes up, so does satisfaction. Strangely enough, satisfaction isn't found in the absence of challenge, but as the natural by-product of a challenge that has been faced and conquered. The steep climb that accompanies hard work, with its scramble and rapid learning, tends to be our happy place. It is in striving that we feel joyful and most alive.

Furthermore, is it possible that this messy space – where our task outsizes our capability – is where we are at our best? The research my colleagues and I have done shows that we tend to do our best thinking and work when we are in the process of mastering something challenging, rather than when we've finally achieved mastery. Why is this? Because when we are in the process of learning new things and overcoming challenges, we engage our creative energies. It is in the climb that we feel on top of the world.

Unfortunately, the converse is also true: job satisfaction plummets for those shielded and walled off from real challenge. According to an oft-cited Gallup poll, 70 per cent of American workers claim to either hate their jobs or to be completely disengaged from them. Another poll found that 63 per cent of American workers report having high levels of stress at work with extreme fatigue and feelings of being out of control.

Is it really the amount of work that leads to stress? Or is it a toxic combination of too much busywork and too little challenging work that is to blame? What looks like apathy and burnout is more likely the exhaustion of being under-utilised. Today, many organisations build campuses with luxury amenities and conveniences; however, the single most effective way for organisations to ensure a satisfied workforce is to provide their employees with mentally challenging work.

Here's the point: as technology advances and offers greater simplicity and ease, we need to maintain healthy levels of mental challenge and struggle in our work. The human mind is built for challenge and wired for growth. While we don't need more work, we do need constant opportunities to do harder work. We need to leave the comfort of sure knowledge and face new challenges that put us in the role of apprentice rather than master.

We not only need strategies to ensure high levels of challenge, we also need practices that emphasise learning over knowing. Being able to shift back into learning mode is essential; while technology promises ease of automation, it also portends the prospect of obsolescence. For professionals working in STEM (science, technology, engineering, maths) or anyone working in a field related to or highly infused with science and technology, acquired knowledge doesn't last long.

Based on the rate at which knowledge is increasing and the rate at which knowledge is decaying, it has been calculated that only about 15 per cent of what we know today is likely to be relevant in five years. Of course, the real kicker here is that we don't even know which 15 per cent this is. Truly, the critical skill of this century is not what you know but how fast you can learn.

So how do we find comfort in the fundamentally uncomfortable? How do we thrive with what feels more like chaos than progress? The following are a set of concrete strategies to help us struggle productively and joyfully. The first three are intended for professionals for their own development while the last three are for managers wanting to help their teams embrace new challenges.

1. Sign up for a stretch

If you can do your current job with ease, it might be time to dial up the intensity level at work. Try to 'disqualify' yourself, meaning, take on a new challenge, a job you aren't yet qualified for. As you size the challenge, look for an assignment that offers a sudden increase in difficulty rather than a gentle stretch or incremental skill development. In her *New York Times* article 'How to Become a Super-ager,' Lisa Feldman Barrett wrote, 'you must expend enough effort that you feel some "yuck".'

When we learn to push past the temporary unpleasantness of intense effort, we develop the necessary mindsets to tackle oversized challenges that are not of our choosing. When we linger too long on a professional plateau, a part of us dies inside. When we step out of our comfort zone and onto a learning curve, we feel alive again. We feel human – perhaps at our most human – vulnerable, in need of community, striving, learning and growing. Yet leaving the comfort of the known world is not a comfortable process. We cling to the security of our expertise, even when we know it to be ephemeral and fragile. We go kicking and screaming into the dark night of the unknown.

As you leave the comfort of work you are well qualified for, remember – if you have a job you are qualified for there is nothing to learn. And taking a job that you aren't qualified for doesn't necessitate a change of employment or even a new assignment; just submit to a new challenge and put yourself squarely at the bottom of a new learning curve.

2. Toss out your scripts

Dr C.K. Prahalad, of the University of Michigan's Stephen M. Ross School of Business, was considered to be the greatest management thinker of his time (twice listed in the top slot on the Thinkers50 ranking). He was also a terrible fire hazard to the university because his courses were so perpetually oversubscribed that students lined the halls just trying to get in earshot of one of his lectures.

When C.K. was a tenured professor, his wife, Gayatri, found a stack of his teaching notes in the trash bin of their home office. She recovered this most precious resource and she returned it to C.K. later that night. He thanked her but admitted, 'I actually threw those away on purpose because my students deserve my best thinking and fresh thinking every semester.' If you want to deepen and refresh your thinking, throw away your notes – your stump speeches, your handy scripts, your stale templates. While you will lose the comfort of familiarity, you will also rediscover the joy of creation.

3. Admit what you don't know

Leaders guiding their organisations in times of change or chaos can feel pressured to project confidence and capability. However, it is in these moments that the best leaders become learners. While I was at Oracle Corporation in the mid-1990s, I worked closely with the company's top executives as they set a new strategy for the internet age. When it came time to communicate the strategy to the mid-level managers, the feedback was brutal: the strategy was unclear and not compelling.

After several attempts to revise the strategy, the feedback wasn't any better. When I reminded the three top executives how important it was for them to clarify the strategy, Jeff Henley, the CFO (and my boss's boss), became agitated and blurted out, 'Liz, you don't need to beat us up. We know we need to fix this. The problem is that we don't know how to do it.' He explained matter-of-factly, 'We've never run a twenty-five-billion-dollar company before, so this is new to us.'

The president and the CTO nodded. I went slack-jawed. It hadn't occurred to me that these executives, whom I held in the highest esteem, were learning on the job, too. Jeff continued, 'If you could help us learn how to do this, now, that would be useful.'

I arranged for some rapid learning that enabled the executives to re-architect the strategy. The new strategy received accolades from the next level down and the once-beleaguered executives were now ebullient, exchanging high fives like an excited group of teenagers.

In fast times, everyone is winging it, even those at the top. When facing new challenges, don't pretend to know the route. Let people know you're learning (albeit quickly). Activate the mentor gene in others and enlist their support as you navigate the unknown.

4. Stretch your team

When a team is experiencing fatigue, managers often assume the role of team representative, taking responsibility for solving the hardest problems, removing obstacles and attempting to ease burdens. While attempting to serve their teams, these leaders actually do them a disservice. The best leaders don't lighten loads, they lay down intriguing challenges. The challenges need not be a dare to scale a singular, daunting peak. You can build capability in your team by offering a steady diet of challenge. Don't just dole out more work, give harder work – bigger challenges that prompt deep learning and growth.

5. Don't rescue strugglers

Many people are promoted into management positions because they are natural problem-solvers. So, when someone brings you a problem, it is only natural for you to want to fix it. Watching people struggle is its own form of pain from which most leaders seek relief. The next time you see someone struggling, step back and remind yourself that they are learning and jumping in will halt their learning process. When someone brings you a problem that you think they are capable of solving, give it back to them. Ask them how they think it can be solved. Play the role of the coach who pulls a solution from them rather than a being the problem-solver who stands ready to hand out a solution. Train your eye to distinguish between struggling and failing. In cases where there is an imminent danger of terminal failure – a mistake from which there is no return and no opportunity to learn – jump in and contribute. But then, when the threat has cleared, put the other person back in charge.

6. Create safe space for mistakes

The ability to tolerate challenge-based struggling increases when we acknowledge that mistakes are inevitable and permissible. Define a space for experimentation in your team's work by clarifying the aspects of the business or operation where it's OK to fail (i.e. where the ship can take a hit and recover) as opposed to aspects in which failure is simply not an option (i.e., where a blow will sink the ship). Creating and communicating this delineation will be empowering. It can give your team confidence to accept challenges with mettle; it will also signal where they should proceed with caution. This distinction will help you know when to stand back and when to rescue.

The Austrian philosopher Ludwig Wittgenstein claimed, 'I don't know why we're are here, but I'm pretty sure it is not in order to enjoy ourselves.' To be sure, struggle is unpleasant, and failure of any sort is painful. But the sting of learning is like an adolescent growing pain; it is an indicator of progress. As those in the United States Marine Corps like to say, 'Pain is weakness leaving the body.' It is strength under construction.

It is debatable whether the history of human civilisation is a long arc of progress or a cycle of rise and fall. What history certainly shows is that a civilisation resting on its laurels will languish and fall. For while the ancient Greeks and Romans prevailed magnificently in a barbaric world, it was their desire for security and comfort that brought about their ruin.

It is in struggle, not in ease, that we find growth. It is in seeking, not knowing, that we find truth. And when we allow the sting of learning to propel us forward, we find joy in the struggle.

SOCRATES MEETS NETFLIX

Dan Pontefract

In 1997, Reed Hastings sold his company, Pure Software, to Rational Software for $750 million. Shortly thereafter – using the proceeds of the sale – he co-founded Netflix.

Back then it was not the online streaming media empire that it has become today. Anachronistic as it may seem, Netflix was originally a mail-order DVD rental company. Hastings was inspired to establish Netflix when he was fined forty dollars for the late return of a DVD to the Blockbuster video store. Entering 2018, Netflix employed nearly four thousand people, earned revenues close to $9 billion and had morphed not only into an online streaming media service, but a successful entertainment studio, producing hit shows such as *The Crown*, *Master of None* and *Orange is the New Black*. (Blockbuster, incidentally, filed for bankruptcy protection in 2010 and in 2011 it sold its remaining 1,700 stores to satellite television provider Dish Network.)

Netflix is also known for its progressive people and culture practices. For example, its expense policy comprises a mere five words, 'Act in Netflix's best interests.' Annual performance reviews are non-existent: the company prefers frequent coaching conversations. Salaried team members have limitless vacation days, if they choose to take them. Stock options issued to employees contain no vesting period. Perhaps what I appreciate most about Netflix, however, can be found within its values and the way they shape behaviours and skills at the company.

There are nine Netflix values. The first is concerned with critical thinking. Netflix refers to this as 'judgment' and defines it as follows:

- You make wise decisions (people, technical, business, and creative) despite ambiguity.

- You identify root causes and get beyond treating symptoms.

- You think strategically and can articulate what you are, and are not, trying to do.

- You smartly separate what must be done well now and what can be improved later.

These four lines act as an important signal to get critical thinking right. Netflix asks its employees to balance the near and the far, the easy and the hard, the known and the unknown. The company does not want its team members judging ignorantly, but openly. It implores them to seek out the truth – the facts – through reflection and interaction. It also wants them to act, rather than to sit on the fence of indecision. Judgment is so important to Netflix that it is their first value.

Netflix teaches its employees not simply to identify today's information, but to look ahead to the needs of tomorrow. Balance is further established by not only saying 'yes' but 'no' as well. This is the Netflix way. Exercise judgment in both action and reflection. It sounds very philosophical, yet practical.

Socrates – who many consider to be the father of western philosophy – was a man in search of the truth. Ancient Athens was where he honed his critical thinking habits. North-west of the Acropolis was the Athens agora. Most Greek cities had one. Agoras were gathering places found near the city's centre where spiritual, academic, athletic, artistic and political events took place.

Inside the Athens agora and to the south of Panathenaic Way was the Enneakrounos, the public well. Just over three hundred yards away, to the left, was a portico known as the Stoa of Zeus. Socrates was often to be found just past the Monument of the Eponymous Heroes and inside the portico, standing on a wooden crate, thoroughly engaged in a discussion with a gaggle of people. It would sound like they were at odds with one another. It was loud. It seemed like bickering. But that was entirely the point.

Socrates, among other things, was renowned for introducing what is referred to in Greek as *elenchus*, a method of eliciting truth by question and answer. The argumentative dialogue spilling over among the people gathered at the Stoa of Zeus was *elenchus* in action, a dialectical method of critical thinking. It requires the constant asking and answering of questions. With *elenchus*, biases can be overcome, presumptions debunked and points of view both defended and challenged. Dialectical discourse occurs between two or more people who hold differing viewpoints. The aim is to draw out their opinions on a subject, not only to establish the truth but ideally to create a new common ground between the two perspectives.

Back in the Athens agora, according to the writings of Plato, Socrates would invoke *elenchus* frequently. As he sought out the truth, Socrates felt cooperative debate was the way it would materialise. More specifically for Socrates, the *elenchus* allowed him to ascertain if humans were capable of living the good life while simultaneously probing if they knew how they ought to live the good life. This was his quest, the pursuit of truth. The purpose was to expose himself to the unknown and to contrary opinion.

Socrates never believed he possessed all the answers. Rather, the *elenchus* would provide the singular truth imparted by the many opinions he came across. Vulnerability was always key. By being vulnerable, Socrates did not reach conclusions on his own. He used the immense power of other people's belief to define a new truth. The Socratic method of critical thinking creates an endpoint from multiple viewpoints; eventually this allows an informed decision that moves an idea forward.

Which brings us back to Netflix. When you reread those four lines defining Netflix's 'judgment' value, picture yourself at the company's headquarters. Might it be a modern-day agora, where employees are encouraged to invoke *elenchus* every day? At a minimum, Netflix and Socrates provide good food for thought when it comes to assessing your critical thinking habits.

TRUTH IN THE POST-TRUMP WORLD

Kevin Morrell

For many people, Donald Trump's shock victory in the US presidential election of 2016 exemplified a new era of 'post-truth politics'. For them the phrase came to symbolise a new low in public discourse where facts came a distant second to populist appeals. But, post-truth politics is much older than you might think.

During the campaign, Donald Trump declared Barack Obama was 'the founder of Isis' and its 'most valuable player'. Neither statement was true but both were designed to create controversy and stick in the minds of sympathetic voters. A few days later, when it caused a media furore, Trump tweeted, 'THEY DON'T GET SARCASM?'

Trump added that he was merely voicing what others were thinking. 'I don't know, but that's what some people are saying,' he said (even though no one had even suggested it before he did). It was vintage Trump: an outrageous claim followed by an ambiguous disclaimer.

So prevalent did it become that 'post-truth' was Oxford Dictionaries' word of 2016. Defined as, 'Circumstances in which objective facts are less influential in shaping public opinion than appeals to emotion and personal belief,' the phenomenon is associated in many people's minds with the referendum in the UK that led to Brexit that same year and the rise of Trump and other populist politicians. But how old is post-truth politics?

The phrase has been attributed to the journalist David Roberts in a 2010 article in *Grist* magazine, but it has a much longer provenance. One reference point is the 'big lie' propaganda of the 1930s. Political academic Hannah Arendt's 1967 *New Yorker* essay 'Truth and Politics' identified the real danger of this period, 'If the modern political lies are so big that they require a complete rearrangement of the whole factual texture – the making of another reality, as it were, into which they will fit without seam, crack, or fissure ... what prevents these new stories, images and non-facts from becoming an adequate substitute for reality?'

But the phenomenon pre-dates this modern political period too. Almost a century earlier, in the 1850s, there was a US election campaign that was even dirtier than 2016, where the anti-immigration party, the 'know-nothings', actively celebrated ignorance of their own party's clandestine activities.

Further back still, before US independence, the Scottish satirist John Arbuthnot, a friend of Jonathan Swift and Alexander Pope, wrote, 'Falsehood flies, and the truth comes limping after it, so that when men come to be undeceived, it is too late ... like a physician who has found out an infallible medicine after the patient is dead.'

Arbuthnot's observation was prescient. A characteristic of post-truth politics has been how rapidly and shamelessly the untruth can be discarded once it has done its poisonous work. In 2016, the Leave campaign's claim that the UK sent £350 million a week to the EU that could be used to fund the NHS (the patient) was written in large text on the side of a bus and repeated so often that it took on the illusion of fact. Yet already by the morning of the referendum result Nigel Farage, the leader of UKIP, was describing it as a 'mistake', conveniently excusing both the lie and the fact that his own salary as an MEP contributed towards it.

Lying, next to Cleon

Arbuthnot entitled his 1712 essay *The Art of Political Lying*. But the age of post-truth politics began earlier still. Two thousand years earlier, in 350 BC, Aristotle's *Constitution of Athens* referred to a populist demagogue called Cleon. Describing him in a way that Trump's critics might recognise, Aristotle noted that Cleon was 'the cause of the corruption of the democracy by his wild undertakings'.

A closer look at Cleon invites several more parallels with Trump. Like the Donald, Cleon was a businessman who came late to politics. He inherited his wealth from his father in the form of a tannery – a leather factory, the Athenian equivalent of blue-collar work.

Like Trump, too, Cleon rose to power at a time of public dissatisfaction with conventional politicians. The year was 430 BC, a desperate time for Athens, which was at war with Sparta and simultaneously devastated by plague. Cleon turned the divisions within Athenian society to his advantage. The ancient Greek essayist Plutarch describes him as someone who 'catered to the pleasure of the Athenians', with a combination of 'mad vanity', 'versatile buffoonery' and 'disgusting boldness'.

Cleon had a distinctive and shocking communication style, one Athenians had never seen before. While speaking, Cleon would hitch his cloak up and slap his thighs, running and yelling at the crowds. Aristotle says he was 'the first to use unseemly shouting and coarse abuse'. The first, but not the last.

Aside from this radically new style of communication, Cleon's populism was based on attacking two enemies. First, though a member of the 'establishment' himself, he was an anti-establishment figure, pursuing a 'relentless persecution of the upper classes'. Second, he was a flag-waving xenophobe, antagonistic towards Athens' rival and (partly thanks to Cleon himself) bitter enemy Sparta, as well as to the city of Mytilene, which wanted independence from Athens. The Athenian general and historian Thucydides wrote of a speech in which Cleon expressed admiration for Mytilene's 'unassailable' walls.

A later Athenian writer, Lucian, suggests Cleon made money from exploiting his office and that he was 'venal to excess'. He was boastful, bragging that he could win a war against the Spartans by himself. He was thin-skinned and censorious, as well as a litigious bully. Cleon tried – unsuccessfully – to have the satirist Aristophanes prosecuted for writing *The Babylonians*, which he considered a treasonable play – in the process turning Aristophanes into a life-long enemy.

He accused Athenian generals of incompetence (echoes again of Trump) and in establishment-bashing mode tried, again unsuccessfully, to prosecute one of them (Laches). He was held responsible for the eventual exile of another, Thucydides. His antagonistic rhetoric meant that Cleon became the biggest obstacle to normal relations with Sparta and within a year of his death a peace treaty was agreed.

History has certainly not been kind to Cleon – no surprise, perhaps, given that he exiled the most eminent Athenian historian and tried to silence the most influential Athenian satirist (perhaps there is a lesson for modern day post-truth politicians who wish to rein in the media and its satirists). Nowadays Cleon is best known through Aristophanes' play *The Knights* (a far ruder precursor of the US TV show *Saturday Night Live*). *The Knights* has an unusually small cast because it is essentially a relentless assault on the character Paphlagon (obviously Cleon), the 'leather-seller' with a 'gaping arse', a 'perfect glutton for beans' who loudly 'farts and snores', an 'arrant rogue' and 'mud-stirrer' with a 'pig's education' and the 'stink of leather', 'this villain, this villain, this villain! I cannot say the word too often, for he is a villain a thousand times a day'.

Cleon may well have had a front row seat for *The Knights*, where he would have seen Aristophanes playing the part of Paphlagon, presumably because no-one else dared to. Characters were masked but no prop-maker dared make a mask resembling Cleon. We might imagine Cleon later writing a review of *The Knights*: 'a totally one-sided, biased show – nothing funny at all. Unwatchable! The theatre must always be a safe and special place. Apologise!' and so on. What matters is that Aristophanes' contemporaries awarded *The Knights* first prize at the Lenaia festival (something like Athens' equivalent of the Cannes festival).

Cleon's brand of post-truth politics flourished; when life is extremely hard, facts are not as novel or distracting as sensationalism. Some Athenians were won over by the novel spectacle of yelling, coarse abuse and thigh slapping – and distracted by diversionary ranting against Sparta.

Imperfect storms

Critics of such post-truth sensations as Brexit and President Trump could equally say their voters were won over by bus-sized gimmicks (Brexit) and tweet-sized slogans, which helped to paint 'enemy' over the faces of an anonymous 'other'. Populism and appeals to emotion will always work on some people and, when times are bad enough, they will work on enough people.

Timing, of course, plays its part. Arguably, 2016 was a perfect storm with the Brexit result creating momentum for the Trump campaign because millions of people in the UK and the US were desperate for change. But Leave voters and Trump supporters would argue that it is precisely that elitist attitude – assuming that the insiders know best – that caused so many people to become disaffected with the 'establishment truth' to the point of preferring the post-truth version of reality.

Perhaps, too, we shouldn't be so shocked by the leaders we have got over the years. Professor Jeffrey Pfeffer from Stanford University has observed that many of Trump's perceived faults would have been leadership assets in other walks of life. He is 'frequently untruthful and inaccurate in his statements and pays little attention to facts and data', Pfeffer wrote in a LinkedIn blog in December 2016.

> What many observers somehow fail to appreciate is that these qualities are actually typical of leaders in many sectors and, moreover, are not so much faults as fundamental bases for becoming a powerful leader.
>
> Research consistently shows that ... unwarranted self-confidence, self-promotion and self-aggrandisement predict leader emergence – in experiments, in field data, even in the US military. The evidence for the effects ... on group or organisational performance is more equivocal, although one overlooked study of US presidents found that a related trait, fearless dominance, did predict some dimensions of presidential performance such as crisis management, congressional relations and persuasiveness.

As Pfeffer also points out, in his book *Leadership BS*, there is plenty of evidence that lying may be one of the most useful and important traits of leaders.

> People lie all the time with few to no consequences. That includes the tobacco industry executives who testified that they were unaware about the studies their own companies conducted demonstrating the adverse health effects of smoking; the numerous financial industry executives who maintained that their balance sheets were sound as they headed into bankruptcy or had to raise capital at distressed

prices during the 2008 financial crisis and even Apple's late founder, Steve Jobs, about whom the phrase 'reality distortion field' was coined.

Silver linings

Trump was not the first post-truth leader, and he almost certainly won't be the last.

One consolation for those who opposed his term as president and those who were unhappy by the campaign that led to Brexit could be found in the knowledge that Athenians were able to keep Cleon in check using existing governance mechanisms – the courts. They could also take comfort that, after his time in power, Cleon was remembered through the eyes of his bitter enemy Aristophanes.

Cleon's era was horrific yet, like Trump's term and the battles of Brexit and afterwards, it also became a golden age for satire and saw the birth of the discipline of history. Civilisation survived Cleon and, shortly after his death, another kind of Athenian golden age was ushered in, in which Socrates, Plato and Aristotle laid down the basis for western philosophy and civilisation. These great thinkers taught the importance of scepticism and scrutiny and of virtue. They placed the highest premium on the search for knowledge and truth.

In the *Rhetoric*, Aristotle gave us all the tools we need to see through a Cleon. Aristotle wanted rhetoric to be widely understood; politicians' arguments could be evaluated on their merits rather than the wrapper (or the side of a bus) they arrived in. Brave figures like Aristophanes did perpetually fight prejudice and Thucydides fought to record facts. Today we can also maintain an ironic distance, seeing the horror and nonsense that persisted even after Trump, reluctantly, departed office as an aesthetic spectacle. We can continue to support commentators, critics and comics; fiercely reject censorship; respect history; defend our courts (this being absolutely vital) and work hard to keep a sense of humour (and a sense of the ridiculous).

Let's hope we are now, at last, able to raise a smile (and a glass) to post-Trump politics and the post-post-truth era.

THE PHILOSOPHY OF PRICE

Hermann Simon

Prices are the hinges of a market economy. As consumers, we pay them many times a day. As managers we have to make price decisions all the time. But we hardly ever link our price-related activities to philosophy. What does philosophy have to do with price? Why should we look at something as ubiquitous and mundane as price from a philosophical standpoint?

It turns out that viewing price through the lens of classical philosophy reveals some very practical insights that can prevent us from making mistakes, both as buyers and sellers. What I refer to as the 'philosophy of price' can:

- deepen our understanding of price and its effects

- keep us humble (many seemingly modern pricing concepts were first articulated by ancient philosophers)

- help us to solve difficult ethical pricing issues, such as in health care.

In this article I offer insights drawn from classical philosophy that remain surprisingly relevant to twenty-first-century price decisions. I have devoted my life to pricing and describe the journey through the land of price in my book *Confessions of the Pricing Man*. In the first twenty years of my career, I worked as an academic. For the next two decades, I did real-world work as a price consultant. Along the way, my associates and I built the world's leading price consultancy. Simon-Kucher & Partners currently employs more than 1,200 people in thirty-eight offices on six continents.

On price and value

There is one question I have been asked thousands of times during my career: 'What is the most important aspect in pricing?'

My evergreen answer has always been 'value' or 'value to customer'. To be even more precise, the best answer is 'perceived value to customer'. Why do I say that? The customer's willingness to pay a price and, thus, the opportunity of the seller to obtain that price, is nothing but the reflection of the value perceived by the customer. This simple insight, however, is not new. It derives from Latin, which uses the same word, *pretium*, interchangeably for value and for price.

Value = *pretium* = price

Languages contain a lot of philosophical wisdom. This linguistic truth from Latin is the eternal equation of pricing. Value and price must always be balanced. Business-people who adhere to this simple equation avoid making big mistakes in setting their prices. The equation also applies to the buyer, who as the saying goes, 'gets what they pay for'.

The concept of value equals price is so fundamental and universal that I would call it a philosophical equation. It tells us that pricing should not be primarily concerned with price as such, but instead with value. It also teaches us that understanding, creating and communicating value is the key challenge in pricing.

Lesson 1

The most important aspect of price and pricing is value. The essential and eternal equation of pricing is 'value = *pretium* = price'. Understanding, creating, and communicating value is the key challenge for a business.

On 'value in use' and the sharing economy

The eternal equation begs the question, 'What is value?' One of the first known answers to this question comes from the Greek philosopher Socrates (469–399 BC), who said that 'happiness does not come from ownership, but from the use of a product'. In contemporary terminology, we speak of 'value in use'. We can therefore consider Socrates to be the father of a very modern concept: the sharing economy. In the sharing economy, one does not *own* a car, a bicycle or an apartment, one *uses* it – often only for a defined period. The increasingly widespread implementation of the sharing economy is radically transforming entire industries.

Why was this revolutionary Socratic idea not implemented earlier? The answer is obvious. The transactional costs in sharing were too high prior to the arrival of the internet. Selling a car requires just one transaction, say of $30,000. Sharing that same car in hourly increments means thousands of transactions over the life of a car. Offering a car on a per-hour basis or a bicycle on a per-minute basis requires an extremely efficient transaction process and the ability to bring together a critical mass of buyers and sellers. Neither is possible without the internet.

At the same time, Socrates denied the value of ownership. I consider this a flaw. Ownership can have intrinsic value, in addition to or even without 'value in use'. Think of a supercar Ferrari, displayed in front of its owner's house but never driven.

Does the owner derive value from that car? Of course! There are two reasons for this.

Firstly, owning an object is likely to convey more status than sharing it. In his classic *The Theory of the Leisure Class*, published in 1899, Thorstein Veblen described this phenomenon, which is also called the 'snob effect'. A second, very modern argument, is that sharing is always based on an 'incomplete contract'. This concept goes back to Nobel laureate Ronald Coase, who explained why firms exist and own their assets. Coase said that, within a firm, transaction costs can be lower and that sharing, renting or leasing is always based on an incomplete contract. Only ownership grants you the right to do anything with the object in question. You cannot repaint a leased car or an Airbnb apartment, nor can you sell it. But if you own it, you can tear it down, repaint it, sell it, dismantle it or whatever. Ownership has a higher value than an incomplete contract. The issue of incomplete contracts gains new importance with so-called 'smart contracts' and blockchain technology.

Can the value of ownership versus the value of sharing/renting/leasing be observed in real life? I think so. Here is a case based on real prices. Let's say the 'ownership price' of a given BMW 7 Series car is €110,510, while the leasing price per month is €1,231 for a leasing period of three years. Thus, in three years the consumer pays a total of €44,316. Without financing costs, the payback period amounts to eighty-nine months or seven and a half years. If you add financing costs, there is hardly a way for the seller to get the 'ownership price' through leasing. A possible explanation is that ownership plus value in use together create a higher perceived value than mere value in use and that certain consumers are willing to pay the higher ownership price. Socrates may have missed this aspect.

Lesson 2

The basic idea of the sharing economy goes back to Socrates, who said that value does not come from ownership, but from the use of a product ('value in use'). While this may be generally true, ownership can also have intrinsic value, resulting from Veblen ('snob') effects or from complete contracts. The observation of higher ownership prices relative to sharing prices is consistent with this notion. Only the internet has made large-scale application of the sharing economy possible, thanks to radically lower transaction and controlling costs.

On value differentiation

We owe many of the more sophisticated insights on value and price to the Greek philosopher Aristotle (384–322 BC). He observed that value in use can vary among individuals. This is the basis for the ubiquitous price differentiation or price discrimination we experience today. Aristotle also noted that the value in use declines as the quantity of goods increases. This fundamental law is now known as Gossen's Second Law, formulated in 1854 by Hermann Heinrich Gossen (1810–1858). This law is the foundation for non-linear pricing.

Aristotle also mentions that the value of a product can depend on the use of another product. This insight provides a rationale for multi-product pricing and for so-called price bundling. He also observed that the value in use will increase if the product can be consumed conspicuously, which leads us back to the snob – or Veblen – effect. Finally, one can draw a direct line of reasoning between Aristotle and Karl Marx. Aristotle stated that labour as a commodity has value, but does not create value. This essentially contradicts Marx's 'labour value' theory, which we will discuss later.

Lesson 3

Many modern pricing concepts, such as price differentiation, non-linear pricing and price bundling, are rooted in ancient philosophy and can be traced back to Aristotle. Even today, his ideas help us to comprehend the underlying logic behind certain pricing tactics.

On 'just price'

The concept of 'just price' dates back to saint and philosopher Thomas Aquinas (1225–1274). Today we use the term 'fair price' in a similar sense. Aquinas looked at pricing from an economic and an ethical perspective. His ideas were strongly influenced by the Christian tradition against usury and against interest in general. To raise prices in response to increasing demand was theft in his view. Aquinas also explicitly stated that charging higher prices in the wake of natural disasters is unethical.

This latter topic remains highly relevant, as illustrated by the report, *Price gouging after Hurricane Sandy: immoral or law of supply and demand?* This concerns the pricing for power generators during and after a 2012 natural disaster in the USA. Should the seller raise the price after a disaster? If the price is kept constant, the first buyers will buy several generators and resell them at a higher price. Is this just?

We can also look at the case of Uber following a terrorist attack in Australia. The demand for cars surged and the Uber app automatically increased the surcharge. This makes economic sense, because the higher fees attract more cars to the site from which people want to flee. Uber got a very negative media response to that action, however. It is said that Uber now applies manual intervention if demand rises suddenly and sharply.

Very innovative life-saving drugs provide another example. Kymriah, a gene-based therapy offered by Novartis, heals a certain type of leukemia with one injection. What is a just price for this product? In the US, an application of this drug costs up to $475,000. In the UK, the National Health Service covers a price of £220,000, but only for children. In Germany the price is €320,000. Novartis chairman Dr Joerg Reinhardt defended these prices, 'We firmly believe that therapies should be paid on the basis of their value. We are determined to set our prices according to this principle. In the future, costs for a genetic therapy will be justified by their value for the individual patient.'

Would a different price system be more just? What about a system where patients pay 50 per cent of their annual income? A patient who earns $100,000 would pay $50,000. A patient who makes $2 million a year would pay $1 million. While such a system seems unrealistic at first glance, it is also the basis of income taxes – one can consider income tax to be the price for government services.

For public goods, theory suggests that the price paid by a customer should be equal to the marginal utility of that customer. The income percentage can be considered as a proxy for the marginal utility. Is such a life-saving drug a public good?

The concept of 'just price' was later discarded by Spanish scholars and replaced by a more market-oriented approach.

Lesson 4

The concept of just price, which dates back to Aquinas, is considered obsolete today, at least for competitive markets. But the problem remains in certain cases, such as monopolies, extreme demand or very high value such as life-saving drugs. We have no clue what is just in such situations.

On Marxist pricing

Are you a Marxist? You are likely to answer 'no'.

My next question is, 'OK, if you are not a Marxist, why is your pricing Marxist?'

While Marx's theory is totally rejected in labour today, it has survived in pricing. What a strange phenomenon! Let me explain why that is the case.

The most important contribution made to the literature by Karl Marx (1818–1883) was his labour theory of value, according to which only labour creates value. He writes that the 'prices of goods are determined by wages'. Marx allows for differences in productivity and qualifications of workers and, thus, for different values per unit of time. But the core of his theory is that only labour creates value. Consequently, labour costs are the sole base for price calculations.

In modern terminology we call this method 'cost-plus pricing'. Based on my decades of observations around the world, I would claim that 80 per cent of all prices in today's markets are primarily determined on the basis of costs. And all costs are labour costs. Lawyers, consultants and most other service providers charge prices for their time (hourly, daily, monthly rates). If an automotive company buys parts from a supplier, these parts carry labour costs up the value chain.

Lesson 5

Karl Marx's labour value theory is considered completely obsolete. Nevertheless, cost-plus pricing, which is nothing but Marxist pricing, predominates. If one doesn't believe in Marxism, one should get rid of Marxist pricing. Perhaps calling it Marxist will accelerate the eradication of cost-plus pricing.

On 'subjective value'

The so-called 'subjective value' theory, which is generally – but not universally – accepted, could be expressed as, 'Value is in the eye of the beholder.' This is also not new.

Publilius Syrus, who lived in the first century bc, said, 'Everything is worth what a purchaser will pay for it.'

What is this theory's implication for pricing? It is 'value extraction' or, in the modern internet vernacular, 'monetisation'. These terms encompass all variants of price differentiation or price discrimination, across customers, product variants and space and time. The internet has radically improved the opportunities for price differentiation due to better data and much lower costs of implementation.

However, there is a strong and increasing opposition against value extraction. Mariana Mazzucato from the London School of Economics is one of its outspoken critics. 'Things are only getting worse,' she wrote. '"Rent seeking" refers to the attempt to generate income, not by producing anything, but by overcharging above the "competitive price" and undercutting competition by exploiting particular advantages or blocking other companies from entering an industry, thereby retaining a monopoly advantage.'

Her views are seconded by Nobel laureate Joseph Stiglitz, who blames weak regulation and monopolistic practices for 'rent extraction'.

A related key question is whether there is a level playing field between consumers and increasingly sophisticated sellers. I think there is. The reason lies in the much better price-and-value transparency the internet has delivered. Today's consumers have all kinds of price comparison tools at their fingertips. The same increasingly applies to value transparency, thanks to widely used online customer feedback mechanisms.

Marshall McLuhan's 'global village', first described in 1962, has become reality. Understanding value creation and delivery on the one side and value extraction (or monetisation) on the other side becomes critical for buyers and sellers. This applies to B2C markets as well as to B2B markets.

Lesson 6

According to the 'subjective value' theory, value is in the eye of the beholder. Aristotle recognised that values are differentiated and offer opportunities for value extraction and systematic price differentiation. Modern information technology has pushed this trend to an extreme and provoked a backlash against 'value extraction'. This opposition suggests that companies should not overdo price discrimination. On the other hand, increasing price transparency and value transparency contribute to a level playing field between sellers and buyers.

Society and price

A journey through philosophy yields many additional insights on the role of prices in society. I highlight several of them in this last section.

On price and quality

Baltasar Gracián (1601–58), a Spanish philosopher and Jesuit said, 'It is better to be cheated in the price than in the quality.' The same idea resonates in the French proverb, *'Le prix s'oublie, la qualité reste'* ('The price is forgotten, the quality remains'). The English social reformer and philosopher John Ruskin (1819–1900) expressed a similar thought: 'It is unwise to pay too much, but it is worse to pay too little. When you pay too much, you lose a little money – that is all. When you pay too little, you sometimes lose everything because the thing you bought was incapable of doing the thing you bought it to do. The common law of business balance prohibits paying a little and getting a lot – it cannot be done. If you deal with the lowest bidder, it is well to add something for the risk you run, and if you do that you will have enough to pay for something better.'

Price as truce

The French philosopher Gabriel Tarde (1834–1904) interpreted price negotiations as war and the price as truce. Labour union strikes fall clearly into this pattern. But it also describes modern price conflicts such as the 2018 'war' over prices between Nestlé, the world's largest food producer and Edeka, Europe's largest grocery retailer.

Limits of price

The American philosopher Michael J. Sandel asserts in his book *What Money Can't Buy: The Moral Limits of the Markets* that prices have begun to penetrate many sectors of our personal lives. For example, for a price of $85 for a five-year membership, travellers could join PreCheck, a programme run by the Transportation Security Administration (TSA) in the US and take advantage of an expedited security line at airports. Today, more than five million people have registered, more than two hundred US airports and forty-two airlines participate, and 94 per cent of the TSA PreCheck waiting times are less than five minutes.

Entering the USA from abroad costs $14 at the time of writing, the fee for an entry into ESTA (Electronic System for Travel Authorization).

In Afghanistan, mercenaries from private firms earn between $250 and $1,000 per day – the fee depending on the person's qualifications, experience and citizenship. In Iraq and Afghanistan, there were at times more active personnel from private security companies than soldiers from the US Army.

For $6,250, one can hire a surrogate mother from India to carry an embryo. A flat rate for unlimited surrogate mothers in India plus extra arrangements for twins or triplets would cost $60,000.

One can purchase the right to immigrate to the USA for $500,000. Smoking is forbidden in most US hotels and motels. Some facilities charge a fine of two hundred dollars or more for violating this rule. One can consider that fine as the price a guest must pay to buy the 'privilege' to smoke in the room.

More and more we are seeing price stickers on everything, as market and price mechanisms reach deeper into our day-to-day lives. This invasion of pricing into areas historically organised outside of market norms is one of the remarkable changes of our times.

Sandel comments on this trend, 'When we decide that certain goods may be bought and sold, then we decide – at least implicitly – that it is appropriate to treat them as commodities, as instruments of profit and use. But not all goods are properly valued in this way. The most obvious example is human beings.'

Prices, information and God

Who makes prices? According to the book *The Mantle of the Prophet: Religion and Politics in Iran,* by Roy Mottahedeh, the following applies: 'Information about prices is the quickening breath that sustains the life of the bazaar and the mechanism by which these prices adjust to new information on supply and demand is so refined as to seem almost divine. "God sets prices," according to a saying ascribed to the prophet Mohammed and most Islamic jurists agreed that an unseen hand that operated with such efficiency must be the hand of God.' This statement recalls Adam Smith's invisible hand.

Lesson 7

From ancient times through to today, philosophers have contributed valuable insights on pricing. Astute pricers should keep their eyes wide open. Pricing is not a narrow discipline. It benefits from deep, almost philosophical thinking and understanding.

Summary

Philosophy helps both buyers and sellers to understand pricing challenges better. Many concepts which seem modern actually have ancient philosophical roots. But their implementation has only become possible thanks to modern information technology and big data analysis.

The eternal equation of pricing will always remain: value equals *pretium* equals price, an insight expressed in Latin two thousand years ago. While some theories of value and price, such as the 'just price', are generally ignored today, they still apply in certain situations. We don't have solutions for all ethical issues. The widely accepted 'subjective value' theory advocates differentiated value extraction, but increasing opposition suggests that sellers should not overdo price discrimination.

This article provides only a very selective and limited review of the philosophy of price. It is by no means comprehensive. It would be easy to write a lengthy book on this topic. Nonetheless, buyers and sellers ignore the philosophy of price at their own peril.

INTERVIEW WITH HENRY MINTZBERG

Philosophy, balance and new management thinking

Philosophy@work: Henry, as a professor of management studies and a writer on management development, you also created a theory of rebalancing societies. Could you explain the general idea of that theory?

Henry Mintzberg: Sure. The theory of a rebalancing society starts with an imbalance in which the society finds itself. Today, the imbalance in which we all live is characterised by destruction: the destruction of our democracies, our planet and ourselves. Our democracies get destroyed through the political pendulum of left and right and lobbying that is allowing no space for the invisible hand of competing.

Our planet gets destroyed because the energy production, stock farming and other necessary production lines are not sustainable and we keep using our Earth's valuable resources to create more money but no sustainability. As we continue to live in a destructive environment we also destroy ourselves as 'human resources'. We need a change in our current system of destruction and a return to balance. That's why I created the theory of a rebalancing society.

We need a change in our destructive system to come back to balance. Historically speaking, there was already an imbalance around 1989 in eastern Europe, when the communist regimes started collapsing. Due to that much power concentrated upon the public sectors their system collapsed because of a major imbalance. The solution to this imbalance was to develop another system that would provide balance again and was already proven successful by western Europe. From that perspective one can say that capitalism did not triumph; it was the balance that did. But capitalism is not the healing answer to anything – although thirty-two years ago it seemed like it was. Now, we are suffering from the consequences that capitalism brought and humanity is in need of a new, more balanced system once again.

Philosophy@work: So, that means we need to change our system in order to have a society living in balance? That seems like a huge mission. Given the fact that our world is incredibly complex, interconnected and everything moves at a rapid pace – how is it possible to regain balance and where should we start?

Henry Mintzberg: That's a terrific question. There is probably not one way and, rather, many different ways that would create balance improving progresses, but there is a perspective I would like to explain that maybe makes it easier to understand what we could do.

To begin, one must understand that there are always three different sectors in a society. While the public and the private sector are mostly known; many people seem to forget about the sector that I like to call the 'plural sector'. It is sometimes described as the not-for-profit sector or the third sector. Today, many countries struggle with balance, as already said, and that is because of the consequences capitalism brought. In many countries the sector's benefits are imbalanced in favour of their private sector. Some people say that, to regain balance, the public sector must act more straightforwardly and recreate balance by somehow standing up to the private sector. The government could limit the private sector's possibilities, but this solution can't really work as long as public states are dominated by private entitlements.

Other people say that, to regain balance, the private sector should implement more corporate social responsibility but, in my opinion, more corporate social responsibility is not equipped to fight corporate social irresponsibility. Actually, that just leaves the plural sector to regain balance and this is my original point because I think that this sector is capable of making a real change.

First of all, one needs to know what the 'plural sector' is. To me, the plural sector is made up of a variety of human associations. All the associations that are neither public nor private belong to the plural sector: foundations, non-profit organisations, cooperatives and so on. If we count them all together they make up a huge part of society. And especially when we consider that social movements are also a part of the plural sector it becomes clear that this sector has much power to enable balance improving changes within society.

So, to answer your question – within the current situation in society the plural sector is the sector that can change even though we live in a very complex, connected and fast-moving world. The plural sector has the opportunities for change. It is just us who have to actively engage in it and move us and our communities in the direction of balance.

Philosophy@work: The plural sector has the power to rebalance our society? That's interesting.

Henry, you are known for your critique of MBAs and your alternative understanding and practices of management. Could you explain your general opinion on management practices these days and their connection to the balance or imbalance of society?

Henry Mintzberg: Of course. To me, management is the practice of helping to set the course of direction for an organisation. This includes the practice of ensuring that the people work together to achieve the goal the organisation wants to achieve. It is true that the manager is the authority side of organisation, but that doesn't mean that they just decide everything by themself. Organisations are collective action in the pursuit of a common mission.

Considering this, management is also a means to enable collective action and give a sense of a mission. Therefore, the practice of management is quite complex because the manager has to see every person within the working process and make sure that all people are responding to one another. Beyond that, the manager has to translate the goal of the organisation into a mission that speaks to the dynamics of the people who want to achieve the goal. This is probably not exactly the definition of management you would find in a dictionary but I think this is a very helpful way of practising management.

Before getting to the current ways management is performed, first of all I would like to go back in time – to 1916. When I was studying those days, I realised that all the experts described management summarised with the expression 'having control over everything', but that never really suited my own perception of the word 'management'. While authors of the popular literature on management often described the work of managers with the words 'plan', 'organise', 'control' and 'coordinate', I thought that there was nobody who actually observed what managers do because the descriptions above make it seem like managers are only there to control the people around them.

Fortunately, this is not what managers do, and this is actually easy to see because managers spend at least half of their time with people outside their units. Exactly how reality looked like was not really put on paper, so I thought that we needed a new vocabulary and I started participating in the search for a new vocabulary to describe what managers actually do. All of what I just mentioned is an explanation of my thoughts on management and also an alternative way to look at it.

Regarding the current situation of management and its practice, I think it is important to notice that – at least in my view – the actual practice of management doesn't even change. It is, in fact, the style of management that changes and this style of management is always depending on the current situation of society. Nowadays, we have a problem with the style of management because we have a problem with the mentality in our society. Our problem is called 'narcissism' and it increases vastly. Narcissism is also spread within businesses and, in that context, there is the term 'leadership' that I would like to introduce at this point. After the 'having control about everything' notion was presented, mostly in the management literature, the term 'leadership' arose. It all started with an article in the *Harvard Business Review* and, since then, many people seem to think that leadership is superior to management.

In the context of this new term, I think that people sometimes misunderstand that leadership is not a whole different thing to management. Both of them are connected to each other. I like to think of that connection in two phrases:

One: the leader should be managing.

Two: The manager should be leading. But it is part of the narcissism that makes 'small managers' want to be 'real leaders', and is probably pulling them away from doing great work as a manager that leads and a leader that manages.

Narcissism is cutting good management out, but also collective action, communities and gatherings of great minds who want to change this world – and, therefore, narcissism is also a part of the imbalance in our society; or, at least, not letting people come together and rebalance the society. To answer your question. Unfortunately, the current style of management is not helping society rebalance but this is caused by the general problem of narcissism and not a management problem in particular.

Philosophy@work: Narcissism creates damage. That reminds me of a story you wrote. I think it was a story from your book that includes all kinds of bedtime stories for managers. It was about scrambled eggs in an airplane – can you retell it?

Henry Mintzberg: 'Scrambled Eggs' is correct; that is the title of the story you're referring to. All right…

Once, I was taking a flight from Montreal to New York on Eastern Air Lines. At that point Eastern Air Lines was the biggest airline in the world and, during my flight, they served me something they called 'scrambled eggs'.

I told the flight attendant that I've never eaten anything this bad.

She said that she knew and heard that all the time but, although the flight attendants kept telling their bosses about that problem, nothing changed. I thought that those in charge just had to try the scrambled eggs to understand and change something. But, apparently, that did not happen. Some years later I found out why.

After telling this story to a few managers, one from IBM told me another story. The chief executive of Eastern Air Lines – Frank Borman – once came running so late for a flight that first class was already full. The flight attendants bumped a first-class passenger to sit the boss where he was used to sitting. And this was the reason why the scrambled eggs stayed on the plane. Borman never got to taste the scrambled eggs because of his status. His comfort zone made him ignorant to the experiences his customers experienced and I always think that this is the reason why Eastern

Air Lines went bankrupt shortly after.

That story is indeed a good example for narcissism causing damage. Managers shouldn't be blinded by their own pride. They should know what's going on in every square of their organisation. Even if that means they have to eat scrambled eggs.

Philosophy@work: That's an amazing story!

I understand that our system is destructive in general and narcissism in our society – and also in management – all together creates a huge imbalance in our society. For the last question, Henry, I want to focus on all of the imbalance causing threats we face today and want to ask you whether you think that the pandemic is going to function as a wake-up call for society and maybe a wake-up call for a more balanced society.

Henry Mintzberg: I am not sure of calling it a 'wake-up call'. A wake-up call would need to be heard but in our current situation – with many people living within a narcissistic worldview – unfortunately, no one is ever really listening. So, the effects of the pandemic would be more of a wake-up 'signal' or a wake-up 'ring'. But, as long as the narcissists are in control of many things, it is going to be hard for the positive learning effects the pandemic could bring to us.

But I am not saying that there wouldn't be a lot of potential to learn from the pandemic and get out even stronger than drifting in. The pandemic could teach us to be less narcissistic and actually focus on the world around us, the people around us and all the opportunities that would create balance in every aspect of our lives – being aware of imbalance and actively recreate imbalance.

I can't predict anything but I hope that people will learn from the effects of the pandemic. Now, it is a very exciting time to be alive, but it is also a very critical time. It can go any which way and it will go any which way. I think that pessimists predict what they don't like and optimists predict what they do like. So, I would be happy to predict that we are going to have all kinds of collaboration because of the pandemic that creates a more balanced society. But we will have to wait and see if that happens.

A NOTE ON THE AUTHORS

Scott D. Anthony

Scott D. Anthony is a senior partner at Innosight and former managing partner of the firm. Based in the firm's Singapore offices since 2010, he has led Innosight's expansion into the Asia-Pacific region as well as its venture capital activities (Innosight Ventures).

In his more than a decade with Innosight, Scott has advised senior leaders in companies such as Procter & Gamble, Johnson & Johnson, Singtel, Kraft, General Electric, LG, the Ayala Group and Cisco Systems on topics of growth and innovation. He has extensive experience in emerging markets, particularly in India, China and the Philippines.

In 2019, Scott was recognised as the ninth most influential management thinker by Thinkers50, the biannual ranking of global business thinkers. In 2017, he was awarded the Thinkers50 Innovation Award, which recognises the world's leading thinker on innovation.

Scott is co-author of *Eat, Sleep, Innovate: How to Make Creativity an Everyday Habit Inside Your Organisation* (Harvard Business Review Press, October 2020).

Scott is a prolific contributor to Harvard Business Publishing. He is the most published digital author on HBR.org and is Harvard Business Corporate Learning's most in-demand subject matter expert. He is the co-author of the *Harvard Business Review* article 'Breaking Down the Barriers to Innovation' as well as other *HBR* articles such as 'Unite Your Senior Team' and dozens of digital articles for the magazine.

Scott's previous books are *The First Mile: A Launch Manual for Getting Great Ideas into the Market*; *Seeing What's Next: Using the Theories of Innovation to Predict Industry Change* (with Innosight co-founder and Harvard professor Clayton Christensen); *The*

Innovator's Guide to Growth: Putting Disruptive Innovation to Work; The Silver Lining: An Innovation Playbook for Uncertain Times; The Little Black Book of Innovation: How It Works, How to Do It and *Building a Growth Factory*.

He has authored or co-authored numerous articles on innovation and strategy for a variety of publications. His Twitter feed is @ScottDAnthony.

Scott is a featured speaker on topics of innovation and growth. He has delivered keynote addresses on five continents, and has appeared on *Good Morning America*, Channel News Asia, CNBC and Fox Business.

Scott served on the board of directors of Media General (NYSE: MEG) from 2009–2013, helping guide that company through a strategic transformation. In 2013 he joined the board of MediaCorp, Singapore's leading diversified media company. Scott chairs the investment committee for IDEAS Ventures, a SGD ten-million fund Innosight runs in conjunction with the Singapore government that has invested in ten Singapore-based companies and generated a 20 per-cent-plus internal rate of return.

Scott received a BA in economics *summa cum laude* from Dartmouth College and an MBA with high distinction from Harvard Business School, where he was a Baker Scholar.

Ayelet Baron

Through masterfully facilitated guided sessions, books and talks, Ayelet Baron assists people around the globe in their transition to living a healthy life. Recognised as one of the top fifty global female futurists by *Forbes*, she has been described as a force of nature when it comes to envisioning a more humane world. Her work has been inspired by futurist Buckminster Fuller, who reminds us, 'We are called to be the architects of the future, not its victims.'

After a very successful career in Silicon Valley as a global strategist working in every corner of the world, Ayelet chose to write the books she wished she had been able to read when she started on her journey of becoming a conscious architect. Ayelet is passionate about driving sustainable change and being of service to the next generation of healthy creators. She now offers guidance to those who are ready to trek into the unknown through her writing, guided sessions and custom project work.

She is a designer and strategist dedicated to the evolution of the next generation of conscious leaders. Integrating humanities, behavioural science and evolutionary strategy, she envisions a world in which people matter and business plays a greater role in societal value. She has worked with leaders within Fortune 100 organisations, leading NGOs and start-ups. Ayelet has been designing experiences, keynote speaking, and facilitating leadership sessions for decades and has worked in over a hundred countries as a global technology executive.

What makes her approach unique is her personal story of seeking the truth. To that extent, she has worked to gain clarity and ground herself in the reality of doing the right thing for herself and her community. She shares her story openly so others can learn from her lessons and apply it to themselves.

Ayelet was a strategic consultant to Genius 100, inspired by Albert Einstein, a purpose-driven community uniting a hundred global visionaries – from its chair, astronaut Soichi Noguchi, to Col. Chris Hadfield, Marc Benioff, Sir Ridley Scott, Sir Ken Robinson, Paul Allen, Paulo Coelho and many additional visionaries.

Ayelet was the chief strategy and innovation officer for Cisco, co-creating a strategy to take Canada to being the second-largest-revenue country. She also helped the global mobile business in 2003 and held several positions in sales strategy around the world. Ayelet was the first chief diversity and inclusion officer for Cisco in emerging markets and also served on its IT senior executive team where she helped position IT as a strategic business partner.

Prior to Cisco, she had a rich consulting background and also worked as a public opinion pollster.

Dorie Clark

Dorie Clark has been named one of the Top 50 business thinkers in the world by Thinkers50 and was recognised as the No. 1 communication coach in the world by the Marshall Goldsmith Leading Global Coaches Awards. Clark, a consultant and keynote speaker, teaches executive education at Duke University's Fuqua School of Business and Columbia Business School.

Recognised as a 'branding expert' by the Associated Press, *Fortune*, and *Inc.* magazine, she is the author of *Entrepreneurial You* (Harvard Business Review Press), *Reinventing You* and *Stand Out*, which was named the No. 1 leadership book of 2015 by *Inc.* and one of the Top 10 business books of the year by *Forbes*. It was also a *Washington Post* bestseller. Her books have been translated into Russian, Chinese, Arabic, French, Polish, Korean, Spanish, Italian, Vietnamese and Thai.

Clark, whom the *New York Times* described as an 'expert at self-reinvention and helping others make changes in their lives', is a frequent contributor to the *Harvard Business Review*. She consults and speaks for a diverse range of clients, including Google, the World Bank, Microsoft, Morgan Stanley, the Ford Foundation, the Bill and Melinda Gates Foundation and Yale University.

A former presidential campaign spokeswoman, Clark has also taught at Spain's IE Business School, HEC-Paris, Babson College, Smith College Executive Education, UNC's Kenan-Flagler School of Business and more.

She has guest-lectured at universities including Harvard Business School, the Harvard Kennedy School, Stanford University's Graduate School of Business, the University of Pennsylvania's Wharton School of Business, the University of California, Berkeley's Haas School of Business, Georgetown,

NYU, the MIT Sloan School of Management and the University of Michigan.

Her work has been published in the *Harvard Business Review Guide to Getting the Right Job* and the *Harvard Business Review Guide to Networking* and she is quoted frequently in the worldwide media, including on NPR, the BBC and MSNBC. She has been a regular commentator on Canada's CTV and was named one of *Inc.*'s 'one hundred great leadership speakers for your next conference'.

A former New England Press Association award-winning journalist, Clark directed the environmental documentary film *The Work of 1000* and was a producer for a multiple-Grammy-winning jazz album. She is a Broadway investor, as well as a participant in the BMI Lehman Engel Musical Theatre Workshop, widely considered the premiere training ground for musical theatre lyricists and composers.

At age fourteen, Clark entered Mary Baldwin College's 'Programme for the Exceptionally Gifted'. At eighteen, she graduated Phi Beta Kappa from Smith College and two years later received a master of theological studies from Harvard Divinity School. You can download her 'Entrepreneurial You' self-assessment at dorieclark.com/entrepreneur

Erica Dhawan

Erica Dhawan is the world's leading authority on connectional intelligence and the founder and CEO of Cotential. Through speaking, training and consulting, she teaches business leaders innovative strategies that increase value for clients, deliver results and ensure competitiveness.

She is the co-author of the bestselling book *Get Big Things Done: The Power of Connectional Intelligence*.

Erica was named by Thinkers50 the 'Oprah of management ideas' and featured as one of the emerging management thinkers most likely to shape the future of business. She hosts the award-winning podcast *Masters of Leadership*. Erica speaks on global stages ranging from the World Economic Forum at Davos to companies such as Fedex, Pepsico and McGraw Hill Financial.

Erica writes for *Harvard Business Review, Forbes, Fast Company* and the Huffington Post. Erica also serves as a board member to Lufthansa Innovation Hub. Previously, she worked at Lehman Brothers and Barclays Capital.

She has an MPA from Harvard University, an MBA from MIT Sloan and a BS in economics from the Wharton School.

Mark Espositio

Mark Esposito PhD, is recognised internationally as a top global thought-leader in matters relating to the fourth industrial revolution – the changes and opportunities that technology will bring to a variety of industries.

He is co-founder and chief learning officer at Nexus FrontierTech, an AI scale-up firm dedicated to help business become more efficient and competitive by introducing the latest data management science. He was inducted in 2016 by Thinkers50 as one of the thirty most prominent rising business thinkers in the world. He is a global expert on the World Economic Forum and advisor to national governments.

Mark has held academic appointments with some of the world's leading institutions, such as Harvard University, University of Cambridge, Arizona State University's Thunderbird School of Global Management, Hult International Business School and IE Business School.

He has developed and conducted courses in business, government and society and economic strategy and competitiveness for Harvard University's Division of Continuing Education and served as institutes council co-leader on the Microeconomics of

Competitiveness (MOC) programme at the Institute of Strategy and Competitiveness at Harvard Business School under the mentorship of Professor Michael E. Porter.

He equally runs two executive education programmes at Harvard Professional Development designed around his books *Growth Strategies: Identifying Opportunities in Market Trends* and *Artificial Intelligence in Business: Creating Value with Machine Learning*.

His third executive program at Harvard is set to be launched in 2021: 'Fintech and Blockchain'.

He holds fellowships with the Social Progress Imperative and with the Global Federation of Competitiveness Councils in Washington DC, USA. He is a non-resident fellow at the Mohammed Bin Rashid School of Government in Dubai as well as research associate for the University College London Centre for Blockchain Technologies.

He has written hundreds of op-eds and professional publications, over 150 peer review articles, several book chapters, over forty case studies and eleven books. Mark is co-author of the bestseller *Understanding How the Future Unfolds: Using DRIVE to Harness the Power of Today's Megatrends*. The framework contained therein was nominated for the C.K. Prahalad 'Breakthrough Idea Award' by Thinkers50, the most prestigious award in business thought leadership. In 2019, *The AI Republic: Building the Nexus between Humans and Intelligent Automation* was a No. 1 bestseller in the US, UK, France, Germany, Spain and Italy and received global accolades.

Grounded in both humanities and economics, Mark has a BA and an MA in human and social sciences from the University of Turin in Italy, a PhD in business strategy and economics from the International School of Management, on a joint programme with St John's University, New York City. From 2009 to 2010, Mark attended post-doctoral education at Harvard Business School.

In 2018 he graduated from his second doctoral degree with an executive DBA at École des Ponts ParisTech; one of France's oldest and most prestigious *grande écoles*.

He is fluent in six languages and in his non-academic life he holds the rank of master instructor, black belt IV dan, at the International Budo Institute, Canada.

Sydney Finkelstein

Sydney Finkelstein is the Steven Roth professor of management and director of the Leadership Centre at the Tuck School of Business at Dartmouth College. Professor Finkelstein has published over twenty-five books and ninety articles, with several bestsellers, including *Why Smart Executives Fail*, which the *Wall Street Journal* called 'a marvel – a jargon-free business book based on serious research that offers genuine insights with clarity and sometimes even wit'.

Superbosses: How Exceptional Leaders Master the Flow of Talent was published in 2016 and also went on to become a bestseller and one of Amazon's top books of the year. The result of a ten-year research project, *Superbosses* profiles leaders as diverse as Julian Robertson, Alice Waters and Lorne Michaels, who all have one thing in common – they helped spawn some of the best talent in their industries. The book describes what they did and how they did it, offering teachable lessons for leaders of any organisation.

His most recent book is *The Superbosses Playbook*, offering a toolkit of practical exercises and activities to enable any manager to become a superboss.

Professor Finkelstein is a consultant and speaker to senior executives around the globe, as well as an executive coach, focusing on leadership, talent development, corporate governance, learning from mistakes and strategies for growth. He is a fellow of the Academy of Management and listed on

Thinkers50, the world's most prestigious ranking of leadership gurus.

He has been featured in the *Financial Times*, the *Wall Street Journal*, the *Washington Post*, *Harvard Business Review*, *Business Week*, the London *Times*, Toronto *Globe and Mail*, *Inc.*, *Fast Company* and CNBC, is a columnist for the BBC and the host of his new podcast, *The Sydcast*.

Stew Friedman

Stew Friedman is an organisational psychologist at the Wharton School of the University of Pennsylvania, where he has been on the faculty since 1984. He worked for five years in the mental health field before earning his PhD from the University of Michigan. As founding director of the Wharton Leadership Programme, in 1991 he initiated the required MBA and undergraduate leadership courses. He also founded Wharton's Work/Life Integration Project in 1991.

Friedman has been recognised by the biennial Thinkers50 global ranking of management thinkers every cycle since 2011 and was honoured with its 2015 Distinguished Achievement Award as the world's foremost expert in the field of talent. He was listed among *HR* magazine's most influential thought leaders, chosen by *Working Mother* as one of America's most influential men who have made life better for working parents, and presented with the Families and Work Institute's Work Life Legacy Award.

While on leave from Wharton for two and a half years, Friedman ran a fifty-person department as the senior executive for leadership development at Ford Motor Company. In partnership with the CEO, he launched a corporate-wide portfolio of initiatives designed to transform Ford's culture; more than 2,500 managers a year participated. Near the end of his tenure at Ford, an independent research group (ICEDR) said the leadership development course was a 'global benchmark' for leadership development programmes. At Ford, he created Total Leadership, which has been a popular Wharton course since 2001 and is used by individuals and companies worldwide, including as a primary intervention in a multi-year study funded by the National Institutes of Health on improving the careers and lives of women in medicine and by more than 135,000 students in Friedman's first massive open online course (MOOC) on Coursera.

Participants in this programme complete an intensive series of challenging exercises that increase their leadership capacity, performance and well-being in all parts of life, while working in high-involvement, peer-to-peer coaching relationships.

His research is widely cited, including among *Harvard Business Review*'s 'Ideas that Shaped Management' and he has written two bestselling books, *Total Leadership: Be a Better Leader, Have a Richer Life* (2008) and *Leading the Life You Want: Skills for Integrating Work and Life* (2014), now being taught as an MOOC on Coursera.

In 2013, Wharton School Press published his landmark study of two generations of Wharton students, *Baby Bust: New Choices for Men and Women in Work and Family*.

Work and Family – Allies or Enemies? (2000) was recognised by the *Wall Street Journal* as one of the field's best books. In *Integrating Work and Life: The Wharton Resource Guide* (1998), Stew edited the first collection of learning tools for building leadership skills for integrating work and life. His latest book is *Parents Who Lead: The Leadership Approach You Need to Parent with Purpose, Fuel Your Career and Create a Richer Life* (2020).

Winner of many teaching awards, he appears regularly in business media (the *New York Times* cited the 'rock star adoration' he inspires in his students). Friedman serves on a number of boards and is an in-demand speaker, consultant, coach, workshop leader, public policy advisor (to the US Departments of Labour and State, the United Nations and two White House administrations) and advocate for family supportive policies in the private sector.

Follow on Twitter @StewFriedman and LinkedIn, read his fifty-plus digital articles at HBR.org and tune in to his Work and Life show on SiriusXM 132, Business Radio Powered by Wharton (selected episodes now available as free podcasts).

Marshall Goldsmith

Marshall Goldsmith is the only two-time winner of the Thinkers 50 Award for being the No. 1 leadership thinker in the world. He has been ranked as the No. 1 executive coach in the world and a Top 10 business thinker for the past eight years. Dr Goldsmith is the author or editor of thirty-six books, including three that have sold over 2.5 million copies and been listed as bestsellers in twelve countries, including in the *New York Times*. *What Got You Here Won't Get You There* and *Triggers* have been recognised by Amazon.com as two of the Top 100 leadership and success books ever written.

Mark J. Greeven

Dr. Mark J. Greeven is a Chinese-speaking Dutch professor of innovation and strategy. For over a decade he has been collaborating with Chinese innovative companies and entrepreneurial multinationals. Thousands of executives have followed his workshops on innovation, strategy and China.

In 2017 he was ranked as one of Thinkers50's thirty next-generation business thinkers, an annual list that the *Financial Times* dubbed the 'Oscars of management thinking'.

Mark has written *Business Ecosystems in China: Alibaba and Competing Baidu, Tencent, Xiaomi and LeEco* (Routledge, 2017) and co-authored *Pioneers, Hidden Champions, Changemakers and Underdogs: Lessons from China's Innovators* (MIT Press, 2019).

Mark has taught dozens of courses on business ecosystems, innovation, strategy and entrepreneurship at global universities such as IMD Business School, Zhejiang University, Erasmus

University Rotterdam School of Management, Duke University Kunshan, East China Normal University, Emlyon Business School and the Berlin Institute of Technology.

Hal Gregersen

Drucker's keen insight about the power of questions has long been a guiding inspiration for Hal Gregersen. An innovation and leadership guru, Hal is executive director of the MIT Leadership Center and senior lecturer at the MIT Sloan School of Management. While Hal's expertise expands across all areas of innovative leadership, asking the right questions cuts deeply across all of his work. He challenges organisations and individuals to question the way we think and act to build a better, more creative world.

To grasp how leaders find and ask the right questions – ones that disrupt the world – Hal's *Questions are the Answer: A Breakthrough Approach to Your Most Vexing Problems at Work and In Life* (HarperCollins, 2018) builds on more than two hundred interviews with renowned business, technology, education, government, social enterprise and artistic leaders. This question-centric project surfaces crucial insights into how leaders build better questions to unlock game-changing solutions.

The first article from the project, 'Bursting the CEO Bubble: Why Executives Should Talk Less and Ask More' (*Harvard Business Review*, March/April 2017), explores how senior leaders can ask better questions to unlock what they don't know they don't know – before it's too late.

The second article from the project – 'Better Brainstorming: Focus on Questions, Not Answers, for Breakthrough Insights' (*Harvard Business Review*, March/April 2018) – outlines how his unique 'Question Burst' method can help anyone solve problems faster and better by asking nothing but questions about a vexing challenge for four fast and furious minutes. Hal is also founder of the 4-24 Project, an initiative dedicated to rekindling the provocative power of asking the right questions in adults so they can pass this crucial creativity skill onto the next generation.

Putting his insight into practice, he is the creator of a unique executive development experience: 'Leadership and the Lens: Learning at the Intersection of Innovation and Image-Making'. The course draws on Hal's two passions – photography and innovation – to teach participants how to ask radically better questions and change their impact as leaders.

Ranked consistently as one of the world's most influential management thinkers by Thinkers50, Hal regularly delivers inspirational keynote speeches, motivational executive seminars and transformational coaching experiences. He also works with a diverse set of companies to help them master the challenges of innovation and change, from Chanel to IBM to the World Economic Forum.

Anil K. Gupta

Dr Anil K. Gupta is a visiting faculty at the Centre for Management in Agriculture, Indian Institute of Management, Ahmedabad and Indian Institute of Technology, Bombay. He is also the founder of Honey Bee Network, SRISTI, NIF & GIAN Ph.D. (Management), Kurukshetra University India, MSc, Biochemical Genetics 1974 Haryana Agricultural University, Hisar fellow, National Academy of Agricultural Sciences; fellow, the World Academy of Art and Science, California 2001.

His mission is to expand the global as well as local space for innovations at grassroots and college levels; link ideas in informal and formal sectors; ensure recognition, respect and reward for creative people; create knowledge networks for augmenting innovations; and unfold creative potential of individuals, institutions and societies through frugal, flexible and friendly empathetic innovations.

Anders Indset

Anders Indset is one of the world's leading business philosophers and a trusted sparring partner to international CEOs and political leaders. Dubbed a 'rock'n'roll Plato' by European media, he is currently one of the most sought-after intellectuals with his approach to practical philosophy.

Norwegian, based out of Frankfurt, he is a guest lecturer at leading international business schools, a founding partner of the Global Institute of Leadership and Technology (GILT) and advisory board member of the Swiss-based deep tech pioneer Terra Quantum. He is known for his unconventional way of thinking, his provocative theses and his rock-star attitude.

His first international bestseller, *Wild Knowledge: Outthink the Revolution*, was released in Europe in 2017 and has been translated into further languages since, and was also a *Spiegel* bestseller in 2019. *The Quantum Economy: Saving the Mensch with Humanistic Capitalism* entered the *Spiegel* bestseller list and was No. 1 in *Manager* magazine and *Handelsblatt* – it was one of the bestselling business books in the German-speaking region. *The Quantum Economy* has been translated into more than ten languages and the work featured in *The Quantum Economy* was a finalist for the Breakthrough Idea Award of the 2019 Thinkers50 gala. Anders' latest book, *The Infected Mind*, is due to be released in autumn 2021.

Santiago Iñiguez de Onzoño

Santiago Iñiguez de Onzoño is the president of IE University and a recognised influencer in global higher education. In 2019 he was the first recipient of the Founders Award by Thinkers50, the prestigious global ranking of thoughtful leaders in management.

Iñiguez serves on the board of Headspring, a joint venture between IE Business School and the *Financial Times*, offering custom programmes for companies, as well as on the boards of EFMD (European Foundation for Management Development), Renmin University Business School (China), Antai Business School (Jiao Tong University, China), LUISS Business School (Italy), Mazars University (France), the Russian Presidential Academy (RANEPA, Russia) and FGV-EASP Fundaçao Getulio Vargas (Brazil). He is a past chair of the board of AACSB.

Iñiguez is the former dean of IE Business School and has played a leading role in business education. He was described by the *Financial Times* as 'one of the most significant figures in promoting European business schools internationally'. He was the first European appointed as dean of the year by Poets & Quants in 2017.

He is the author of *The Learning Curve: How Business Schools Are Reinventing Education* (2011), *Cosmopolitan Managers: Executive Education That Works* (2016) and *In An Ideal Business: How the Ideas of Ten Female Philosophers Bring Value to the Workplace* (2020), as well as co-editor of *Business Despite Borders: Companies in the Age of Populist Anti-Globalisation* (2018), all published by Palgrave Macmillan (Springer).

Iñiguez is a regular speaker at international conferences and frequently contributes to journals and media on higher education and executive development. He is one of the five hundred global LinkedIn influencers and in 2019 was recognised as the leading Spanish influencer in management by the Mexican magazine *Entrepreneur*.

Iñiguez is a professor of strategic management. He holds a degree in law, a PhD in moral philosophy and jurisprudence (Complutense University, Spain) and an MBA from IE Business School. He was a recognised student at the University of Oxford, UK.

Kriti Jain

Dr Kriti Jain is a leading management expert with a unique interdisciplinary background, specialising in decision-making and risk management, especially in the strategic contexts of top leadership and public policy. Thinkers50 has recognised her as a global thinker with the potential to change the world of theory and practice.

A tenured associate professor at Spain's IE Business School, consistently ranked amongst the best business schools globally, Kriti is a recipient of several prestigious grants from the European Union and Spanish and US governments for her research on decision-making.

She has a PhD in decision sciences from INSEAD and her research work has been published in leading science, management, economics and psychology journals, including *Management Science*, *Harvard Business Review*, *Human Resource Management*, the *Journal of Behavioral Decision Making* and *Journal of Operations Management*.

As a professor, Jain teaches courses and conducts customised training programmes on strategic decision-making, leadership, managing talent and negotiation. Students include business leaders, lawyers, entrepreneurs and doctoral scholars across her various collaborations with business schools and training alliances. The combination of scientific rigour with industry relevance makes these highly sought-after courses.

Before joining full-time academa, Kriti worked with McKinsey on risk management projects, focusing on the energy and materials sector for global clients based in Europe and the Middle East.

She is a champion of diversity and inclusion, especially in emerging markets, and has developed training programmes on female leadership and entrepreneurship, including in collaboration with the United Nations. Her Indian background, combined with work experiences in the US and Europe, provides her with a multi-dimensional lens to address issues of business, education and society. She is on the advisory board of several businesses, is a public speaker and a regular media commentator.

Martin Lindstrom

Martin Lindstrom is the founder and chairman of Lindstrom Company, the world's leading brand and culture transformation group, operating across five continents and more than thirty countries. *Time* magazine has named Lindstrom one of the world's hundred most influential people. For three years running, Thinkers50, the world's premiere ranking resource of business icons, selected Lindstrom to be among the world's Top 50 business thinkers. Lindstrom is a high-profile speaker and author of seven *New York Times* bestselling books, translated into sixty languages. His book *Brand Sense* was critically acclaimed by the *Wall Street Journal* as 'one of the five best marketing books ever published', *Small Data* was praised as 'revolutionary' and *Time* wrote this about *Buyology*: 'a breakthrough in branding'.

Henry Mintzberg

Henry Mintzberg is Cleghorn Professor of Management Studies at the Desautels Faculty of Management, McGill University, Montreal. His work has focused on managers and how they are trained and developed. The author or co-author of fifteen books, Mintzberg is, perhaps, best known for his work on organisational forms – identifying five types: simple structure, machine bureaucracy, professional bureaucracy, the divisionalised form and the adhocracy. He is also credited with advancing the idea of emergent strategy – the idea that effective strategy emerges from conversations within an organisation rather than being imposed from on high.

Cheerfully contrarian, Mintzberg is a long-time critic of traditional MBA programmes. In his first book, *The Nature of Managerial Work* (1973), he challenged the established thinking about the role of the manager and it is one of the few books that actually examine what managers do, rather than discussing what they should do. Other highlights include *The Rise and Fall of Strategic Planning* (1994), *Managers not MBAs* (2004) and *Managing* (2009).

Karl Moore

Dr Karl Moore joined the Desautels Faculty of Management, McGill University, in autumn 2000. He teaches graduate courses in strategy and leadership. He has taught extensively in executive education and MBA programmes with leading universities including Oxford, Stanford, LBS, Harvard Business School, Cambridge, IMD, Darden, Renmin (Bejing), Cornell, INSEAD, Duke, the Drucker School, the Rotterdam School of Management, IIM Bangalore, Queen's and McGill. He was nominated for the 2017 Thinkers50 distinguished achievement awards in the leadership category as a top thinker in the area for his work on introverts/extroverts in the C-suite and millennials. Seven other nominees included faculty from Harvard, MIT, Columbia, Penn and Dartmouth.

He was on the faculty of Oxford University between 1995–2000, where he taught executive education at Green Templeton College and on the MBA and doctoral programmes at the Saïd Business School.

An experienced senior corporate manager prior to joining academia, Dr Moore worked for twelve years in sales and marketing management positions in the high-tech industry with IBM, Bull and Hitachi. He is a cycle director for the Advanced Leadership Programme, a programme chaired by Henry Mintzberg. He also works with Henry as a module director on the international masters for health leadership and the IMPM.

In 2002 he won the faculty teaching award at the MBA level. In 2014 he won the professor of the year award from the McGill alumni association and in 2017 the principal's prize for public engagement through the media, which was a lifetime award.

Dr Moore's publications include twenty-nine refereed journal articles, ten books or edited volumes, fourteen chapters in books, thirty-one executive articles and dozens of conferences papers. His research has received more than 3,500 Google Scholar citations and has been published in a number of leading journals including *SMJ*, *JIBS*, *Human Relations*, *Management International Review*, *Business History*, *Marketing Management*, *World Business*, *Across the Board*, *Leader to Leader*, *Strategy + Business*, *European Business Forum*, *Chief Executive*, the *Academy of Management Executive*, *Journal of Applied Behavioural Science*, *Policy Options*, *Marketing Research* and the *Journal of Brand Management*. He is on the editorial boards of *Management International Review* and the *Journal of Management History*. He was an associate editor of the Academy of Management Perspectives from 2012 to 2016. Karl is a past division chair of the management history division of the Academy of Management. Karl was elected to an MA (Oxon) in 1995.

His current research is on millennials and introvert/ambivert/ extrovert leaders. *It's OK, Boomer: How to Effectively Work with Millennials/Generation Z* is due in autumn from the McGill/Queens Press. His next book, his eleventh, will be *Introvert/Ambivert/ Extrovert Leaders in the C-Suite*.

On the history side of globalisation and international business, he and co-author historian David Lewis have published articles in *Business History* and the *Management International Review* on international business in the ancient world. Their book, *Origins of Globalisation*, was published by Routledge in April 2009. It received worldwide press attention.

From 2007–2016, Karl did a weekly video cast for the *Globe and Mail*, Canada's national newspaper, where he interviewed CEOs and leading business professors from the top universities in the world.

In March 2011 he started a weekly blog, Rethinking Leadership, for *Forbes*. It can be read at: blogs.forbes.com/karlmoore

In spring 2014, he started a radio show, *The CEO Series*, on CJAD where he interviewed a CEO for an hour. He has done over thirty interviews including with Prime Minister Justin Trudeau,

Montreal Canadins CEO Geoff Molson, Bombardier CEO Alain Bellemare and *Quiet* author Susan Cain. The show website is soundcloud.com/cjad800/sets/the-ceo-series

Many of the interviews are featured as weekly articles in the *Globe and Mail*, and in French in *Les Affaires*.

He has been a consultant to leading global firms including Nokia, Air Canada, Lufthansa, British Airways, IBM, HP, Shell, Volvo, Accenture, Lilly, Pfizer and Regis McKenna. Articles on his research and op-ed pieces written by him have appeared in the *Financial Times*, the *New York Times*, the *Los Angeles Times*, the *Independent*, the *Guardian*, *Les Echoes*, the *Australian Financial Review*, *Het Financielle Dagblad*, the *Globe and Mail*, the *National Post*, *La Presse*, the *Montreal Gazette* and other leading papers. He is a regular guest in the media and appears on CNN, BBC, CBC, CTV and Global Television. Karl has given over 3,200 interviews in his career.

The winter 2006 issue of *Business Strategy Review*, published by the London Business School, identified Karl among a group of the world's greatest business thinkers. Others on the list of about twenty include Charles Handy, Philip Kotler, Gary Hamel, Warren Bennis and Rosabeth Moss Kanter.

Kevin Morrell

Professor Kevin Morrell researches the ways that organisations and individuals contribute to the public good. His interests branch out to such fields as strategy, sustainability and leadership. He is known globally for his work on the evidence-based approach to business research and for his research on understanding careers and employee retention.

He is professor of strategy and director of the Centre for Organisations and Society, Durham University Business School, and head of the strategy and international business group at WBS. He specialises in understanding public sector organisations. He is the author of *Organization, Society and Politics: An Aristotelian*

Perspective and co-author of *The Ethical Business* and *The Realities of Work.*

Gianpiero Petriglieri

Gianpiero Petriglieri is an associate professor of organisational behaviour at INSEAD and an expert on leadership and learning in the workplace. He directs the Management Acceleration Programme, the school's flagship executive education programme for emerging leaders, and is the academic director of the INSEAD Initiative for Learning Innovation and Teaching Excellence.

Gianpiero's award-winning research and teaching focus on what it means, and what it takes, to become a leader. He is particularly interested in the development and exercise of leadership in the age of nomadic professionalism, in which people have deep bonds to work but loose affiliations to institutions and authenticity and mobility have replaced loyalty and advancement as hallmarks of virtue and success.

Gianpiero's research has appeared in leading academic journals such as the *Administrative Science Quarterly, Academy of Management Annals, Academy of Management Learning & Education, Organization Studies* and *Organization Theory.* He also writes essays regularly for the *Harvard Business Review* and *Sloan Management Review.* His work has been featured in a range of media including the BBC, *Financial Times, The Economist,* the *Guardian, New York Times,* the *Wall Street Journal, Washington Post, Quartz, Vox, Le Figaro* and *El Pais,* and he is listed among the fifty most influential management thinkers in the world by Thinkers50.

Building on his research, Gianpiero has contributed to refining a unique approach to experiential leadership development that aims to accelerate the development of individual leaders as well as to strengthen leadership communities within and across organisations. Alongside the Management Acceleration Programme, he designs and directs customised leadership development programmes for multinationals in a variety of industries. He also speaks widely on how to live, lead and learn on the move without losing one's roots.

Dan Pontefract

Dan Pontefract is a leadership strategist, keynote speaker and bestselling author. He founded the Pontefract Group in 2014.

The four books he authored, *Lead. Care. Win*, *Open to Think*, *The Purpose Effect* and *Flat Army*, were all critically acclaimed and bestsellers.

His third book, *Open To Think*, is the 2019 Get Abstract international book of the year and the 2019 Axiom Business Book Award silver medal winner in the leadership category.

A renowned speaker, Dan has presented at four different TED events and also writes for *Forbes* and *Harvard Business Review*. Dan is an adjunct professor at the University of Victoria's Peter B. Gustavson School of Business and has garnered more than twenty industry awards over his career.

Previously chief envisioner and chief learning officer at TELUS – a Canadian telecommunications company with revenues of $14 billion and 50,000 employees – he launched the Transformation Office, the TELUS MBA and the TELUS Leadership Philosophy, all award-winning initiatives that dramatically helped to increase the company's employee engagement to record levels of nearly 90 per cent. Prior to TELUS, he held senior roles at SAP, Business Objects and BCIT.

Megan Reitz

Megan Reitz is professor of leadership and dialogue at Ashridge, where she speaks, researches, consults and supervises on the intersection of leadership, change, dialogue and mindfulness. She is on the Thinkers50 list of global business thinkers and is ranked in *HR* magazine's most influential thinkers listing. She has presented her research to audiences throughout the world and is the author of *Dialogue in Organizations* and *Mind Time*. Her new book, with *Financial Times* Publishing, is called *Speak Up*.

Her passion and curiosity centres on the quality of how we meet, see, hear, speak, learn with and encounter one another in organisational systems. Her research and publications, featured in *Harvard Business Review* and *Forbes* magazine, explore the neuroscience of leadership, the links between mindfulness and leadership capacities for the twenty-first century, and the capacity to 'speak truth to power' and enable others to do the same.

Before joining Ashridge, Megan was a consultant with Deloitte, surfed the dot-com boom with boo.com and worked in strategy consulting for the Kalchas Group, now the strategic arm of Computer Science Corporation. She was educated at Cambridge University and has a PhD from Cranfield School of Management. She is an accredited executive coach with Ashridge and the School of Coaching.

Hermann Simon

Hermann Simon is the founder and honorary chairman of Simon-Kucher & Partners. He is an expert in strategy, marketing and pricing. He is the only German in the Thinkers50 hall of fame of management thinkers. In German-speaking countries, he has been continuously voted the most influential living management thinker since 2005. The magazine *Cicero* ranks him in the top one hundred of the five hundred most important intellectuals.

Before committing himself entirely to management consulting, Simon was a professor of business administration and marketing at the Universities of Mainz (1989–1995) and Bielefeld (1979–1989). He was also a visiting professor at Harvard Business School, Stanford, London Business School, INSEAD, Keio University in Tokyo and the Massachusetts Institute of Technology. Between 1995 and 2009 he was CEO of Simon-Kucher & Partners.

Professor Simon has published over thirty-five books in twenty-seven languages, including worldwide bestsellers *Hidden Champions* (Boston: 1996; cover story of *BusinessWeek* in 2004) and *Power Pricing* (New York: 1997), as well as *Manage for Profit, Not for Market Share* (Boston: 2006). *Hidden Champions of the Twenty-First Century, Success Strategies of Unknown World Market Leaders* (New York: 2009) investigates the strategies of little-known market leaders. *Confessions of the Pricing Man* was published by Springer, New York in 2015. *Price Management* was published in 2019.

Simon was and is a member of the editorial boards of numerous business journals, including the *International Journal of Research in Marketing, Management Science, Recherche et Applications en Marketing, Décisions Marketing* and *European Management Journal*, as well as several German journals. For several decades he regularly wrote columns for the German business monthly *Manager Magazin*. As a board member of numerous foundations and corporations, Professor Simon has gained substantial experience in corporate governance. From 1984 to 1986 he was the president of the European Marketing Academy (EMAC). Simon is co-founder of the first Special Purpose Acquisition Company (SPAC) listed on the German stock exchange in Frankfurt and the first search fund in Germany.

A native of Germany, Simon studied economics and business administration at the universities of Bonn and Cologne. He received his diploma (1973) and his doctorate (1976) from the University of Bonn. Simon has received numerous international awards and holds honorary doctorates from IEDC Business

School of Bled (Slovenia), the University of Siegen (Germany) and Kozminski University, Warsaw (Poland). He is an honorary professor at the University of International Business and Economics in Beijing. In China, the Hermann Simon Business School is named after him.

Henry Stewart

Henry Stewart is founder and chief happiness officer of Happy Ltd., originally set up as Happy Computers in 1987. Inspired by Ricardo Semler's book *Maverick!*, he has built a company that has won multiple awards for having some of the best customer service in the UK and being one of the country's best places to work.

Henry was listed under the 'Guru Radar' of the Thinkers50 list of the most influential management thinkers in the world. 'He is one of the thinkers who we believe will shape the future of business,' explained list compiler Stuart Crainer.

His first book, *Relax*, was published in 2009. His second book, *The Happy Manifesto*, was published in 2013 and was shortlisted for business book of the year.

Haiyan Wang

As managing partner of the China India Institute, Haiyan Wang is responsible for overseeing the organisation's strategic direction, research and all programme activities.

Haiyan is the co-author of three books, *The Silk Road Rediscovered*, *Getting China and India Right* and *The Quest for Global Dominance* (second ed.). She co-authors a monthly column for *Bloomberg BusinessWeek* and blog for *Harvard Business Review*.

Haiyan has been listed by Thinkers50 under the 'Guru Radar' and shortlisted for the 2013 Global Solutions award and 2011 Global Village award. She has also been named a 'new guru' by the *Economic Times*.

Haiyan's opinion pieces have appeared in top international media such as the *Wall Street Journal*, *Wired*, the *Financial Times*, the *Economic Times*, *China Daily*, the *Times of India* and *Chief Executive* magazine.

A native of China, Haiyan spent the last twenty years consulting for and managing multinational business operations in China and the US in several different industry sectors. Drawing on her leading research and broad international experience, Haiyan speaks at global conferences, such as Summer Davos, the *Economist* conference, TEDx, the Brookings Institution and the Asia Society, on global trends, smart globalisation and emerging markets.

Caroline Webb

Caroline Webb is an executive coach, author and speaker who specialises in showing people how to transform their life and work for the better by applying insights from the behavioural sciences (behavioural economics, psychology and neuroscience). Her book *How to Have a Good Day: Harness the Power of Behavioural Science to Transform Your Working Life* has been published in fourteen languages and over sixty countries so far. It was hailed by *Forbes* as one of their 'must-read business books', by *Fortune* as one of their top 'self-improvement through data' books, and by *Inc.* magazine as one of the 'best fifteen leadership and personal development books of the past five years'. The book also won plaudits from publications as diverse as the *Financial Times*, *Time* and *Cosmopolitan* magazine.

She is also a senior advisor to McKinsey, where she was previously a partner. During her twelve years at McKinsey & Company, Caroline specialised in helping leaders achieve transformational change in their organisations and teams. She co-founded McKinsey's leadership practice, designed the firm's approach to transforming top team dynamics, led the firm's work on organisational effectiveness in the healthcare sector and drove the expansion of the firm's work on personal leadership effectiveness. She also founded and remains faculty of McKinsey's flagship leadership development course for senior female executives.

Caroline spent the 1990s working in public policy as an economist at the UK's central bank, the Bank of England. She worked closely with the monetary policy committee as author of the *Inflation Report* and was involved in global economic forecasting and institution building in post-communist Europe.

Caroline is a frequent contributor to *Harvard Business Review* and she has also written on behavioural change topics for the World Economic Forum, *Fast Company*, Quartz, *Business Insider*, Huffington Post and *Wired*. Her work has also been widely featured in national and international media over the years, including in *The Economist*, the *Financial Times*, the *Washington Post*, the *New York Times*, the *Guardian, Inc.*, *Forbes*, *Fortune* and on BBC radio.

She sits on the advisory board of Ethical Systems and OpenMind, two non-profit organisations dedicated to improving the quality of discourse and behaviour in business and education. She is also a founding fellow of the Harvard-affiliated Institute of Coaching, one of Marshall Goldsmith's 'one hundred coaches' and a member of the Silicon Guild. She has degrees in economics from Cambridge and Oxford Universities. Caroline splits her time between New York and London and travels frequently to give speeches and run workshops for clients around the world.

Robin Weninger

Robin Weninger is managing director of the Global Institute of Leadership and Technology (GILT), an educational company with the goal of putting education at the heart of every organisation in order to cope with an ever more complex and uncertain world.

He is an advisory board member at Zigurat Innovation and

Technology Business School and Nuclio Digital School, Barcelona. He is also a lecturer at the Frankfurt School of Finance and Management and the International School of Management. As former managing director of the German Tech Entrepreneurship Center (GTEC), he is now serving as an expert on educational topics. Robin is also a member of the advisory board of several EU-funded innovation projects under the H2020 framework. The World Economic Forum recognised Robin as a 'global shaper' in 2015 and as a 'European digital leader' in 2017.

In his work, Robin focuses on leading and guiding organisations through their challenges of change through the application of educational and entrepreneurial frameworks, technology and business models. He also deals with behavioural design and complex systems theory to better utilise network and spillover effects to scale organisations for impact.

Robin is always keen to support initiatives that change the world for the better and leave sustainable footprints for the future of education and work.

Liz Wiseman

Liz Wiseman is a researcher and executive advisor who teaches leadership to executives around the world. She is the author of *New York Times* bestseller *Multipliers: How the Best Leaders Make Everyone Smarter*, *The Multiplier Effect: Tapping the Genius Inside Our Schools* and *Wall Street Journal* bestseller *Rookie Smarts: Why Learning Beats Knowing in the New Game of Work.*

She is the CEO of the Wiseman Group, a leadership research and development firm headquartered in Silicon Valley, California. Her clients include Apple, AT&T, Disney, Facebook, Google, Microsoft, Nike, Salesforce, Tesla and Twitter. Liz has been listed in the Thinkers50 rankings and, in 2019, was recognised as the top leadership thinker in the world.

She has conducted significant research in the field of leadership and collective intelligence and writes for *Harvard Business Review*, *Fortune* and a variety of other business and leadership journals. She is a frequent guest lecturer at BYU and Stanford University and is a former executive at Oracle Corporation, where she worked as the vice president of Oracle University and as the global leader for human resource development.

SOURCES

Happiness at work

Social Funds, www.socialfunds.com/funds/profile.
  cgi?sfFundId=1126

Superboss leadership: a new model for the twenty-first century

Boris Groysberg and Katherine Connolly, 'The 3 things CEOs worry about the most', *Harvard Business Review*, 16 March 2015, www.hbr.org/2015/03/the-3-things-ceos-worry-about-the-most

The Talent Challenge: Adapting to Growth, PWC, www.pwc.com/gx/en/services/people-organisation/publications/ceosurvey-talent-challenge.html

C. Ronald Blankenship, interview by author

Andy Samberg, interview by author

Lee Clow, interview by author

Tom Carroll, interview by author

Kyle Craig, interview by author

Stevan Alburty, interview by author

Character actor Dick Miller, quoted in Beverly Gray, *Roger Corman: An Unauthorized Life* (Los Angeles: Renaissance Books, 2000), 51

Clive Thompson, 'End the Tyranny of 24/7 Email,' *New York Times*, 28 August 2014 (accessed 31 December 2014)

John Griffin, interview by author

Miles Davis, with Quincy Troupe, *Miles: The Autobiography of Miles Davis* (New York: Simon & Schuster, 1989), 273

Tom Shales and James Andrew Miller, *Live from New York; An Uncensored History of Saturday Night Live* (Boston: Little, Brown and Company, 2002), 345

Alice Waters, interview by author

David Murphy, interview by author

Kyle Craig, interview by author

Juhani Poutanen, interview by author

'The Best Advice I Ever Got,' *Fortune*, 6 July 2009, 45, www.archive.fortune.com/galleries/2009/fortune/0906/ gallery.best_advice_i_ever_got2.fortune/7.html (accessed 2 January 2015)

Gayle Ortiz, interview by author

Chase Coleman, interview by author

Michael Gross, *Genuine Authentic* (New York: HarperCollins Publishers, 2003), 219

Stan Lee and George Mair, *Excelsior!: The Amazing Life of Stan Lee* (New York: Simon & Schuster, 2002), 154

Mark Evanier, *Kirby: King of Comics* (New York: Abrams, 2008), 16

Jim Downey, SNL writer, interview by author

Quoted in John Colapinto, 'When I'm Sixty-Four: Paul McCartney Then and Now,' *New Yorker*, 4 June 2007, 63

Mark Dippé, interview by author

The philosophy of the hidden champions

Theodore Levitt, *The Globalization of Markets*, Harvard Business Review, May/June 1983, 92–102

Hermann Simon, *Hidden Champions – Speerspitze der deutschen Wirtschaft*, Zeitschrift für Betriebswirtschaft 60 (9/1990), 875-890

Hermann Simon, *Hidden Champions – Lessons from 500 of the World's Best Unknown Companies* (Cambridge: Harvard Business School Press, 1996); *Hidden Champions of the 21st Century* (New York: Springer, 2009)

Arthur Schopenhauer, *The World as Will and Representation* (Cambridge: Cambridge University Press, 2014)

Marvin Bower, *The Will to Manage: Corporate Success Through Programmed Management* (New York: McGraw-Hill, 1966); Marvin Bower, *The Will to Lead: Running a Business with a Network of Leaders* (Cambridge: Harvard Business School Press, 1997)

Doris B. Wallace and Howard E. Gruber, *Creative People at Work,*

Twelve Cognitive Case Studies (New York/Oxford: Oxford University Press, 1989)

Eugene T. Gendlin, *Focusing* (New York: Bantam Books, 1982); Daniel Goleman, *Focus: The Hidden Driver to Excellence* (New York: Harper, 2013)

Peter F. Drucker, *Adventures of a Bystander* (New York: Harper & Row, 1978), 255

Friedrich von Schiller, *Wilhelm Tell, Part 3* (translated from German)

Ralph Waldo Emerson, *Selected Essays* (Harmondsworth: Penguin American Library, 1982)

Søren Kierkegaard, *Fear and Trembling* (Cambridge: Cambridge University Press, 2006)

Justin Steinberg, *Spinoza's Political Psychology: The Taming of Fortune and Fear* (Cambridge: Cambridge University Press, 2018)

Laurence Chang, *Wisdom for the Soul* (Washington: Gnosophia, 2006)

Christopher Freeman, *The Economics of Industrial Innovation*, 2nd ed. (Cambridge: MIT Press, 1982)

Robert Maurer, *The Spirit of Kaizen: Creating Lasting Excellence One Small Step at a Time* (New York: McGraw Hill Education, 2012)

Theodore Levitt, Editorial, *Harvard Business Review*, November–December 1988, 9

Immanuel Kant, *Critique of Pure Reason* (Cambridge: Cambridge University Press, 1999)

Edward de Bono, *Lateral Thinking* (New York: Harper Collins, 2015)

Hopkins, Jasper (ed.), *Complete Philosophical and Theological Treatises of Nicholas of Cusa*, 2 vol. (Minneapolis: A.J. Banning Press, 2001)

Paul R. Lawrence and Jay W. Lorsch, *Organization and Environment: Managing Differentiation and Integration*, (Homewood, Ill.); Richard D. Irwin 1977, revised edition published by Harvard Business School Press, 1986

Barry Johnson, *Polarity Management – Identifying and Managing Unsolvable Problems* (Amherst, Mass.: HRD Press, 1992)

Saint Augustine, *Confessions* (Oxford: Oxford University Press, 1991)

Warren Bennis, *Why Leaders Can't Lead* (San Francisco: Jossey-Bass, 1989)

On the nobility of guiding Goliath

Shai Bernstein, Emanuele Colonnelli, Xavier Giroud and Benjamin Iverson, 'Bankruptcy Spillovers', National Bureau of Economic Research working paper #23162, February 2017, www.nber.org/papers/w23162.pdf

Scott D. Anthony, 'The New Corporate Garage,' *Harvard Business Review*, September 2012, www.hbr.org/2012/09/the-new-corporate-garage

Clayton M. Christensen, 'How Will You Measure Your Life?' *Harvard Business Review*, July–August 2010, www.hbr.org/2010/07/how-will-you-measure-your-life

The fourth industrial revolution will change business, work and the planet: brace for impact

R. Boyd, N. Stern and B. Ward (2015). 'What will global annual emissions of greenhouse gases be in 2030 and will they be consistent with avoiding global warming of more than 2°C?', ESRC Centre for Climate Change Economics and Policy; Grantham Research Institute on Climate Change and the Environment, www.lse.ac.uk/GranthamInstitute/wp-content/uploads/2015/05/Boyd_et_al_policy_paper_May_2015.pdf

'Economic benefit', Smart Manufacturing Leadership Coalition (SMLC), 2016, www.smartmanufacturingcoalition.org/economic-benefit

Mark Esposito and Terence Tse, 'DRIVE: the Five Megatrends that Underpin the Future, Business, Social and Economic Landscapes', *Thunderbird International Business Review*, 2017, 1–9

Ganesh Hegde, 'Industry 4.0 and the Evolution of Semiconductor Manufacturing', 14 July 2017, blog.appliedmaterials.com/industry-40-and-evolution-semiconductor-manufacturing

Global e-Sustainability Initiative (GeSI), 'ICT solutions for twenty-first-century challenges', www.smarter2030.gesi.org

IDG Enterprise marketing, 'State of the network 2016', February 2016, www.idg.com/tools-for-marketers/state-of-the-network-2016

Peter Lacy and Jakob Rutqvist, *Waste to Wealth: the Circular Economy Advantage* (Accenture, Palgrave Macmillan, 2015)

Peter Lowes, Frank Cannata, Subodh Chitre and Jason Barkham, 'Automate this: the business leader's guide to robotic and intelligent automation', Deloitte, 2017, www2.deloitte.com/content/dam/Deloitte/us/Documents/process-and-operations/us-sdt-process-automation.pdf

James Macaulay, Lauren Buckalew and Gina Chung, 'Internet of things in logistics. DHL and Cisco', 2015, discover.dhl.com/content/dam/dhl/downloads/interim/full/dhl-trend-report-internet-of-things.pdf

Diego Alejo Vázquez Pimentel, Iñigo Macías-Aymar and Max Lawson, 'Reward work, not wealth', Oxfam, January 2018, d1tn3vj7xz9fdh.cloudfront.net/s3fs-public/file_attachments/bp-reward-work-not-wealth-220118-en.pdf

David Schatsky, Navya Kumar and Sourabh Bumb, 'Intelligent IoT: Bringing the power of AI to the Internet of Things', Deloitte, 12 December 2017, www2.deloitte.com/insights/us/en/focus/signals-for-strategists/intelligent-iot-internet-of-things-artificial-intelligence.html?id=us:2pm:3ad:lookagainfy18:eng:greendot:em:3772:cn:aiiot:custom:custom:51580719

'Robot revolution – global robot & AI primer', Bank of America Merrill Lynch, 2015, www.bofaml.com/content/dam/boamlimages/documents/ PDFs/robotics_and_ai_condensed_primer.pdf

United Nations, Department of Economic and Social Affairs, population division, 'World Population Prospects: The 2017 Revision', New York: United Nations, 2017

World Economic Forum, 'Technology and innovation for the future of production: accelerating value creation, March 2017,

www3.weforum.org/docs/WEF_White_Paper_Technology_
Innovation_Future_of_Production_2017.pdf

When work meets philosophy: a template for wise leadership from Plato's *Republic* and *Symposium*

Allan Bloom, *The Republic of Plato*, second edition (Basic Books, 1991), 228 (550e)

Ibid., xxi

Plato, *The Symposium* (translated by Walter Hamilton, Penguin Classics, 1951), 78

The joy of struggle

John Stuart Mill, autobiography, vol. XXV, part 1, chapter 5, The Harvard Classics (New York: P.F. Collier & Son, 1909–14)

Edwin A. Locke, *Handbook of Principles of Organisational Behaviour*, 2nd ed., (UK: John Wiley & Sons, Ltd, 2009), 139

Research shows that those who are the least challenged are 40 per cent less challenged than the average and those who are the most challenged are 36 per cent more challenged than the average. Additionally, 39 per cent cite workload as the top cause of stress; Nikki Blacksmith and Jim Harter, 'Majority of American workers not engaged in their jobs,' Gallup, 28 October 2011; Sharon Jayson, 'Burnout up among employees,' *USA Today*, 24 October 2012

David R. Schilling, 'Knowledge doubling every 12 months, soon to be every 12 hours,' Industry Tap, 19 April 2013; 'Quick facts and figures about biological data,' ELIXIR, 2011; Brian Goldman, 'Doctors make mistakes. Can we talk about that?' TED, November 2011; Brett King, 'Too much content: a world of exponential information growth,' Huffington Post, 18 January 2011

Edward N. Wolff, 'The growth of information workers in the US economy', Communications 48, no. 10 (2005)

D. L. Bosworth, 'The rate of obsolescence of technical knowledge: a note,' *Journal of Industrial Economics*, 26, no. 3 (1978); Lionel Nesta, 'Knowledge and productivity in the world's largest manufacturing corporations,' *Journal of Economic Behavior & Organization* (2011); J. Allen and R. van der Velden, 'When do skills become obsolete and when does it matter?,' in A. de Grip, Jasper van Loo and Ken Mayhew, eds., *The Economics of Skills Obsolescence* (Amsterdam and Boston: JAI, 2007)

Lisa Feldman Barrett, 'How to become a "super-ager",' *New York Times*, 31 December 2016

The philosophy of price

Hermann Simon, *Confessions of the Pricing Man* (New York: Springer Nature, 2016)

Socrates, *Euthydemos*

Lucas Pfisterer and Stefan Roth, 'Value creation in usage processes – investigating the micro-foundations of value-in-use', *Marketing – Journal of Research and Management*, 3/2018

Aristotle (384–322 BC) is often named as the father of the sharing economy. But actually the pioneer was Socrates. The lives of these two philosophers did not overlap. Plato, the mentor of Aristotle (427–348 BC), overlapped with both Socrates and Aristotle.

Thorstein Veblen, *The Theory of the Leisure Class* (Routledge, 2017)

Ronald H. Coase, *The Firm, the Market and the Law* (Chicago: University of Chicago Press, 1990)

Aristotle, *Politics*, Book I; see also, Edward W. Younkins, 'Aristotle and Economics', www.quebecoislibre.org/050/050915-11.htm, accessed 27 September 2018.

Hermann Heinrich Gossen (1854), *Entwicklung der Gesetze des menschlichen Verkehrs und der daraus fließenden Regeln für menschliches Handeln* (Braunschweig: F. Vieweg)

Georg Tacke, *Nichtlineare Preisbildung: Höhere Gewinne durch Differenzierung* (Wiesbaden: Gabler, 1989)

RH Tawney, *Religion and the Rise of Capitalism – On Aquinas and Just Price* (New York: Penguin, 1948), 40

David Futrelle, 'Post-Sandy price gouging: economically sound, ethically dubious', *Time*, 2 November 2012, www.business.time.com/2012/11/02/post-sandy-price-gouging-economically-sound-ethically-dubious

Frankfurter Allgemeine Zeitung, translation by author, 17 October 2018, 22

Paul A. Samuelson, 'The Pure Theory of Public Expenditure'

Luis de Molina, *A Treatise on Money* (Grand Rapids: Christian's Library Press, 2015)

Karl Marx, *Wages, Prices and Profits* (Moscow: Foreign Languages Publishing House, 1951), 28

Mariana Mazzucato, *The Value of Everything* (London: Penguin Books, 2018), 57

Madhavan Ramanujam and Georg Tacke, *Monetising Innovation: How Smart Companies Design the Product Around the Price* (Hoboken: Wiley, 2016)

Mariana Mazzucato, *The Value of Everything* (London: Penguin Books, 2018), 57

Aphorismen, www.aphorismen.de/zitat/6535

John Ruskin, 'Gesetz der Wirtschaft', www.iposs.de/1/gesetz-der-wirtschaft

Michael J. Sandel, *What Money Can't Buy: The Moral Limits of Markets* (New York: Farrar, Straus and Giroux, 2012)

Roy Mottahedeh, *The Mantle of the Prophet* (London: OneWorldPublications, 2000), 34

INDEX

Unbound is the world's first crowdfunding publisher, established in 2011.

We believe that wonderful things can happen when you clear a path for people who share a passion. That's why we've built a platform that brings together readers and authors to crowdfund books they believe in – and give fresh ideas that don't fit the traditional mould the chance they deserve.

This book is in your hands because readers made it possible. Everyone who pledged their support is listed below. Join them by visiting unbound.com and supporting a book today.

Bayram Alagoez

Faizan Ali

Lluis Altes

Quentin Ankri

Rowinda Appelman

Adrian Ashton

Kenneth Auchenberg

Elena Badia

Martin F Bauer

Susi Billingsley

Jacques Brechtendorf

Alessandro Broccolo

Stephen Bruce

Angelina Bryant

David Burkus

Anna Carolina Campos

Patricia Cherio

Robert Chivelli

David Christie

Goran Cvetkovic

Domenico Dargenio

Geoffrey Darnton

Gianluigi de Bernardi

Esther-Mirjam de Boer

Kathrine Decorzant

Mynia Deeg

Dr. Anke Diederichsen

Michael Dorn

Stefan Duller

Moriz Eberhardt

Helmut Erler

Michael Esser

Tina Feria

Yves Froppier

Molly Ganley

Rocio Pilar Gil de Garate
  Hernandez

Estelle Graf

Philipp Greiner

Miriam Greis

Katharina Hammerschmidt

Maileen Hampton

Nick Hixson

Eilif Hjelseth

Valéria Horváth

Anne-Lena Jost

Jamal Khan

Dan Kieran

Michael Kirmes

Timo Klein

Miriam Korth

Markus Kreuter

Martin Kudlac

Andreas Kuehne

Simone Langenheder

Bruno Larceem

Melanie Leach

Wolfgang Lehmacher

Richard Little

Andre Lopes

Johana Lopez

Kelli Loveless

Miinu Lumiaho

Tony Martignetti

Linda Julianna Matula

Brian Mcleish

Lisa Merchelio

Gemma Milne

John Mitchinson

Carlo Navato

Boris Neretin

Julio Pacheco

Margret Paul

Mevan Peiris

Claudine Perlet

Bernardo Perrone

Justin Pollard

Giovanni Porcellana

Beth Porter

Tom Poupard

Antonio Ramirez

Ramona

Jochen Reitzl

Manuel Rivoir

Gabriele Rizzi

Robyn Roscoe

Carol Sayles

Philippe Schaeffer

Markus Schobel

Mia Schönhaus

Ludwig Schreier

Marc Schuster

Stig Skilbred

Keno Specht

Wendy Staden

Katherine Starks

Michel Stromann

Mike Stuart

Christopher Swarat

Aleksandra Temereva

Thinkers50

Ante Todoric

Anne-Sophie Tombeil

Fabrice Tortey

Anne-Marie Turcotte

Alfredo Uribe

Manuela van der Glas

Ruud van der Glas

Jurgen van der Vlugt

Nhat Vuong

Lindsay Watt

Robin Weninger

Markus Werner

Beatrice Willmers

David Wohde

Herby Wolfsdorf

Brigitte Zermann

Jan Zimmermann